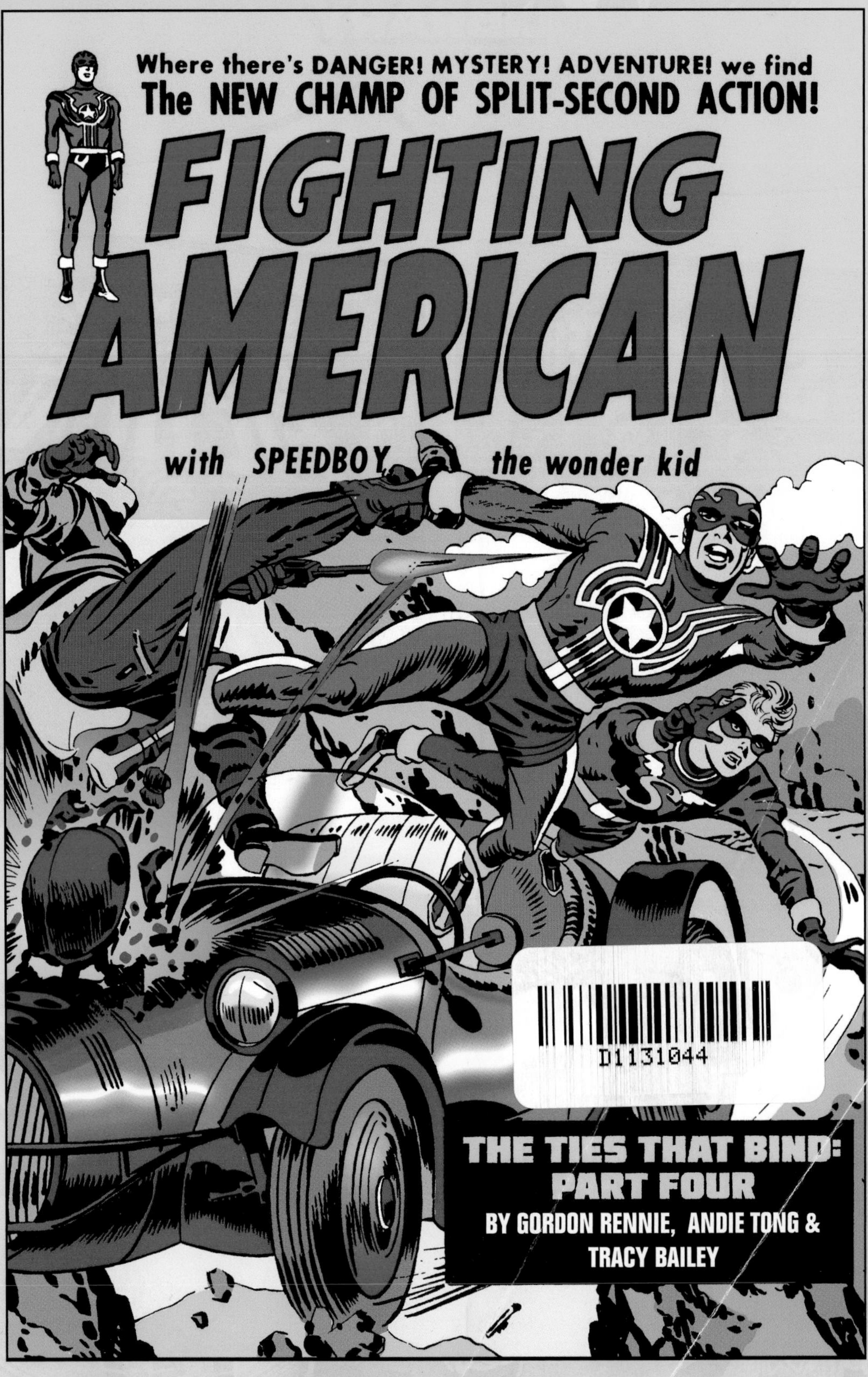
Where there's DANGER! MYSTERY! ADVENTURE! we find
The NEW CHAMP OF SPLIT-SECOND ACTION!
FIGHTING AMERICAN
with SPEEDBOY the wonder kid
THE TIES THAT BIND: PART FOUR
BY GORDON RENNIE, ANDIE TONG & TRACY BAILEY

ISSUE FOUR COVER B ART BY JACK KIRBY, JOE SIMON, COLORS BY DML

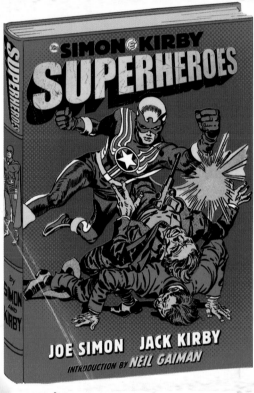
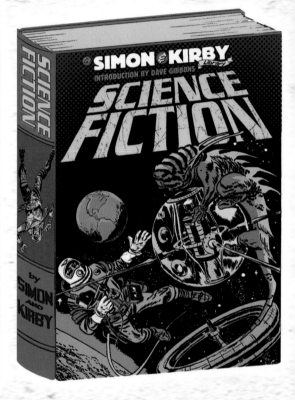

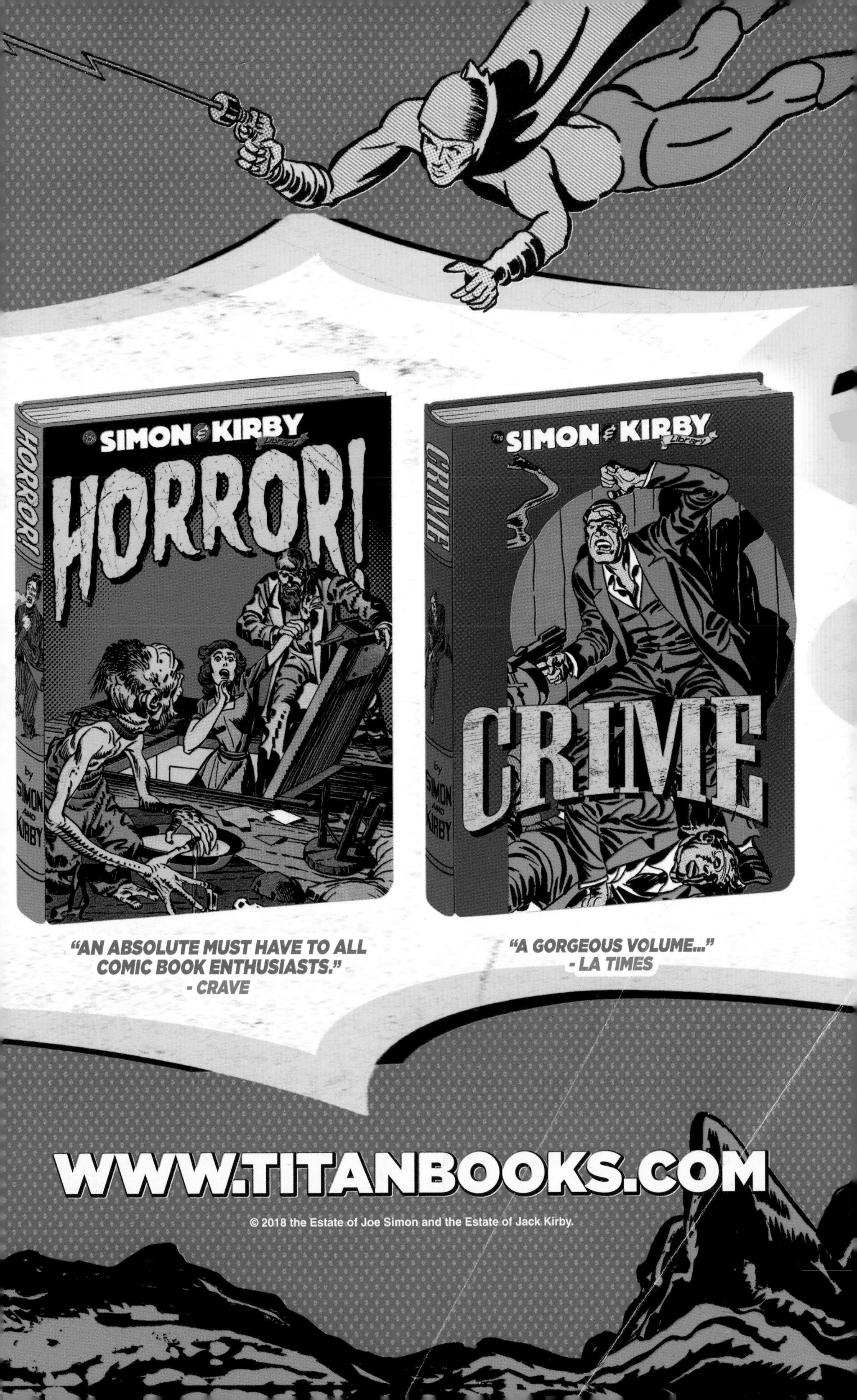
The SIMON & KIRBY Library
HORROR!
by SIMON AND KIRBY
The SIMON & KIRBY Library
CRIME
by SIMON AND KIRBY
"AN ABSOLUTE MUST HAVE TO ALL COMIC BOOK ENTHUSIASTS."
- CRAVE
"A GORGEOUS VOLUME..."
- LA TIMES
WWW.TITANBOOKS.COM
© 2018 the Estate of Joe Simon and the Estate of Jack Kirby.

BIOS

GORDON RENNIE is an award-winning comics and video games writer. For more than 20 years, he has been one of the most prominent writers for *2000AD* and the *Judge Dredd Megazine*. On *Dredd* alone he has collaborated with legendary artists like *Judge Dredd* co-creator Carlos Ezquerra, Ian Gibson, Cam Kennedy, and *The Walking Dead*'s Charlie Adlard.

His other strips for *2000AD* include *Jaegir, Absalom, Missionary Man, Necronauts, Rogue Trooper,* and *Caballistics, Inc.*

Outside of *2000AD*, his work includes *Doctor Who, Department of Monsterology, Warhammer,* the award-winning *Robert Burns Witch-Hunter* graphic novel, and the *Fighting American* series for Titan Comics, continuing the adventures of the character created by the legendary Joe Simon and Jack Kirby, creators of *Captain America.*

Gordon has worked on numerous video games, including *Call of Duty, Star Wars,* and *Alien Vs. Predator.*

ANDIE TONG has been a professional artist since 2000 when he worked on his first graphic novel, *The Architect*, written by Mike Baron. Throughout his career he has drawn *Spectacular Spiderman, Teenage Mutant Ninja Turtles, Masters of the Universe, Starship Troopers,* and *The Batman Strikes.* He also drew *Tron: Betrayal,* a prequel to the 2010 movie *Tron: Legacy,* and three volumes of Tor books' graphic novel series *The Eye of the World.* In 2013, he drew three books for HarperCollins starring Batman and the Justice League and he illustrated *The First Law: The Blade Itself.* In 2015, he illustrated the Disney book *Zodiac Legacy*, written by Stan Lee and Stuart Moore. For Titan Comics he drew the much lauded *Tekken* series.

FIGHTING AMERICAN

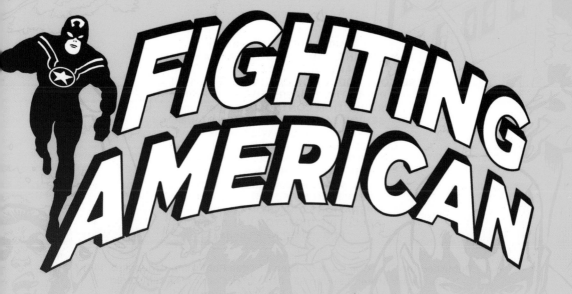

FIGHTING AMERICAN:
THE TIES THAT BIND
ISBN 9781785863837

FIGHTING AMERICAN CREATED
BY JOE SIMON & JACK KIRBY

TITANCOMICS

SENIOR EDITOR Martin Eden
MANAGING/LAUNCH EDITOR Andrew James
ART DIRECTOR Oz Browne
SENIOR PRODUCTION CONTROLLER Jackie Flook
PRODUCTION SUPERVISOR Maria Pearson
PRODUCTION **CONTROLLER** Peter James
SENIOR SALES MANAGER Steve Tothill
PRESS OFFICER Will O'Mullane
COMICS BRAND MANAGER Chris Thompson
ADVERTISING MANAGER Michelle Fairlamb
HEAD OF RIGHTS Jenny Boyce
PUBLISHING MANAGER Darryl Tothill
PUBLISHING DIRECTOR Chris Teather
OPERATIONS DIRECTOR Leigh Baulch
EXECUTIVE DIRECTOR Vivian Cheung
PUBLISHER Nick Landau

Published by Titan Comics, a division of Titan Publishing Group, Ltd. 144 Southwark Street, London SE1 0UP. Titan Comics is a registered trademark of Titan Publishing Group Ltd.
Originally published in single comic form as Fighting American: The Ties That Bind #1-4. FIGHTING AMERICAN © 1954, 2018 JOSEPH H. SIMON AND THE ESTATE OF JACK KIRBY.

A CIP Catalogue for this title is available from the British Library.

First Edition September 2018

10 9 8 7 6 5 4 3 2 1

Printed in Spain.

www.titan-comics.com
BECOME A FAN ON FACEBOOK.COM/COMICSTITAN
FOLLOW US ON TWITTER@COMICSTITAN

For rights information contact Jenny Boyce:
jenny.boycet@titanemail.com

FIGHTING AMERICAN

THE TIES THAT BIND

WRITER: **GORDON RENNIE**

ARTIST: **ANDIE TONG**

COLORIST: **TRACY BAILEY**

LETTERER: **SIMON BOWLAND**

EDITOR: **DAVID LEACH**

TITAN®
COMICS

THE STORY SO FAR

In 1954, NELSON FLAGG took part in an experimental US Military procedure that saw his mind transferred into the enhanced and revitalized body of his dead brother, JOHNNY FLAGG, to become America's first and only super hero, FIGHTING AMERICAN!

Soon after, FIGHTING AMERICAN and his sidekick, SPEEDBOY, found themselves marooned in time, 63 years later, in the 21st Century.

With the architect of their predicament, MADAME CHAOS, now safely behind bars, FA and SB have begun the mammoth task of tracking down all of the stolen PROFESSOR DYLE TWISTER tech that she sold on the Dark Web to every whack-job, fanatic, terrorist and weirdo she could find. Meanwhile, one of FA's old 1950s enemies (also brought from the 1950s), the notorious DOUBLE HEADER, is now the head of the FBI and starting to make life difficult for our two-fisted men of action.

Now read on…

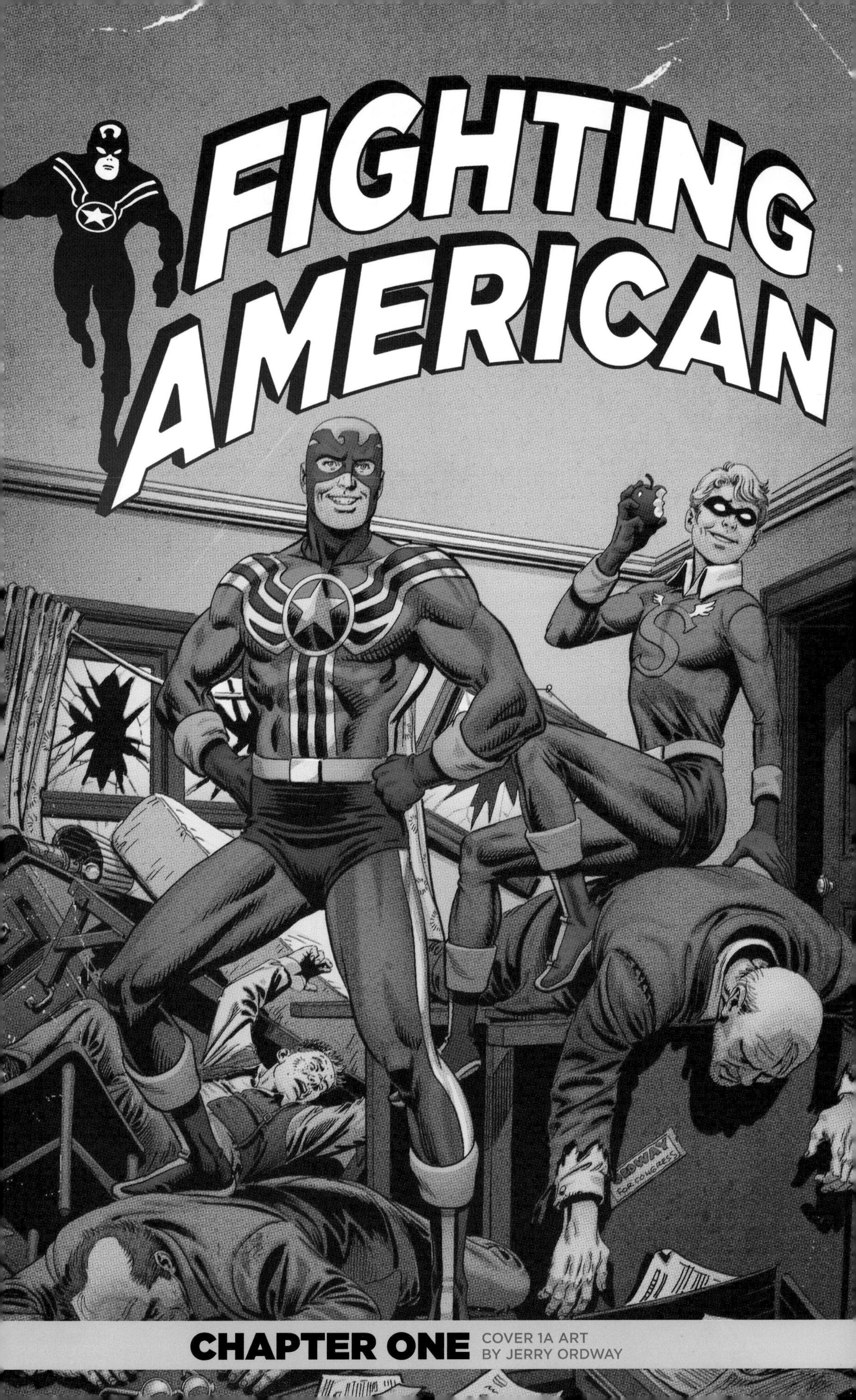
FIGHTING AMERICAN
FOR CONGRESS

CHAPTER ONE COVER 1A ART BY JERRY ORDWAY

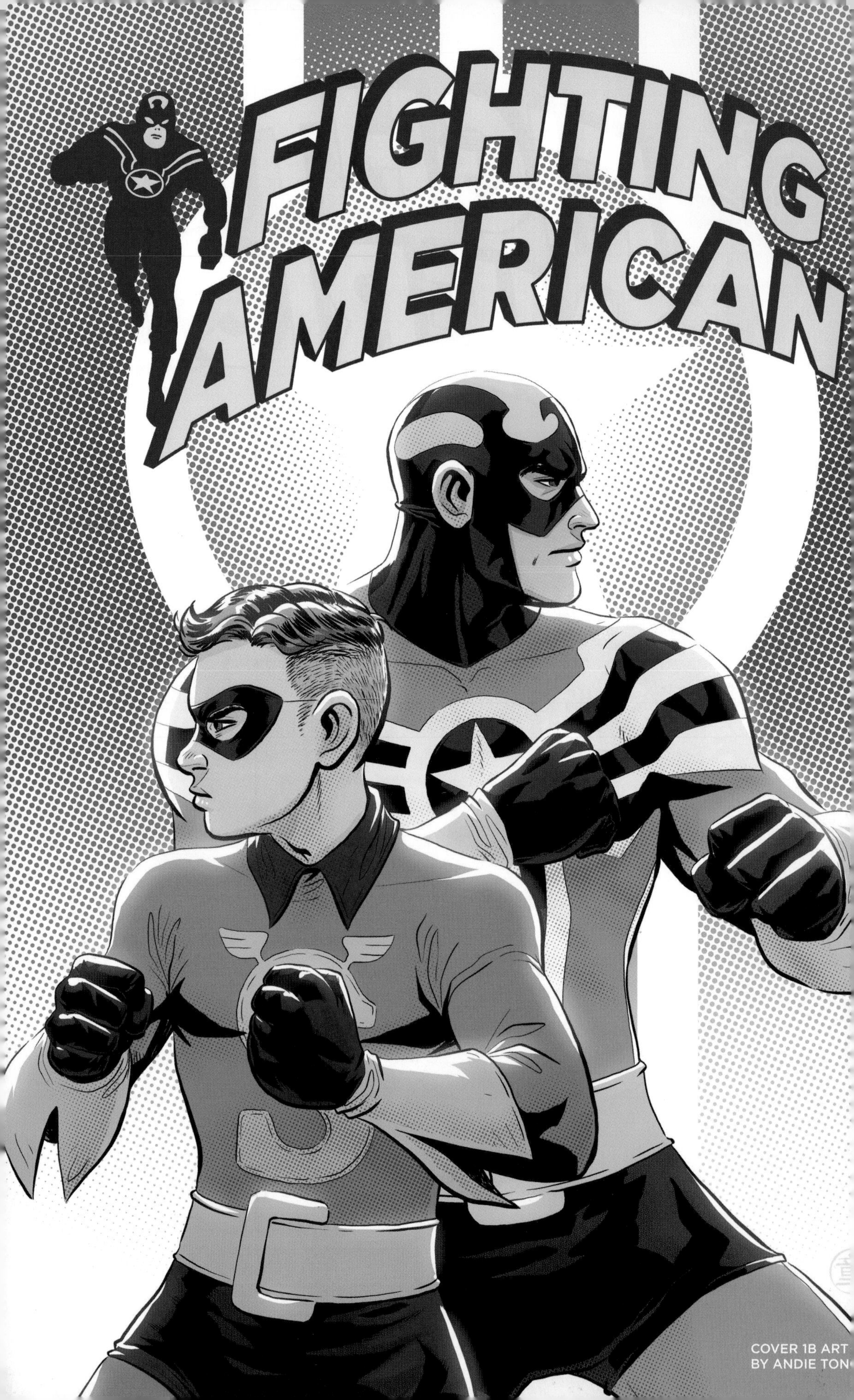
FIGHTING
AMERICAN

COVER 1B ART
BY ANDIE TON

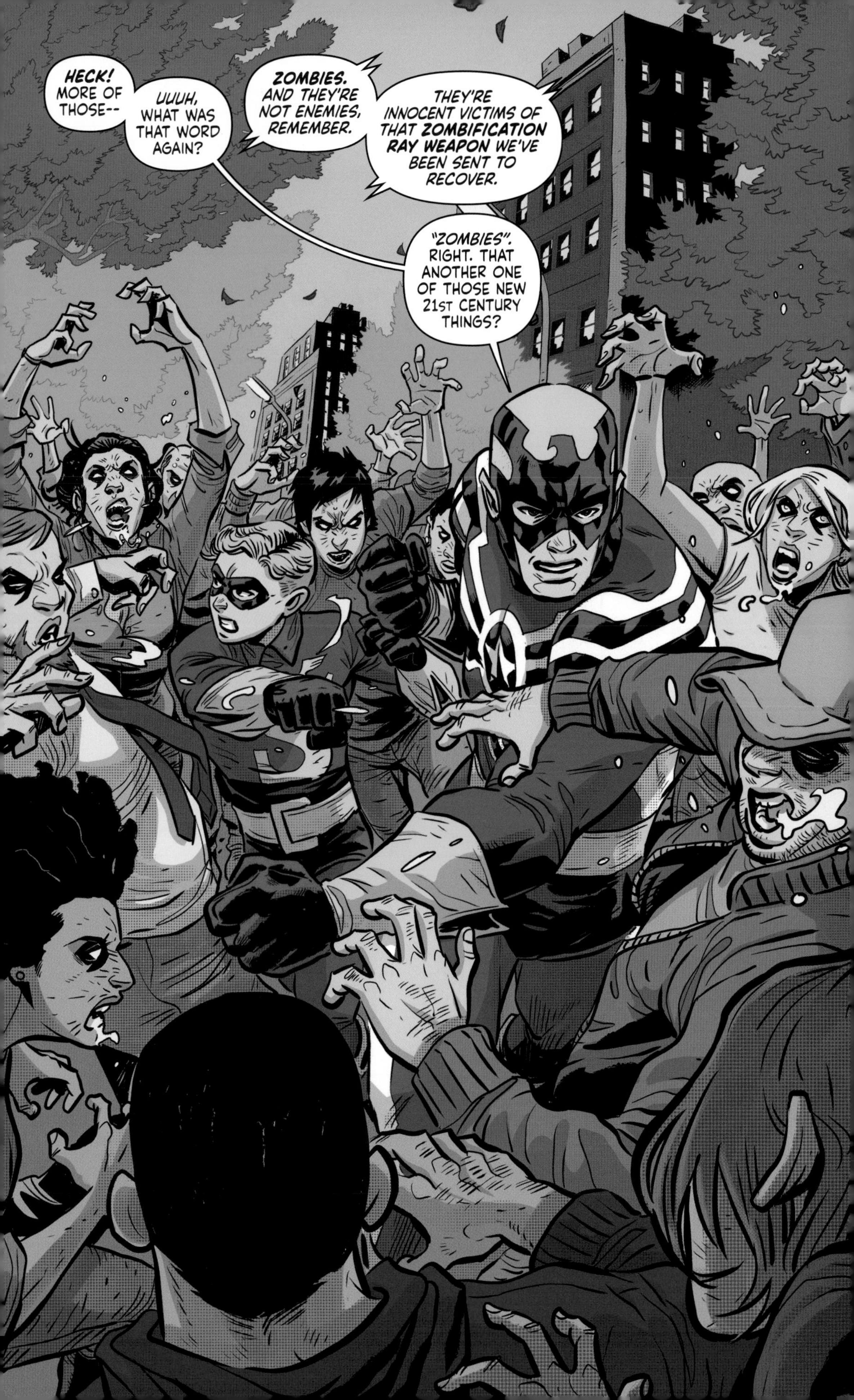
HECK! MORE OF THOSE--
UUUH, WHAT WAS THAT WORD AGAIN?
ZOMBIES. AND THEY'RE NOT ENEMIES, REMEMBER.
THEY'RE INNOCENT VICTIMS OF THAT ZOMBIFICATION RAY WEAPON WE'VE BEEN SENT TO RECOVER.
"ZOMBIES". RIGHT. THAT ANOTHER ONE OF THOSE NEW 21ST CENTURY THINGS?

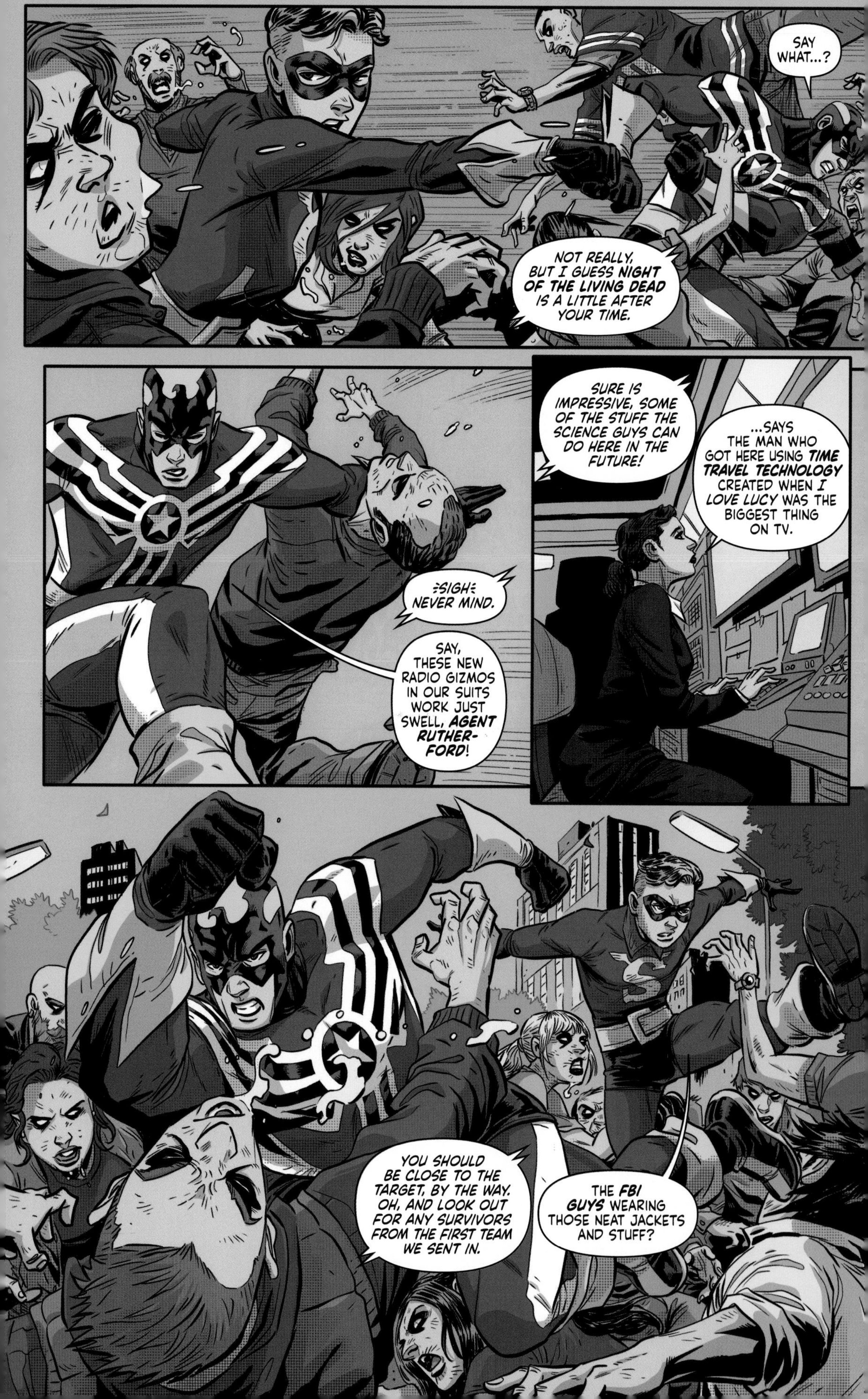
SAY WHAT...?
NOT REALLY, BUT I GUESS NIGHT OF THE LIVING DEAD IS A LITTLE AFTER YOUR TIME.
SIGH NEVER MIND.
SAY, THESE NEW RADIO GIZMOS IN OUR SUITS WORK JUST SWELL, AGENT RUTHER-FORD!
SURE IS IMPRESSIVE, SOME OF THE STUFF THE SCIENCE GUYS CAN DO HERE IN THE FUTURE!
...SAYS THE MAN WHO GOT HERE USING TIME TRAVEL TECHNOLOGY CREATED WHEN I LOVE LUCY WAS THE BIGGEST THING ON TV.
YOU SHOULD BE CLOSE TO THE TARGET, BY THE WAY. OH, AND LOOK OUT FOR ANY SURVIVORS FROM THE FIRST TEAM WE SENT IN.
THE FBI GUYS WEARING THOSE NEAT JACKETS AND STUFF?

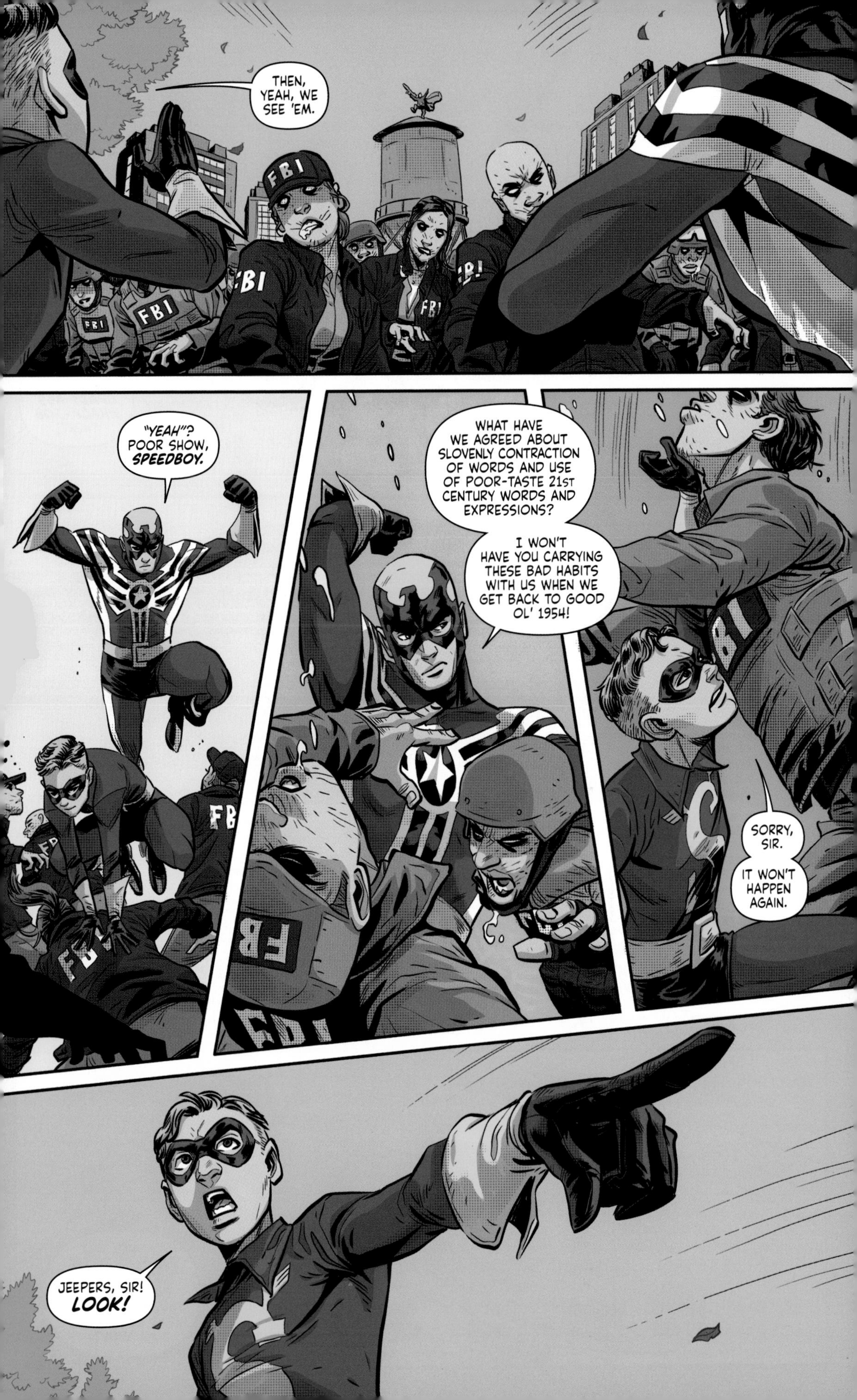
THEN, YEAH, WE SEE 'EM.
FBI
"YEAH"? POOR SHOW, SPEEDBOY.
WHAT HAVE WE AGREED ABOUT SLOVENLY CONTRACTION OF WORDS AND USE OF POOR-TASTE 21ST CENTURY WORDS AND EXPRESSIONS?
I WON'T HAVE YOU CARRYING THESE BAD HABITS WITH US WHEN WE GET BACK TO GOOD OL' 1954!
SORRY, SIR.
IT WON'T HAPPEN AGAIN.
JEEPERS, SIR! LOOK!

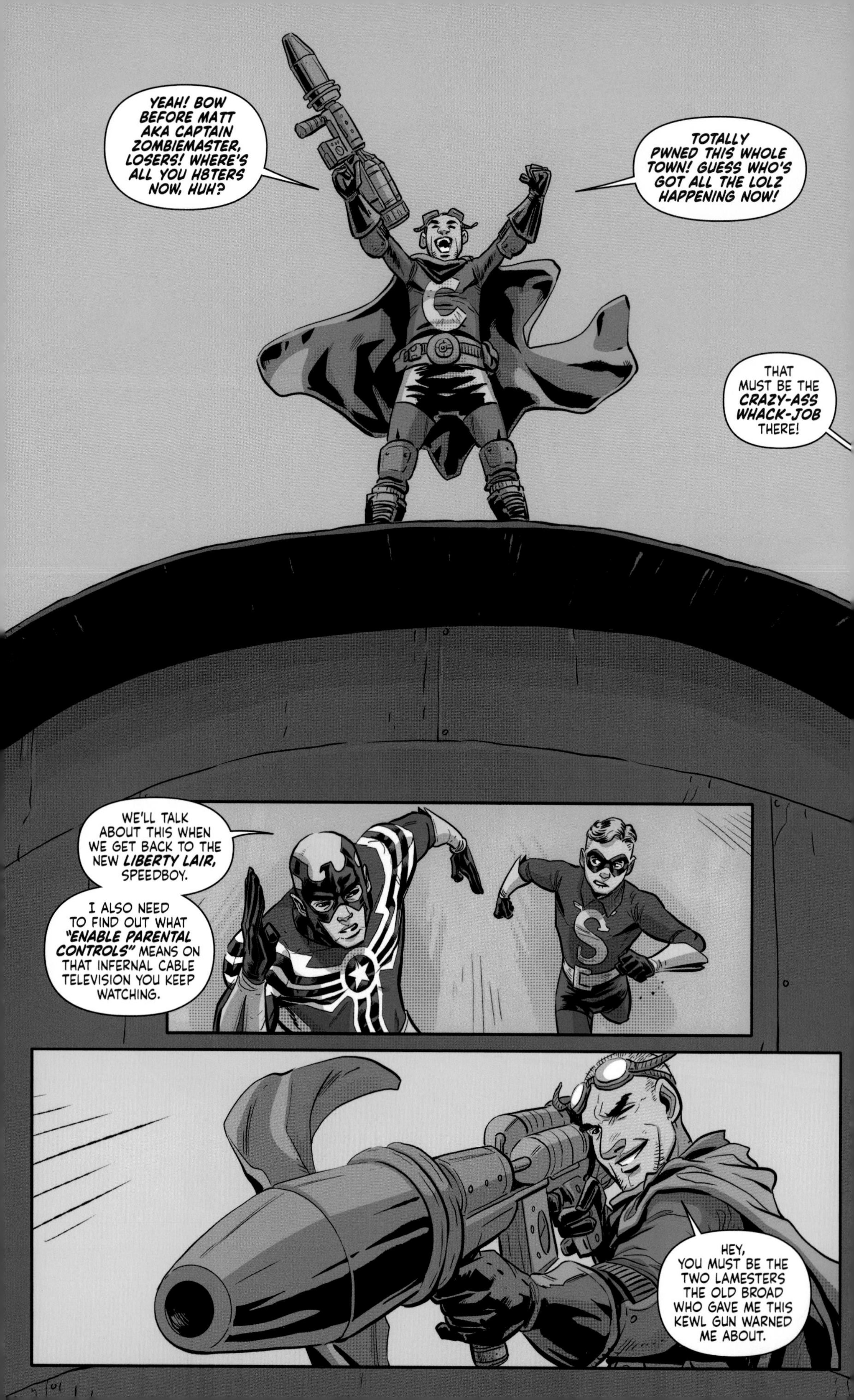
YEAH! BOW BEFORE MATT AKA CAPTAIN ZOMBIEMASTER, LOSERS! WHERE'S ALL YOU H8TERS NOW, HUH?
TOTALLY PWNED THIS WHOLE TOWN! GUESS WHO'S GOT ALL THE LOLZ HAPPENING NOW!
THAT MUST BE THE CRAZY-ASS WHACK-JOB THERE!
WE'LL TALK ABOUT THIS WHEN WE GET BACK TO THE NEW LIBERTY LAIR, SPEEDBOY.
I ALSO NEED TO FIND OUT WHAT "ENABLE PARENTAL CONTROLS" MEANS ON THAT INFERNAL CABLE TELEVISION YOU KEEP WATCHING.
HEY, YOU MUST BE THE TWO LAMESTERS THE OLD BROAD WHO GAVE ME THIS KEWL GUN WARNED ME ABOUT.

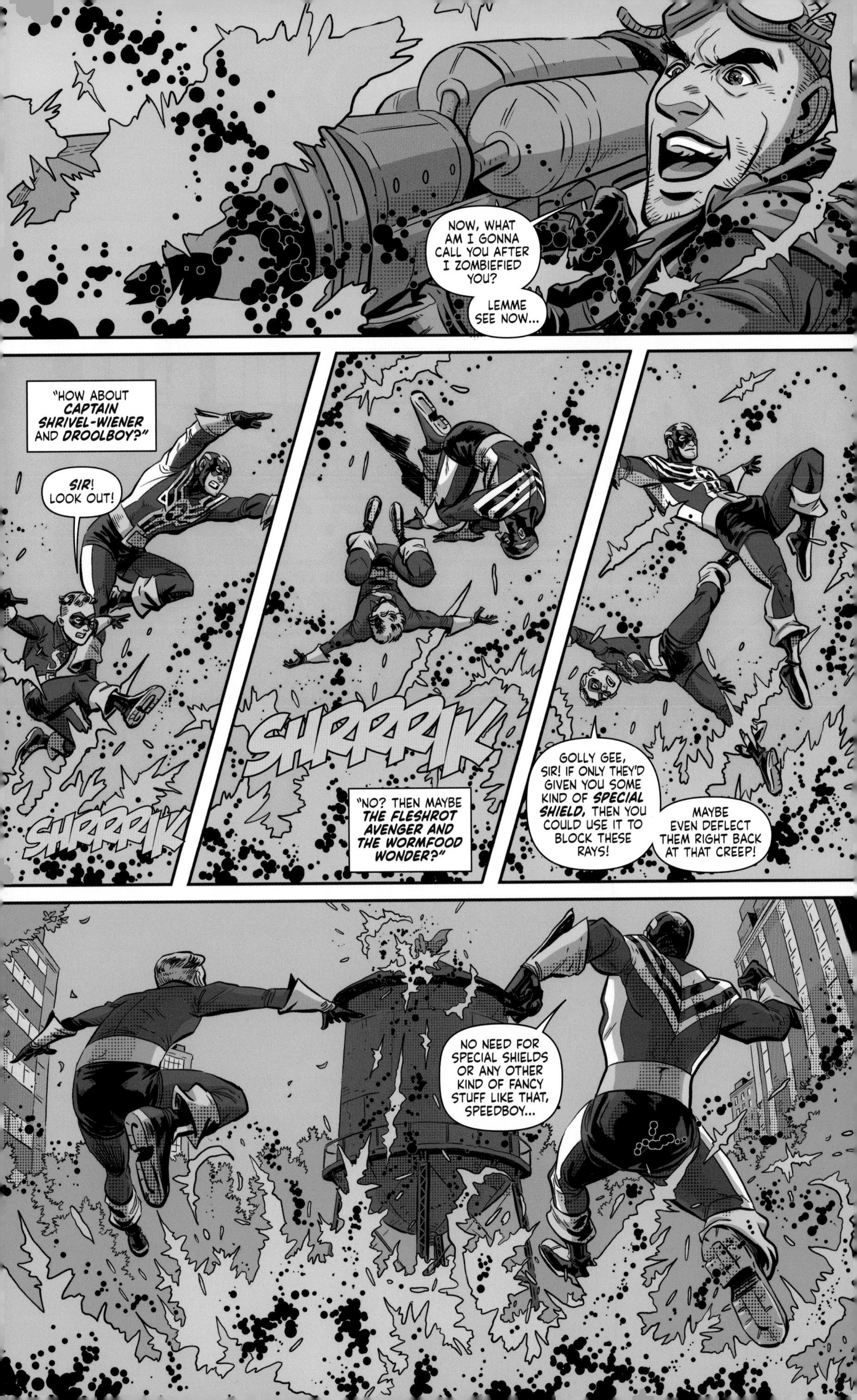

NOW, WHAT AM I GONNA CALL YOU AFTER I ZOMBIEFIED YOU?
LEMME SEE NOW...
"HOW ABOUT CAPTAIN SHRIVEL-WIENER AND DROOLBOY?"
SIR! LOOK OUT!
SHRRRIK
SHRRRIK
"NO? THEN MAYBE THE FLESHROT AVENGER AND THE WORMFOOD WONDER?"
GOLLY GEE, SIR! IF ONLY THEY'D GIVEN YOU SOME KIND OF SPECIAL SHIELD, THEN YOU COULD USE IT TO BLOCK THESE RAYS!
MAYBE EVEN DEFLECT THEM RIGHT BACK AT THAT CREEP!
NO NEED FOR SPECIAL SHIELDS OR ANY OTHER KIND OF FANCY STUFF LIKE THAT, SPEEDBOY...

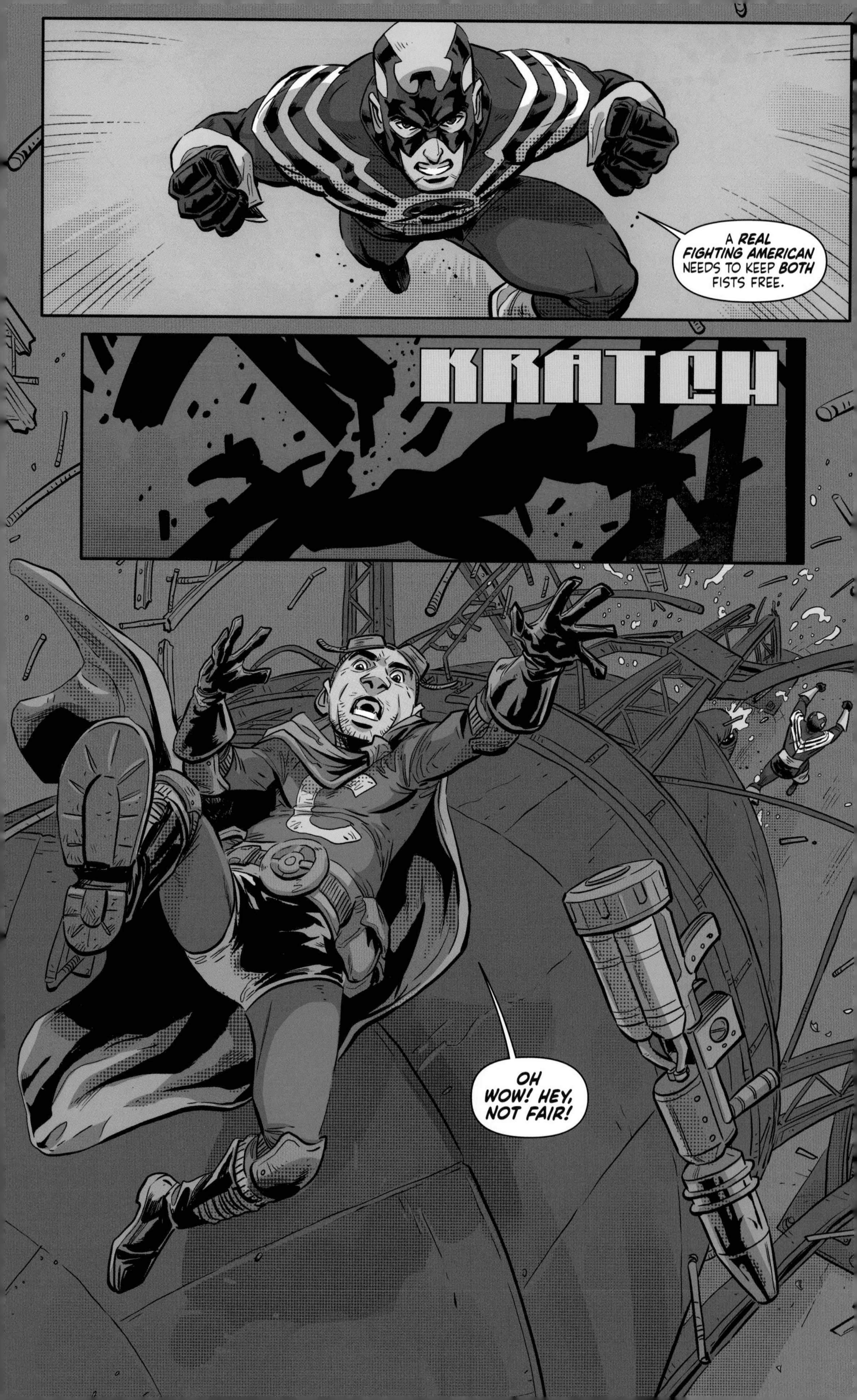
A REAL FIGHTING AMERICAN NEEDS TO KEEP BOTH FISTS FREE.
KRATCH
OH WOW! HEY, NOT FAIR!

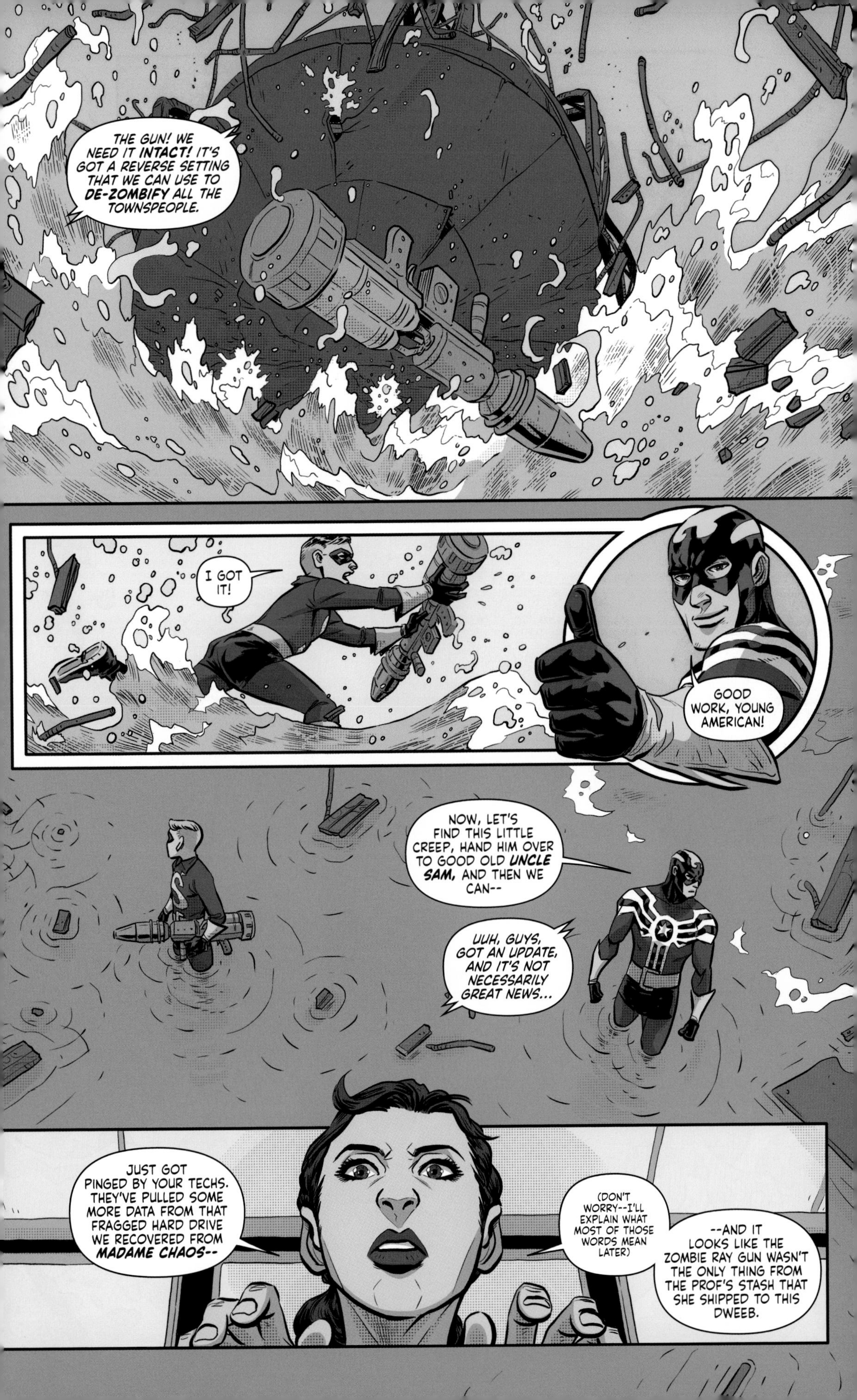
THE GUN! WE NEED IT INTACT! IT'S GOT A REVERSE SETTING THAT WE CAN USE TO DE-ZOMBIFY ALL THE TOWNSPEOPLE.
I GOT IT!
GOOD WORK, YOUNG AMERICAN!
NOW, LET'S FIND THIS LITTLE CREEP, HAND HIM OVER TO GOOD OLD UNCLE SAM, AND THEN WE CAN--
UUH, GUYS, GOT AN UPDATE, AND IT'S NOT NECESSARILY GREAT NEWS...
JUST GOT PINGED BY YOUR TECHS. THEY'VE PULLED SOME MORE DATA FROM THAT FRAGGED HARD DRIVE WE RECOVERED FROM MADAME CHAOS--
(DON'T WORRY--I'LL EXPLAIN WHAT MOST OF THOSE WORDS MEAN LATER)
--AND IT LOOKS LIKE THE ZOMBIE RAY GUN WASN'T THE ONLY THING FROM THE PROF'S STASH THAT SHE SHIPPED TO THIS DWEEB.

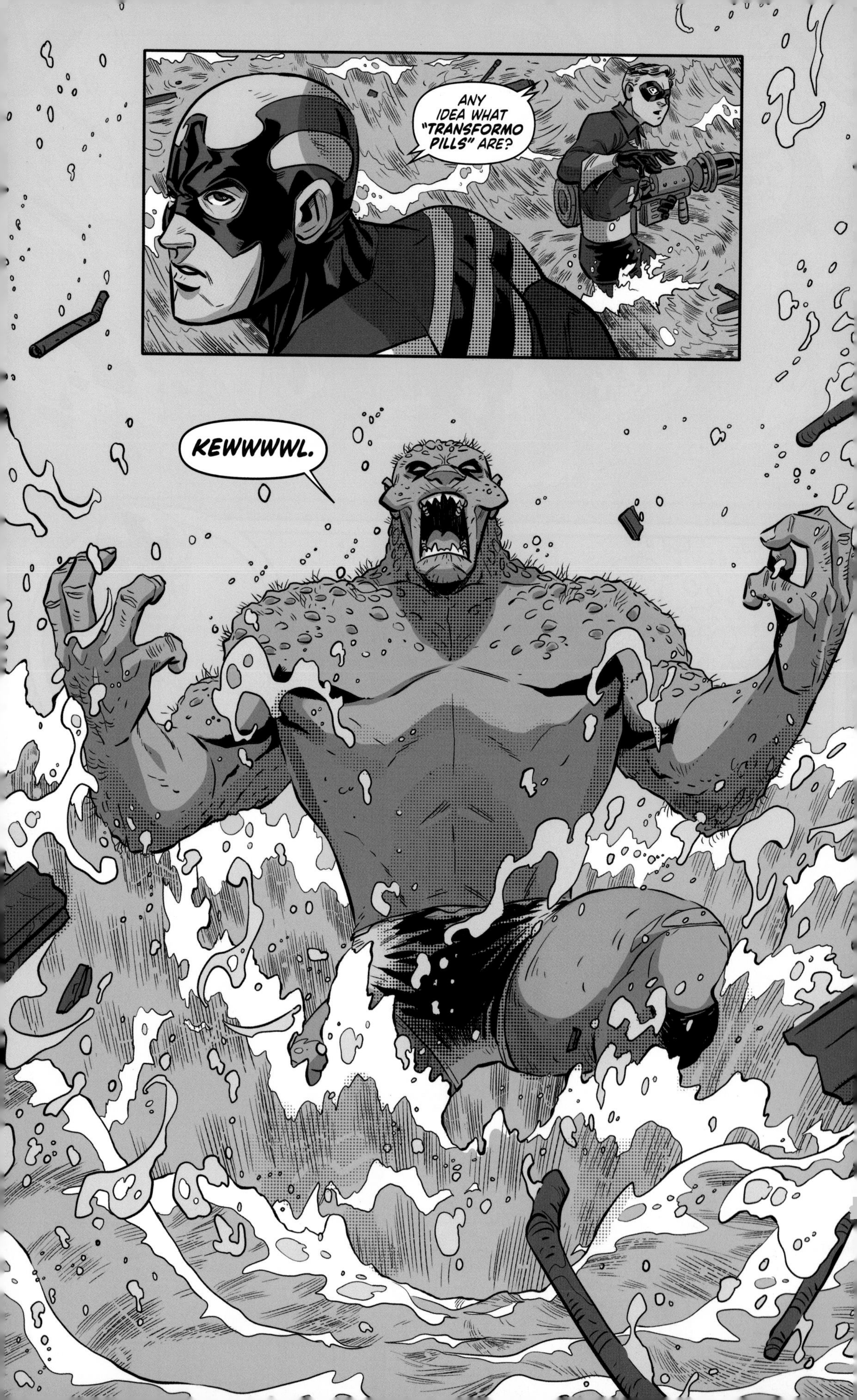
ANY IDEA WHAT "TRANSFORMO PILLS" ARE?
KEWWWWL.

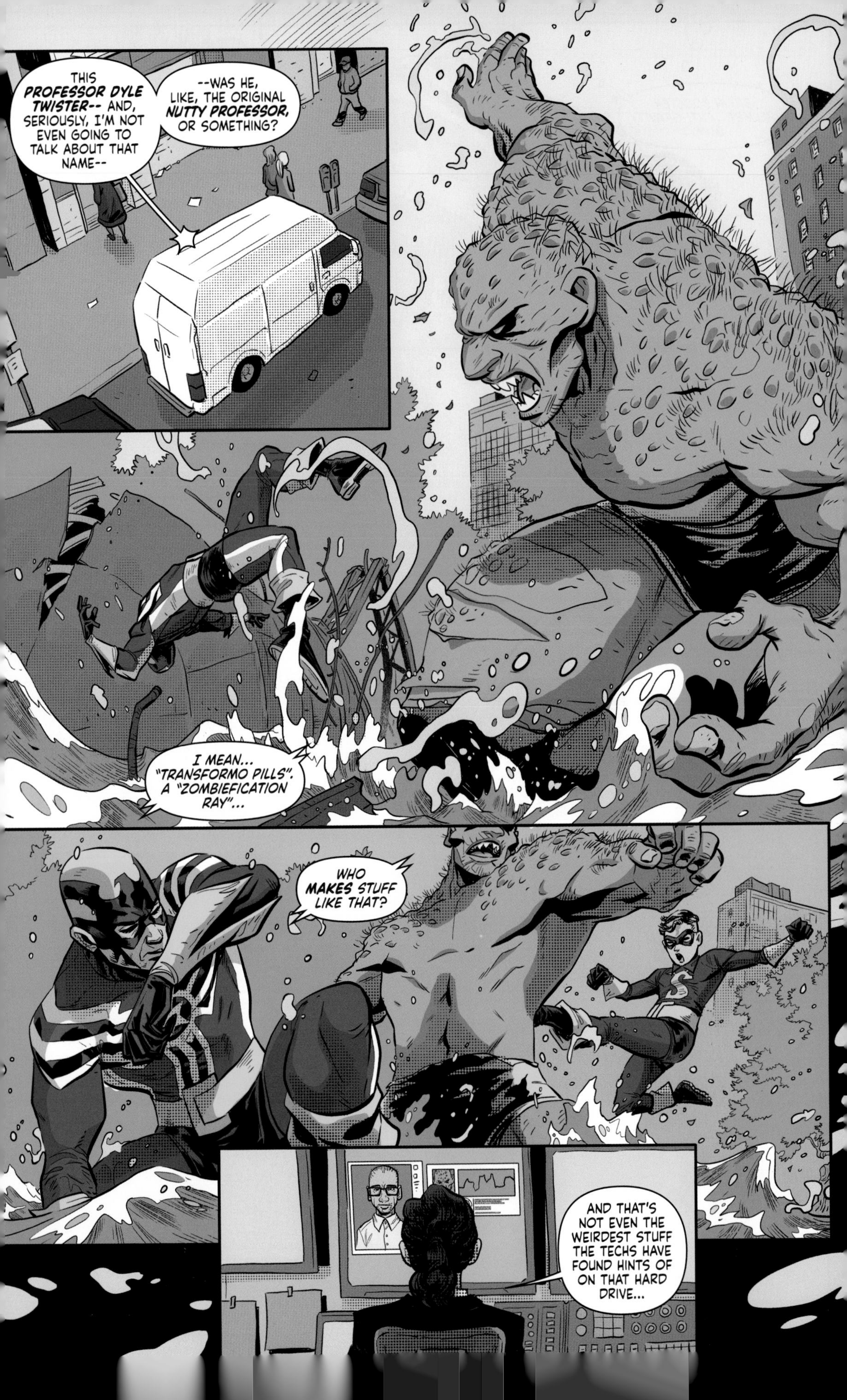
THIS PROFESSOR DYLE TWISTER-- AND, SERIOUSLY, I'M NOT EVEN GOING TO TALK ABOUT THAT NAME--
--WAS HE, LIKE, THE ORIGINAL NUTTY PROFESSOR, OR SOMETHING?
I MEAN... "TRANSFORMO PILLS". A "ZOMBIEFICATION RAY"...
WHO MAKES STUFF LIKE THAT?
AND THAT'S NOT EVEN THE WEIRDEST STUFF THE TECHS HAVE FOUND HINTS OF ON THAT HARD DRIVE...

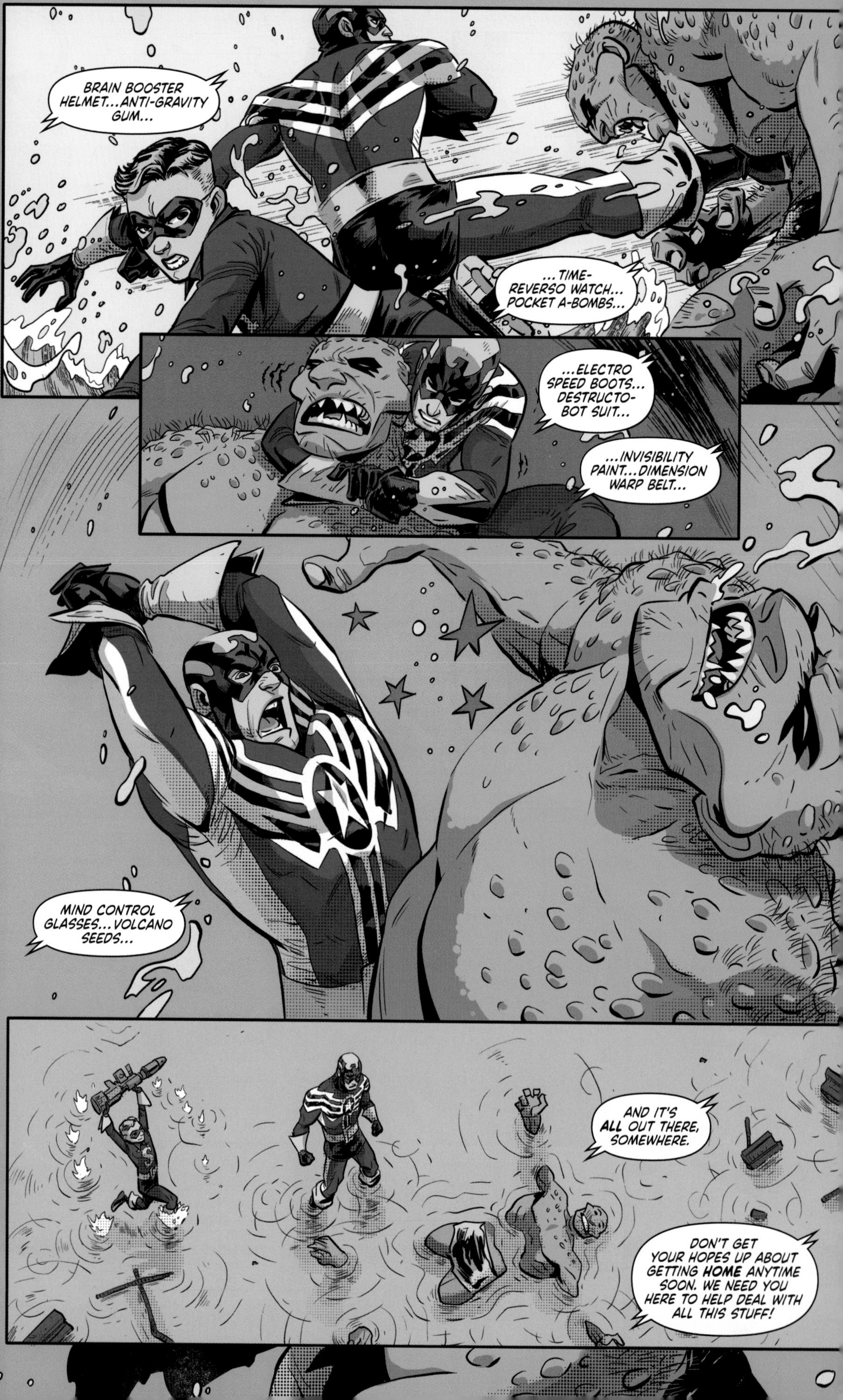
BRAIN BOOSTER HELMET...ANTI-GRAVITY GUM...
...TIME-REVERSO WATCH... POCKET A-BOMBS...
...ELECTRO SPEED BOOTS... DESTRUCTO-BOT SUIT...
...INVISIBILITY PAINT...DIMENSION WARP BELT...
MIND CONTROL GLASSES...VOLCANO SEEDS...
AND IT'S **ALL** OUT THERE, SOMEWHERE.
DON'T GET YOUR HOPES UP ABOUT GETTING **HOME** ANYTIME SOON. WE NEED YOU HERE TO HELP DEAL WITH ALL THIS STUFF!

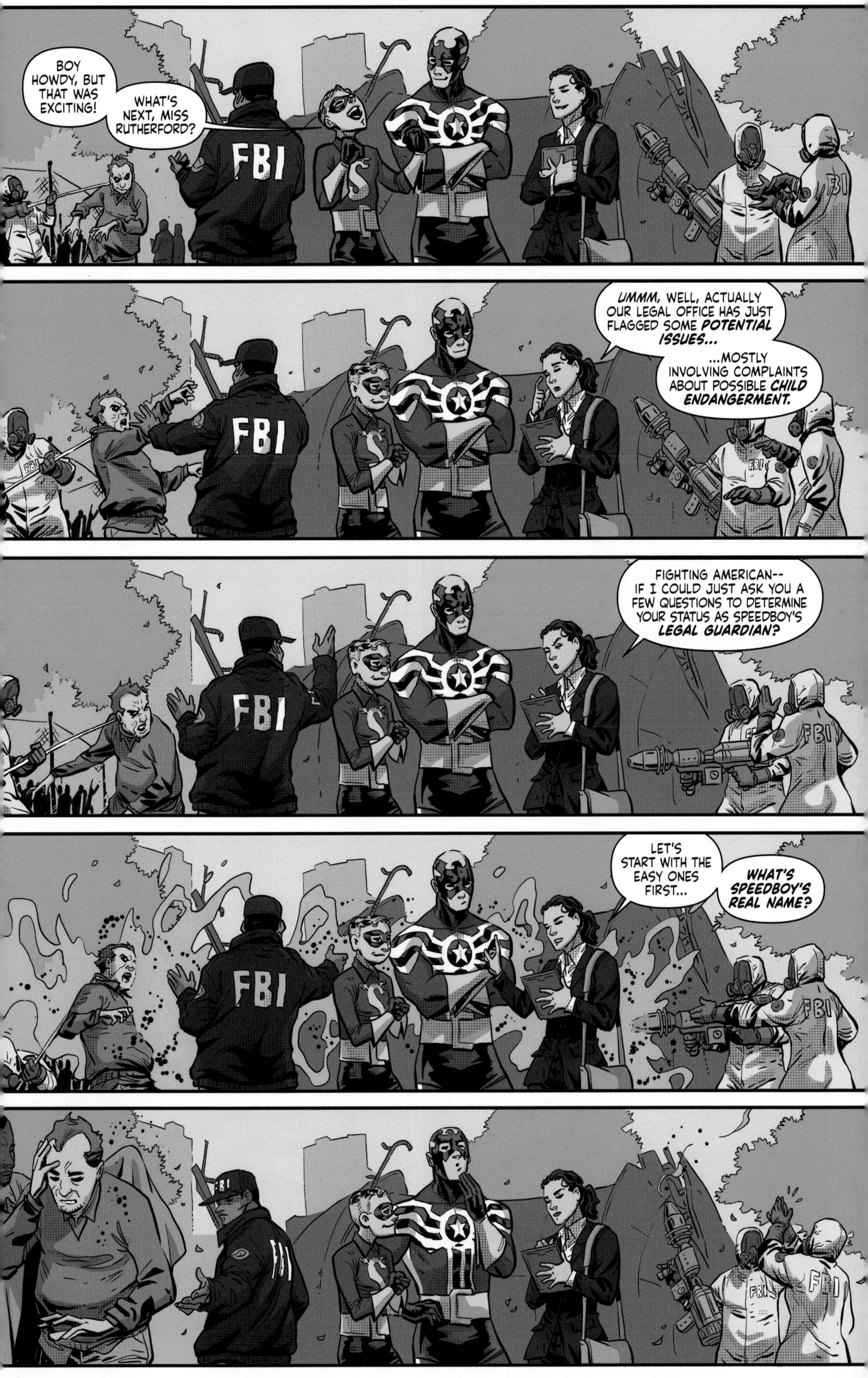
BOY HOWDY, BUT THAT WAS EXCITING!
WHAT'S NEXT, MISS RUTHERFORD?
FBI
UMMM, WELL, ACTUALLY OUR LEGAL OFFICE HAS JUST FLAGGED SOME POTENTIAL ISSUES...
...MOSTLY INVOLVING COMPLAINTS ABOUT POSSIBLE CHILD ENDANGERMENT.
FBI
FIGHTING AMERICAN-- IF I COULD JUST ASK YOU A FEW QUESTIONS TO DETERMINE YOUR STATUS AS SPEEDBOY'S LEGAL GUARDIAN?
FBI
LET'S START WITH THE EASY ONES FIRST...
WHAT'S SPEEDBOY'S REAL NAME?
FBI
FBI

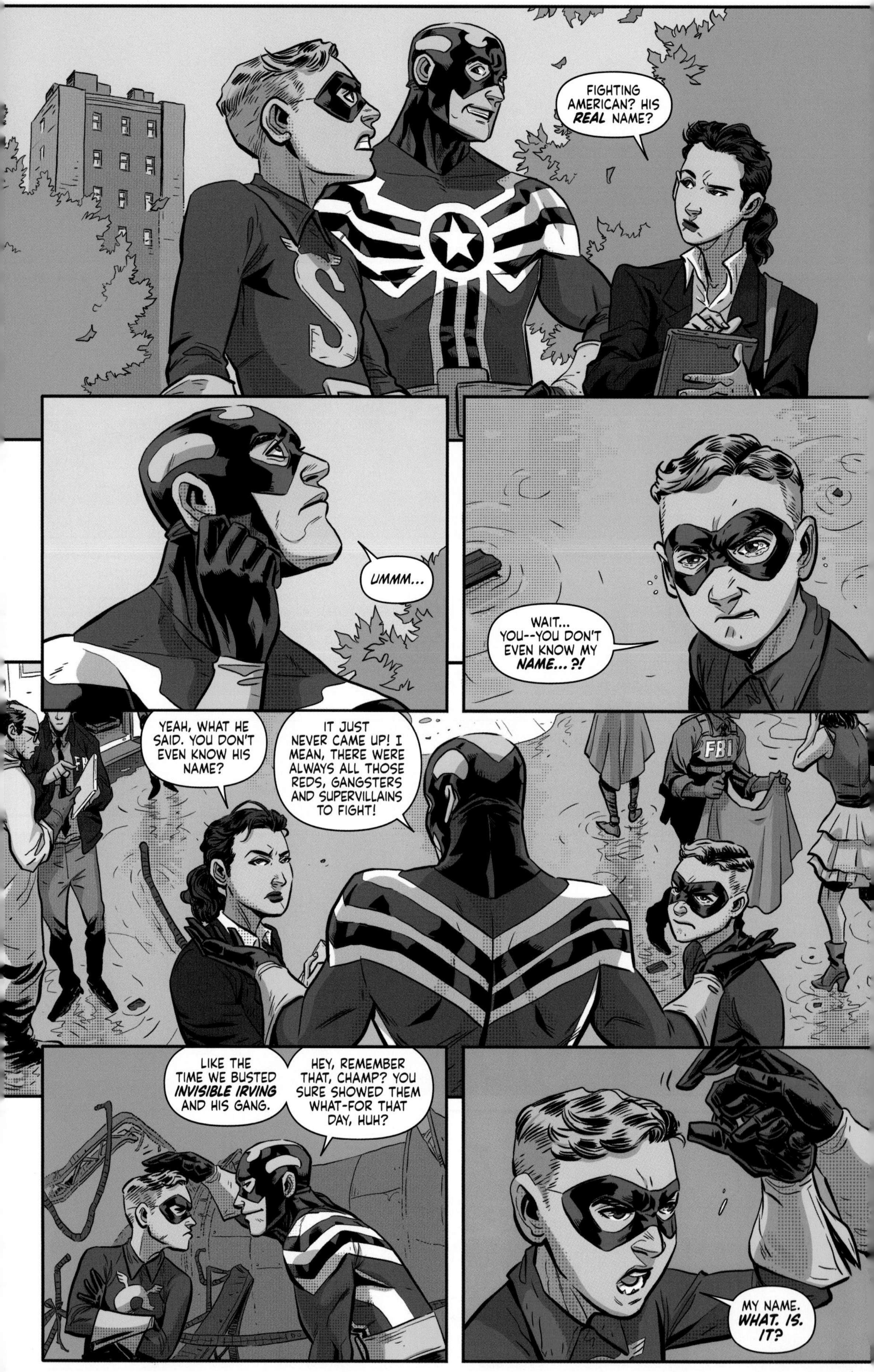
FIGHTING AMERICAN? HIS REAL NAME?
UMMM...
WAIT... YOU--YOU DON'T EVEN KNOW MY NAME...?!
YEAH, WHAT HE SAID. YOU DON'T EVEN KNOW HIS NAME?
IT JUST NEVER CAME UP! I MEAN, THERE WERE ALWAYS ALL THOSE REDS, GANGSTERS AND SUPERVILLAINS TO FIGHT!
FBI
LIKE THE TIME WE BUSTED INVISIBLE IRVING AND HIS GANG.
HEY, REMEMBER THAT, CHAMP? YOU SURE SHOWED THEM WHAT-FOR THAT DAY, HUH?
MY NAME. WHAT. IS. IT?

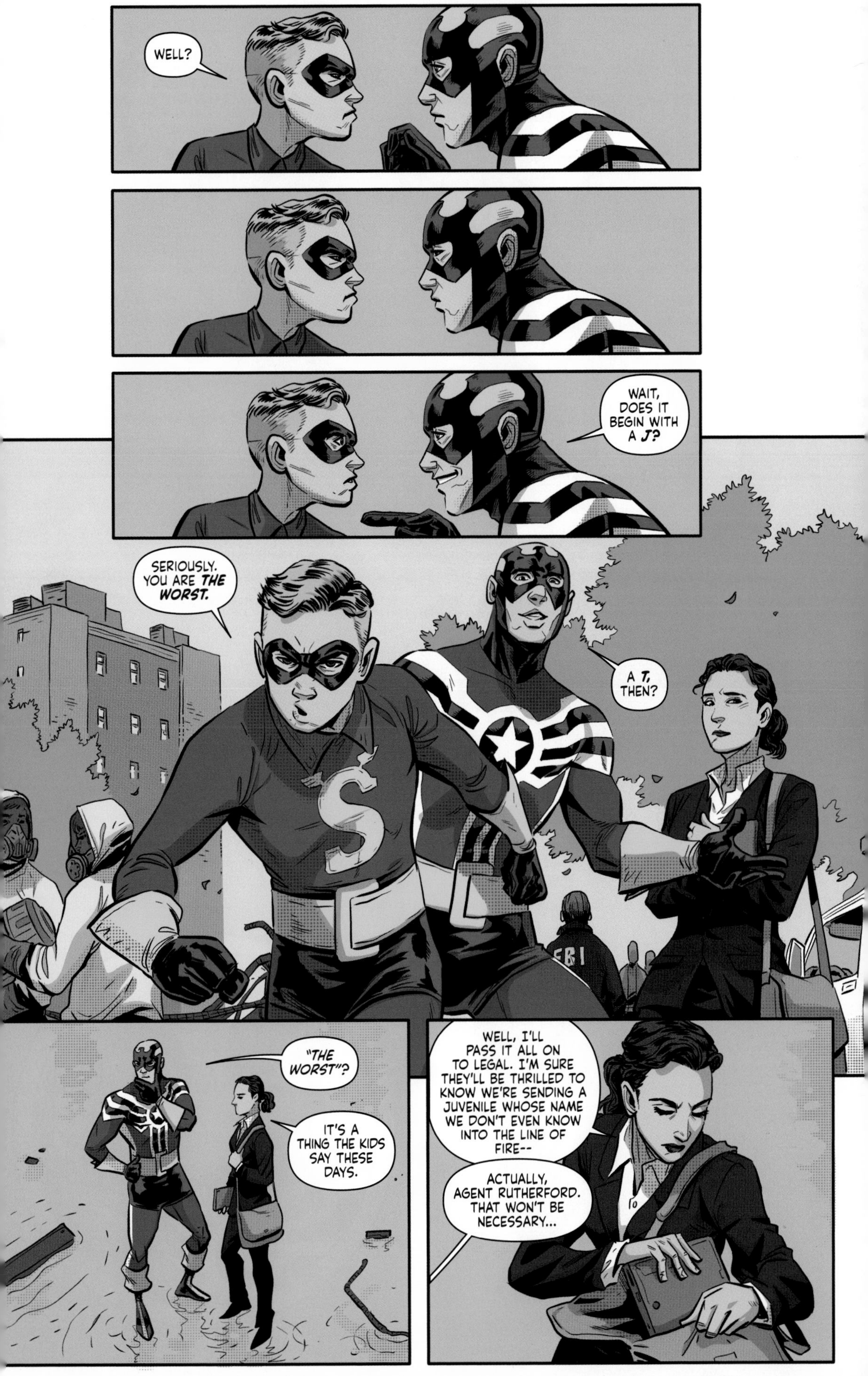
WELL?
WAIT, DOES IT BEGIN WITH A *J?*
SERIOUSLY. YOU ARE ***THE WORST.***
A *T,* THEN?
FBI
"THE WORST"?
IT'S A THING THE KIDS SAY THESE DAYS.
WELL, I'LL PASS IT ALL ON TO LEGAL. I'M SURE THEY'LL BE THRILLED TO KNOW WE'RE SENDING A JUVENILE WHOSE NAME WE DON'T EVEN KNOW INTO THE LINE OF FIRE--
ACTUALLY, AGENT RUTHERFORD. THAT WON'T BE NECESSARY...

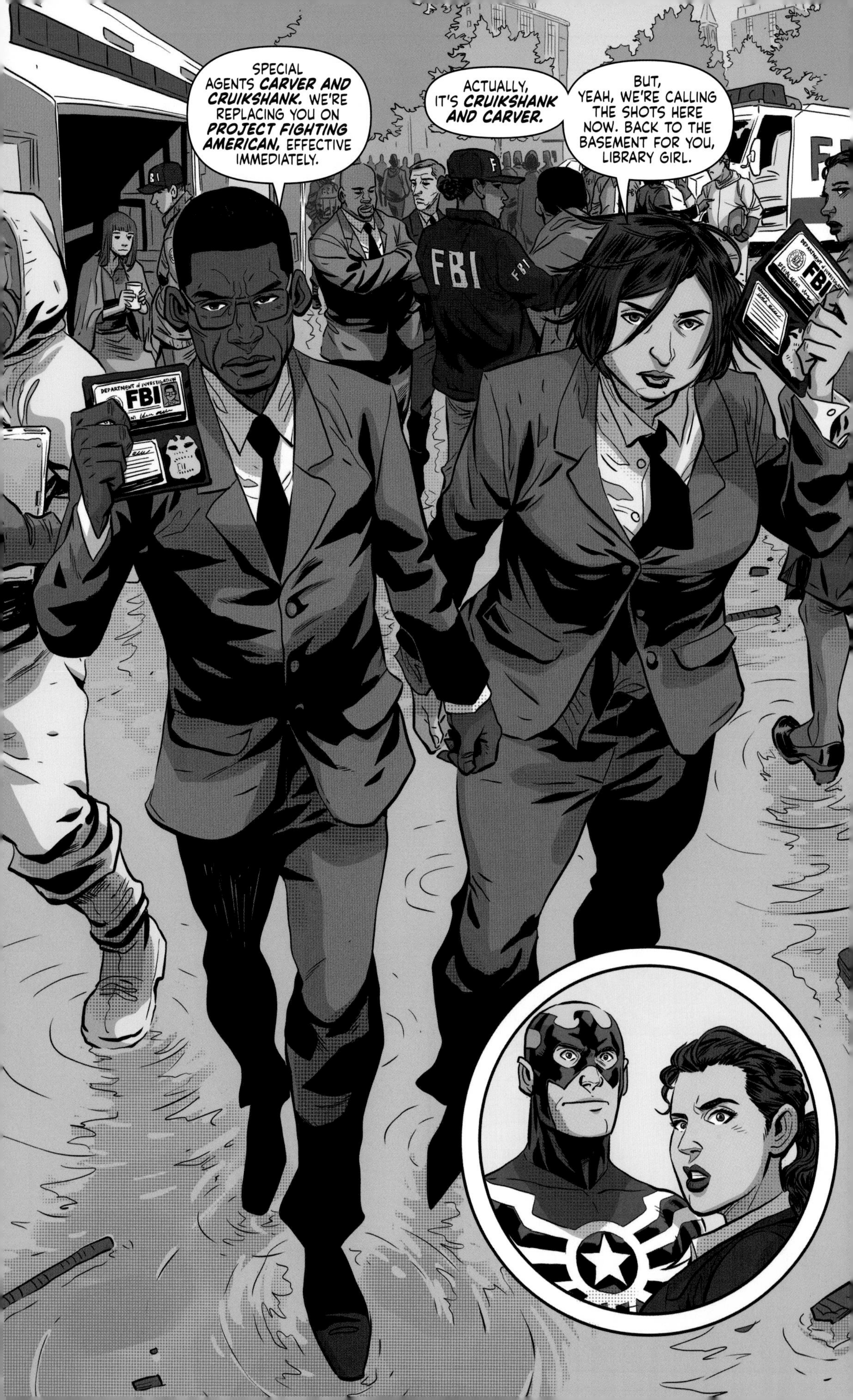
SPECIAL AGENTS CARVER AND CRUIKSHANK. WE'RE REPLACING YOU ON PROJECT FIGHTING AMERICAN, EFFECTIVE IMMEDIATELY.
ACTUALLY, IT'S CRUIKSHANK AND CARVER.
BUT, YEAH, WE'RE CALLING THE SHOTS HERE NOW. BACK TO THE BASEMENT FOR YOU, LIBRARY GIRL.
FBI

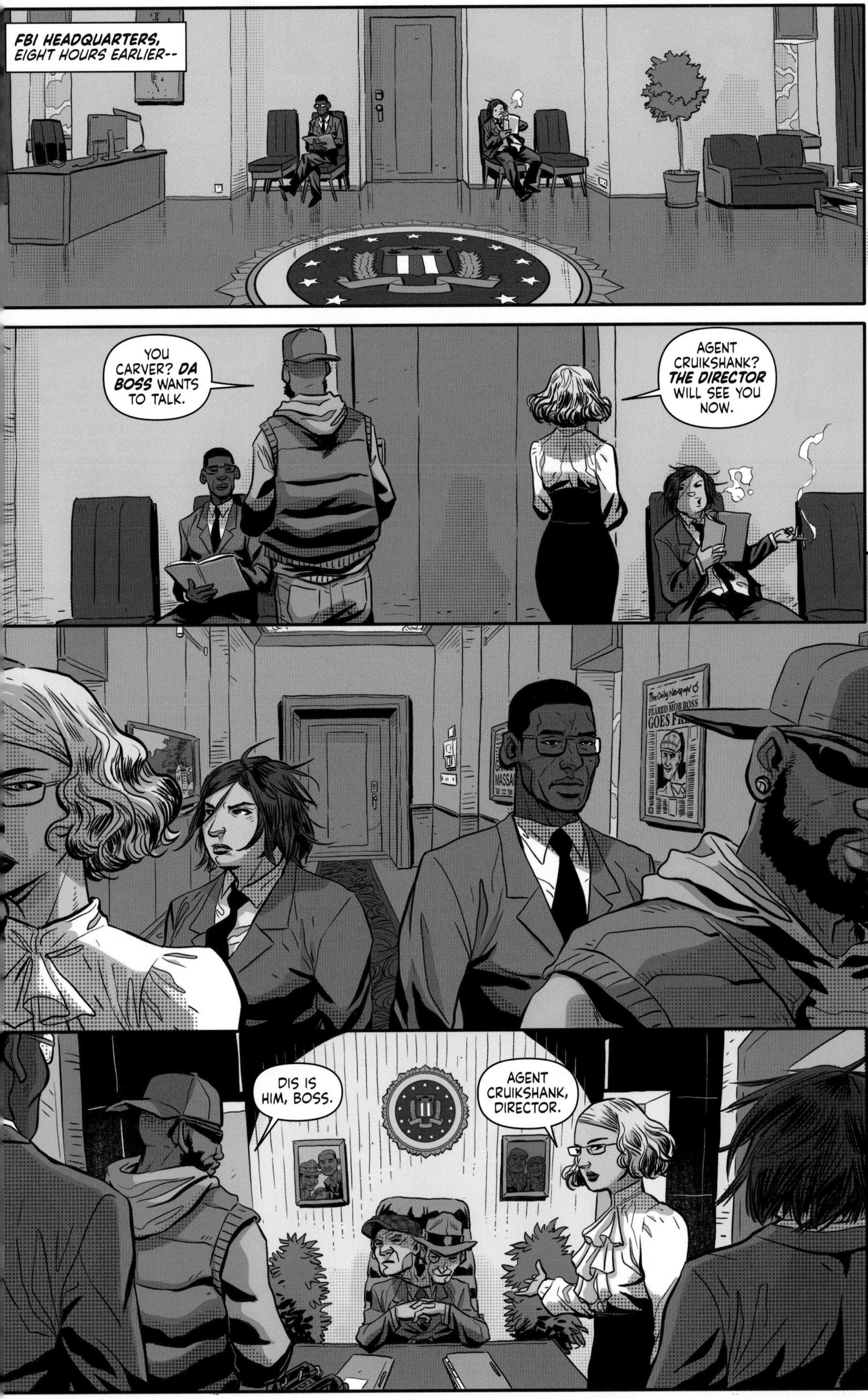
FBI HEADQUARTERS, EIGHT HOURS EARLIER--
YOU CARVER? DA BOSS WANTS TO TALK.
AGENT CRUIKSHANK? THE DIRECTOR WILL SEE YOU NOW.
The Daily Newspaper
FEARED MOB BOSS GOES FR
DIS IS HIM, BOSS.
AGENT CRUIKSHANK, DIRECTOR.

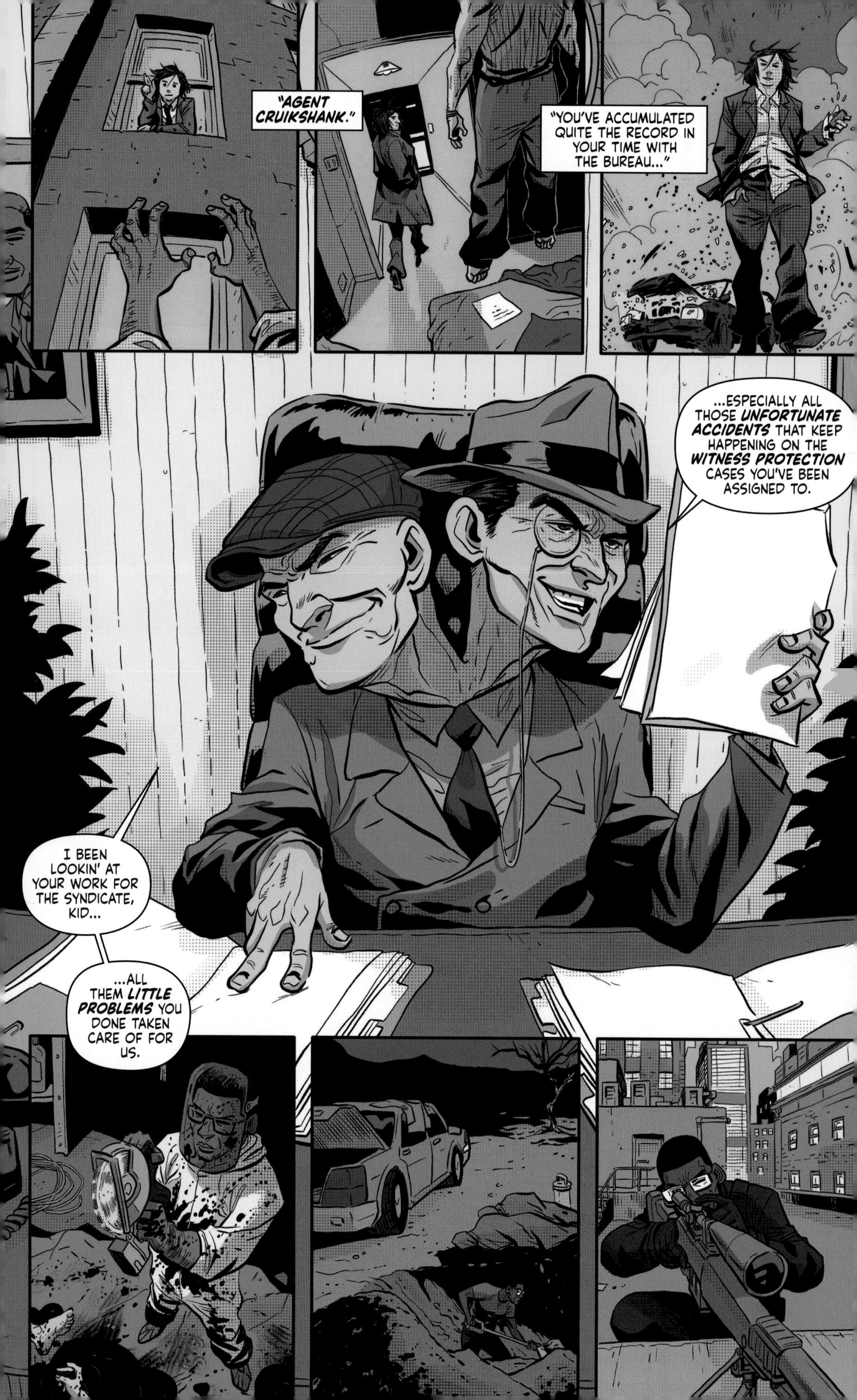
"AGENT CRUIKSHANK."
"YOU'VE ACCUMULATED QUITE THE RECORD IN YOUR TIME WITH THE BUREAU..."
...ESPECIALLY ALL THOSE UNFORTUNATE ACCIDENTS THAT KEEP HAPPENING ON THE WITNESS PROTECTION CASES YOU'VE BEEN ASSIGNED TO.
I BEEN LOOKIN' AT YOUR WORK FOR THE SYNDICATE, KID...
...ALL THEM LITTLE PROBLEMS YOU DONE TAKEN CARE OF FOR US.

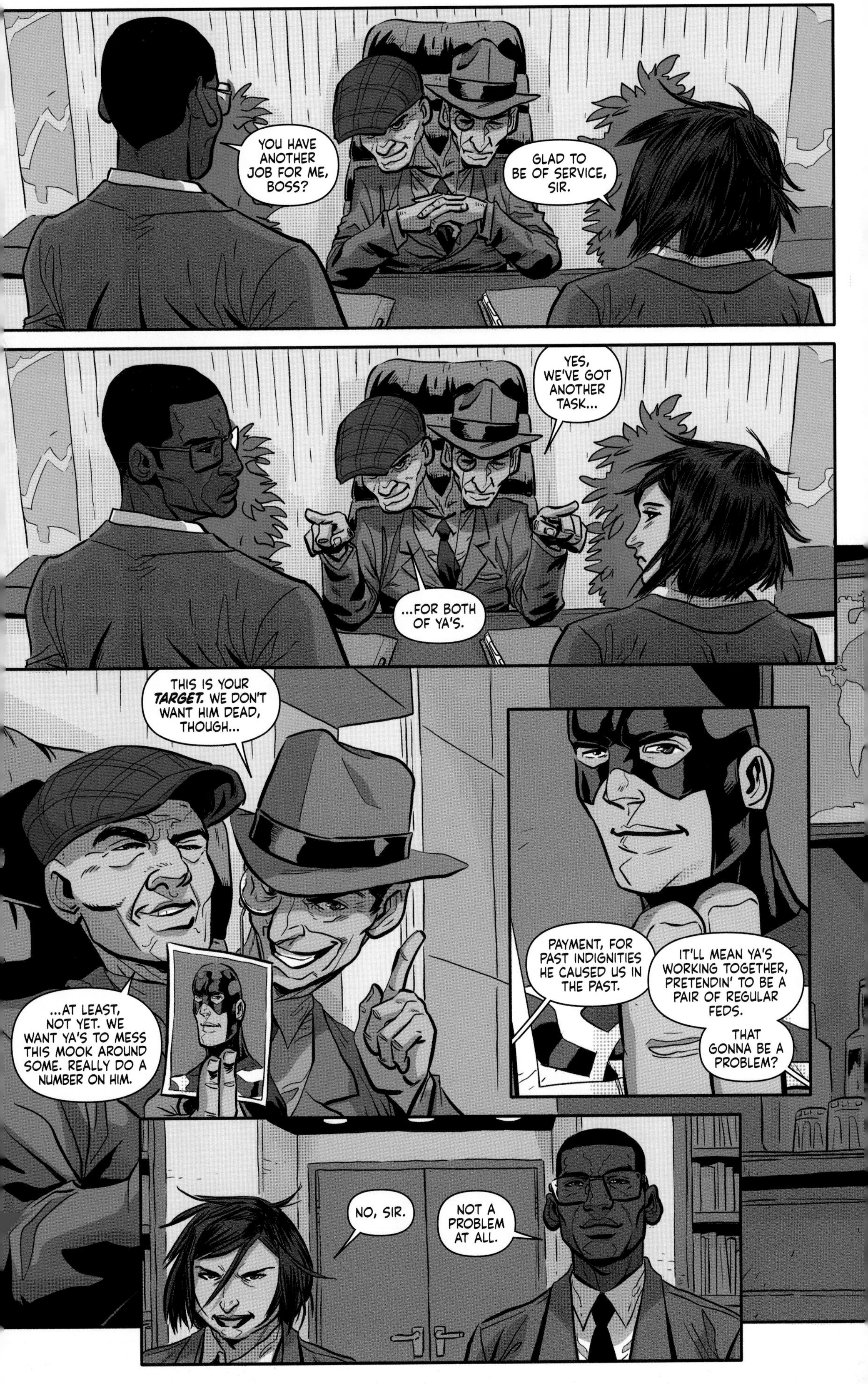
YOU HAVE ANOTHER JOB FOR ME, BOSS?
GLAD TO BE OF SERVICE, SIR.
YES, WE'VE GOT ANOTHER TASK...
...FOR BOTH OF YA'S.
THIS IS YOUR *TARGET.* WE DON'T WANT HIM DEAD, THOUGH...
...AT LEAST, NOT YET. WE WANT YA'S TO MESS THIS MOOK AROUND SOME. REALLY DO A NUMBER ON HIM.
PAYMENT, FOR PAST INDIGNITIES HE CAUSED US IN THE PAST.
IT'LL MEAN YA'S WORKING TOGETHER, PRETENDIN' TO BE A PAIR OF REGULAR FEDS.
THAT GONNA BE A PROBLEM?
NO, SIR.
NOT A PROBLEM AT ALL.

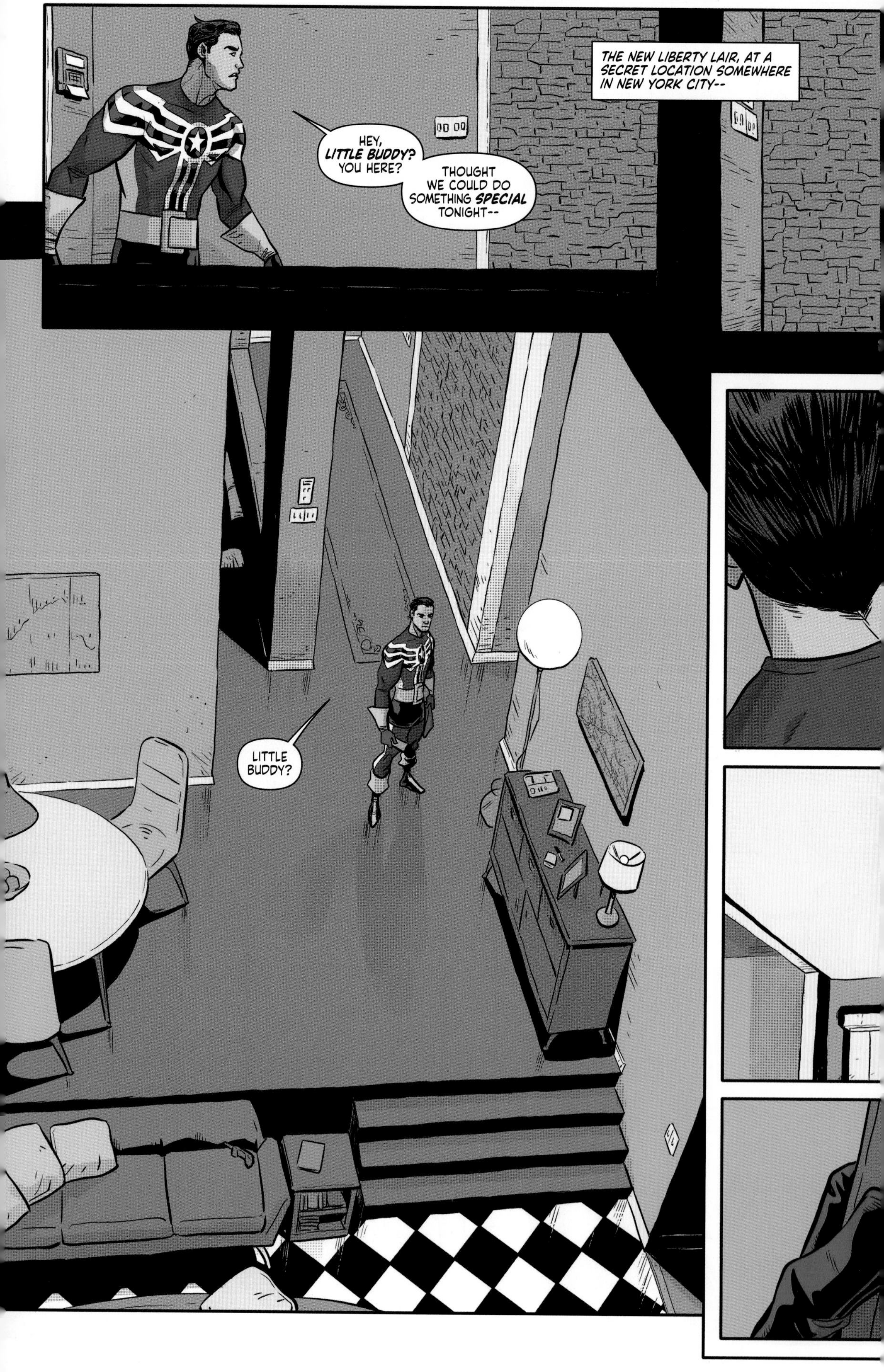
THE NEW LIBERTY LAIR, AT A SECRET LOCATION SOMEWHERE IN NEW YORK CITY--
HEY, LITTLE BUDDY? YOU HERE?
THOUGHT WE COULD DO SOMETHING SPECIAL TONIGHT--
LITTLE BUDDY?

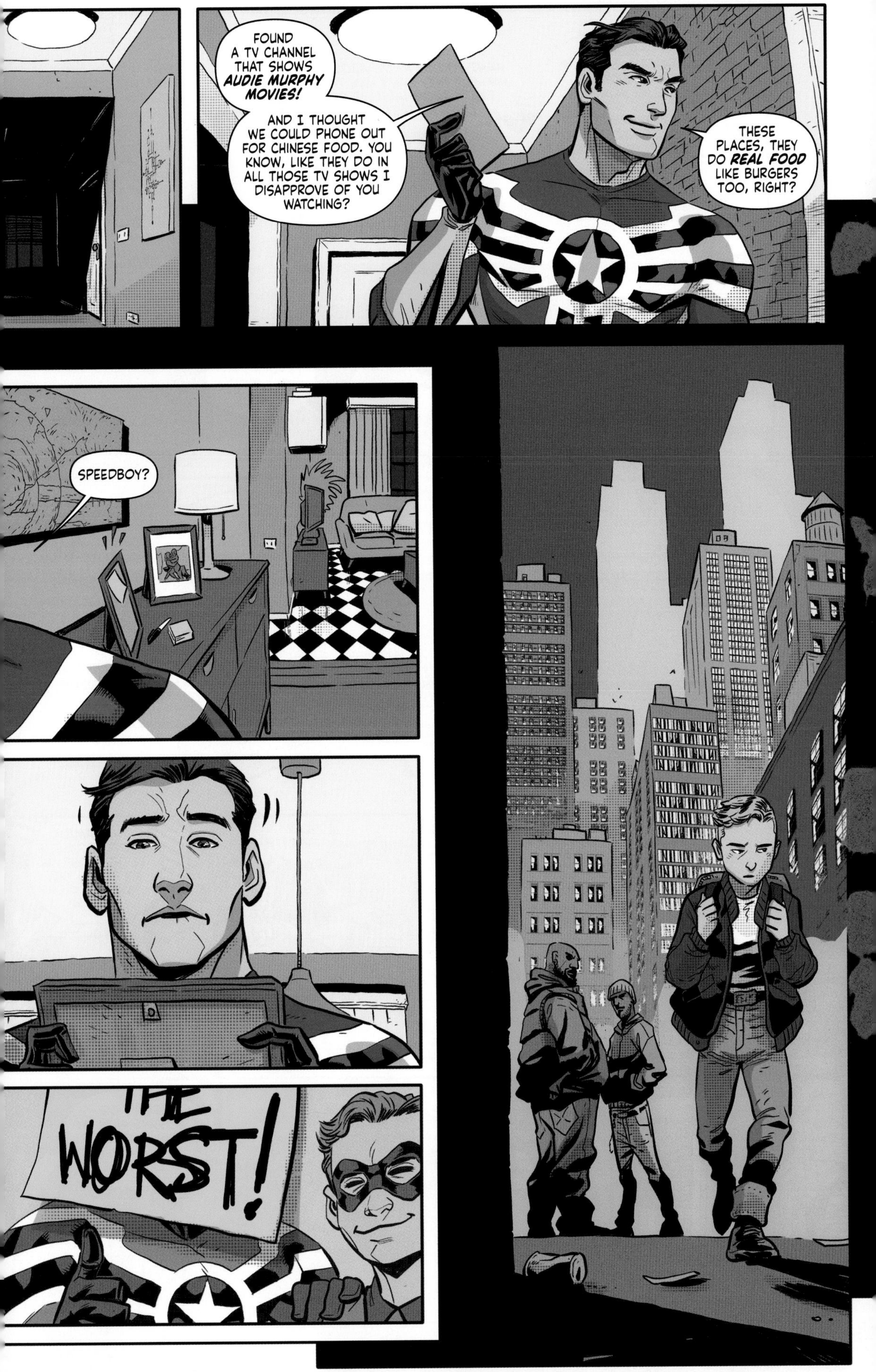

FOUND A TV CHANNEL THAT SHOWS ***AUDIE MURPHY MOVIES!***
AND I THOUGHT WE COULD PHONE OUT FOR CHINESE FOOD. YOU KNOW, LIKE THEY DO IN ALL THOSE TV SHOWS I DISAPPROVE OF YOU WATCHING?
THESE PLACES, THEY DO ***REAL FOOD*** LIKE BURGERS TOO, RIGHT?
SPEEDBOY?
THE WORST!

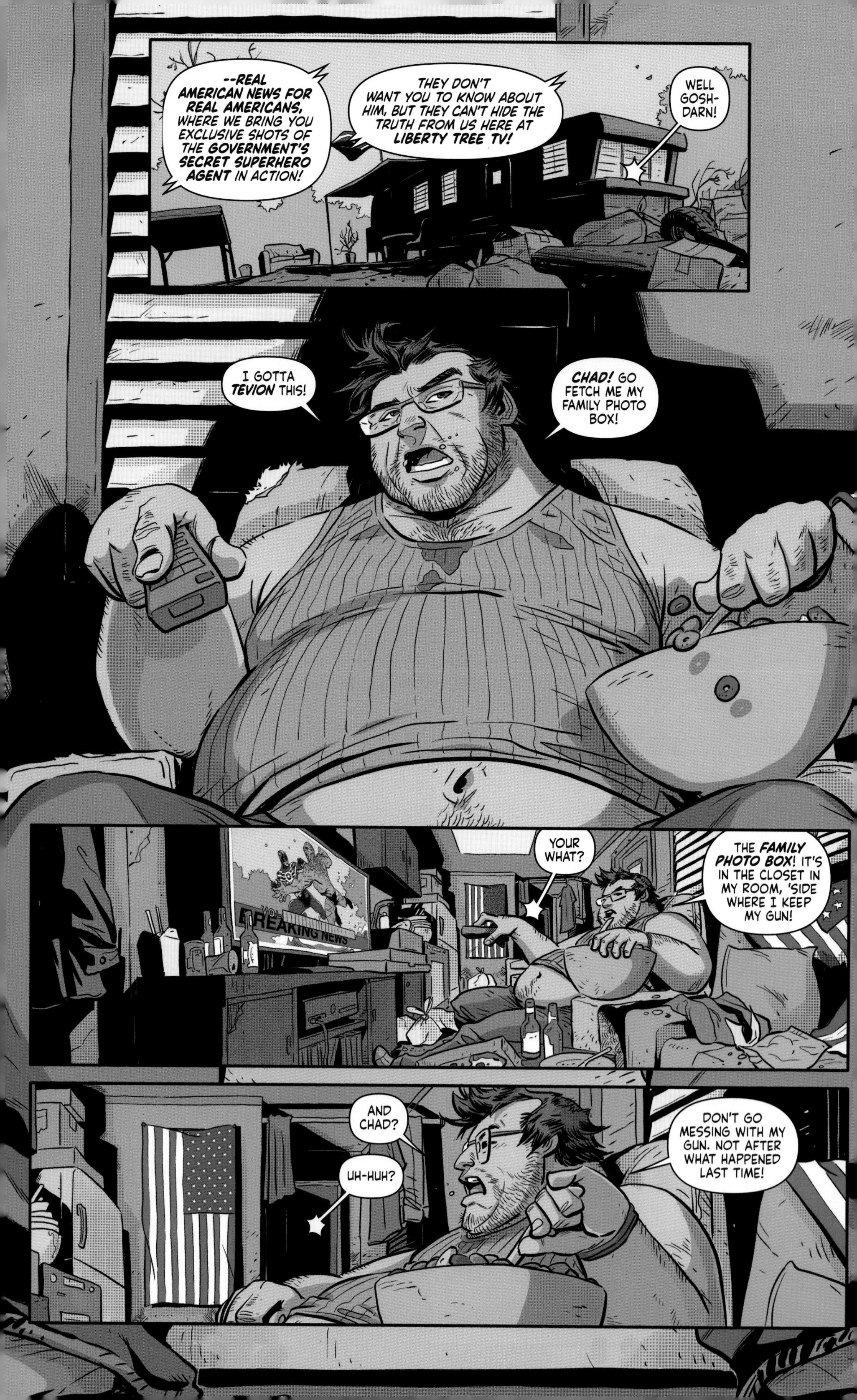
--REAL AMERICAN NEWS FOR REAL AMERICANS, WHERE WE BRING YOU EXCLUSIVE SHOTS OF THE GOVERNMENT'S SECRET SUPERHERO AGENT IN ACTION!
THEY DON'T WANT YOU TO KNOW ABOUT HIM, BUT THEY CAN'T HIDE THE TRUTH FROM US HERE AT LIBERTY TREE TV!
WELL GOSH-DARN!
I GOTTA TEVION THIS!
CHAD! GO FETCH ME MY FAMILY PHOTO BOX!
YOUR WHAT?
THE FAMILY PHOTO BOX! IT'S IN THE CLOSET IN MY ROOM, 'SIDE WHERE I KEEP MY GUN!
BREAKING NEWS
AND CHAD?
UH-HUH?
DON'T GO MESSING WITH MY GUN. NOT AFTER WHAT HAPPENED LAST TIME!

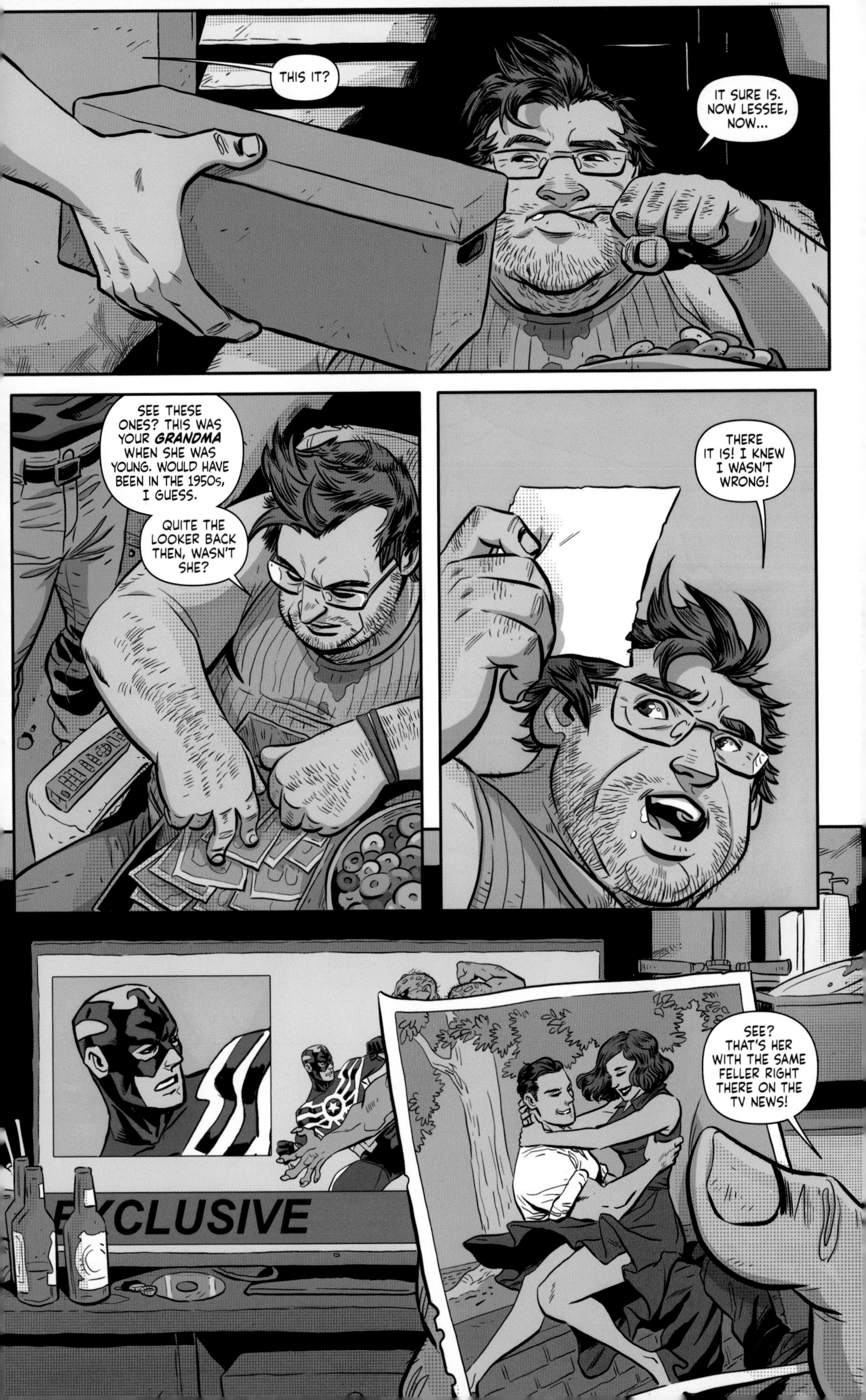
THIS IT?
IT SURE IS. NOW LESSEE, NOW...
SEE THESE ONES? THIS WAS YOUR GRANDMA WHEN SHE WAS YOUNG. WOULD HAVE BEEN IN THE 1950s, I GUESS.
QUITE THE LOOKER BACK THEN, WASN'T SHE?
THERE IT IS! I KNEW I WASN'T WRONG!
EXCLUSIVE
SEE? THAT'S HER WITH THE SAME FELLER RIGHT THERE ON THE TV NEWS!

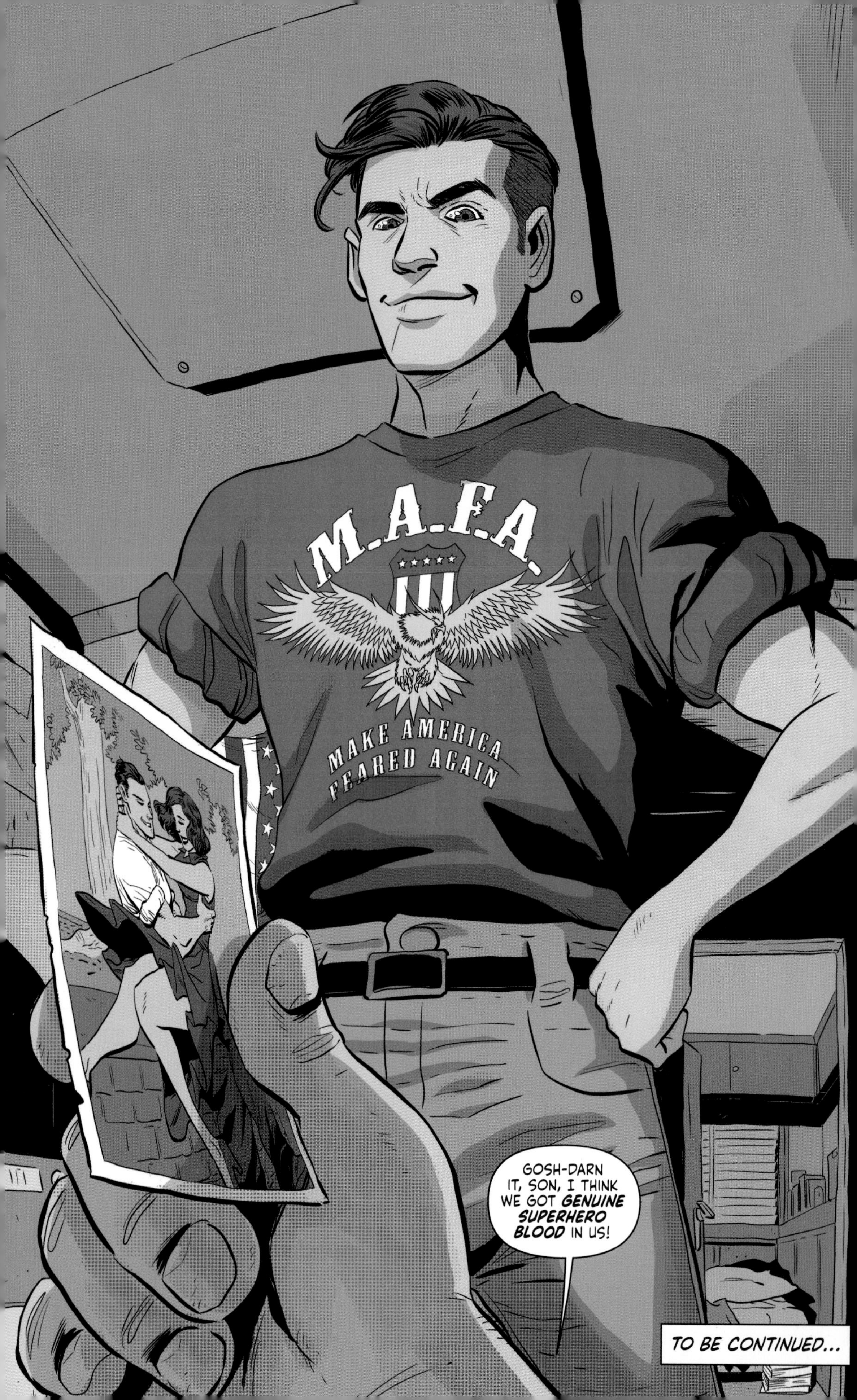
M.A.F.A.
MAKE AMERICA FEARED AGAIN
GOSH-DARN IT, SON, I THINK WE GOT GENUINE SUPERHERO BLOOD IN US!
TO BE CONTINUED...

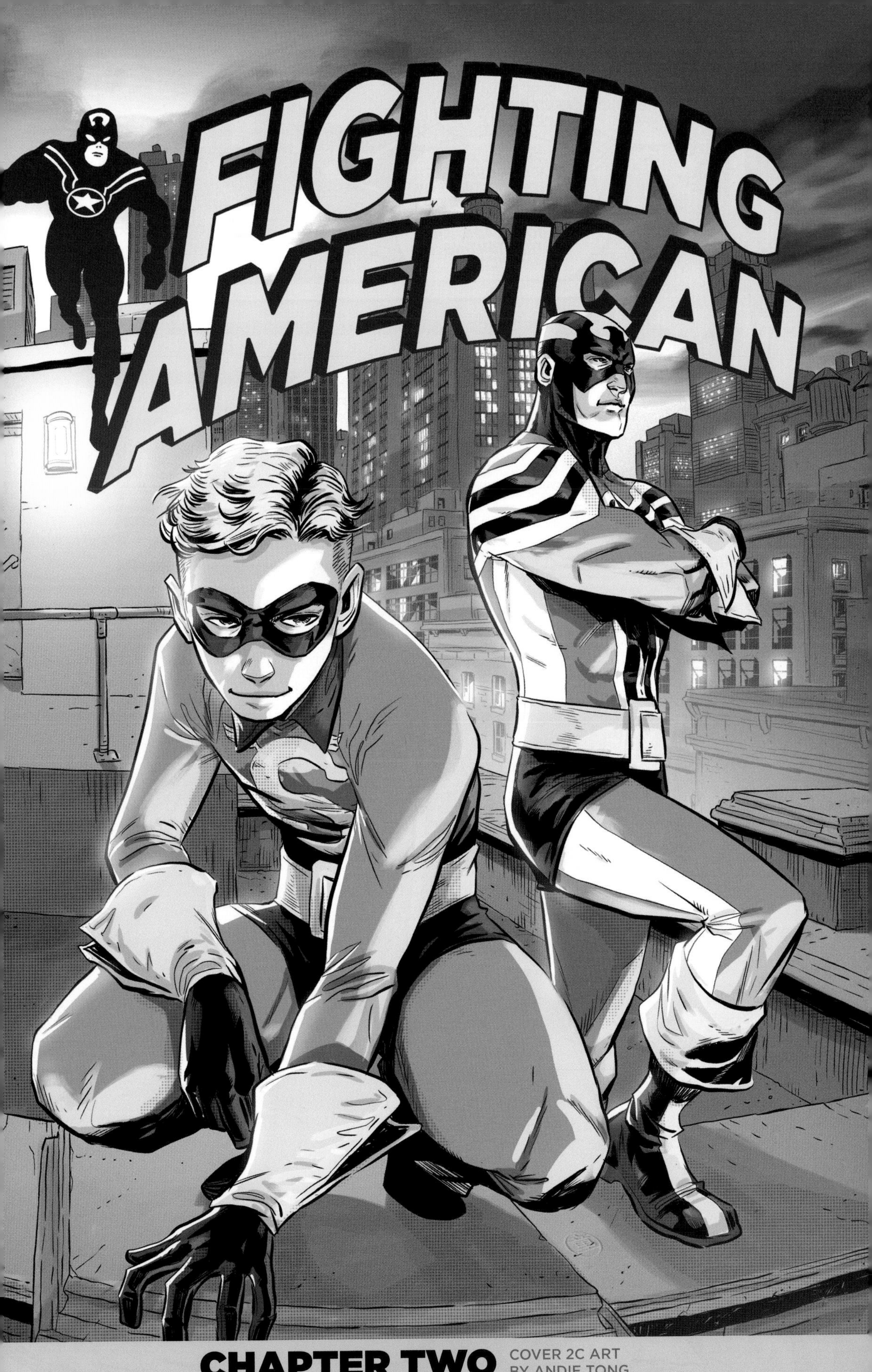
FIGHTING
AMERICAN

CHAPTER TWO

COVER 2C ART
BY ANDIE TONG

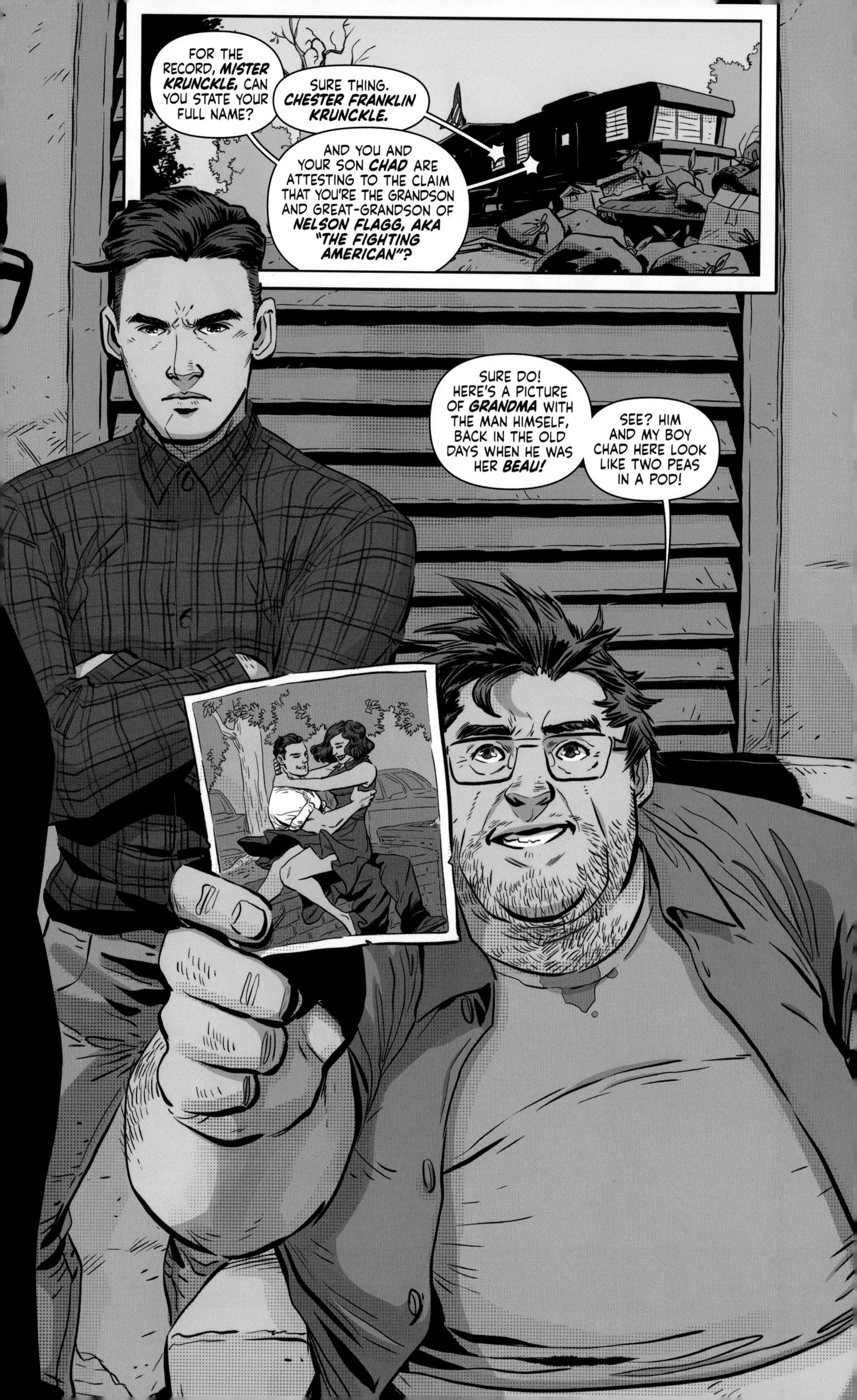
FOR THE RECORD, MISTER KRUNCKLE, CAN YOU STATE YOUR FULL NAME?
SURE THING. CHESTER FRANKLIN KRUNCKLE.
AND YOU AND YOUR SON CHAD ARE ATTESTING TO THE CLAIM THAT YOU'RE THE GRANDSON AND GREAT-GRANDSON OF NELSON FLAGG, AKA "THE FIGHTING AMERICAN"?
SURE DO! HERE'S A PICTURE OF GRANDMA WITH THE MAN HIMSELF, BACK IN THE OLD DAYS WHEN HE WAS HER BEAU!
SEE? HIM AND MY BOY CHAD HERE LOOK LIKE TWO PEAS IN A POD!

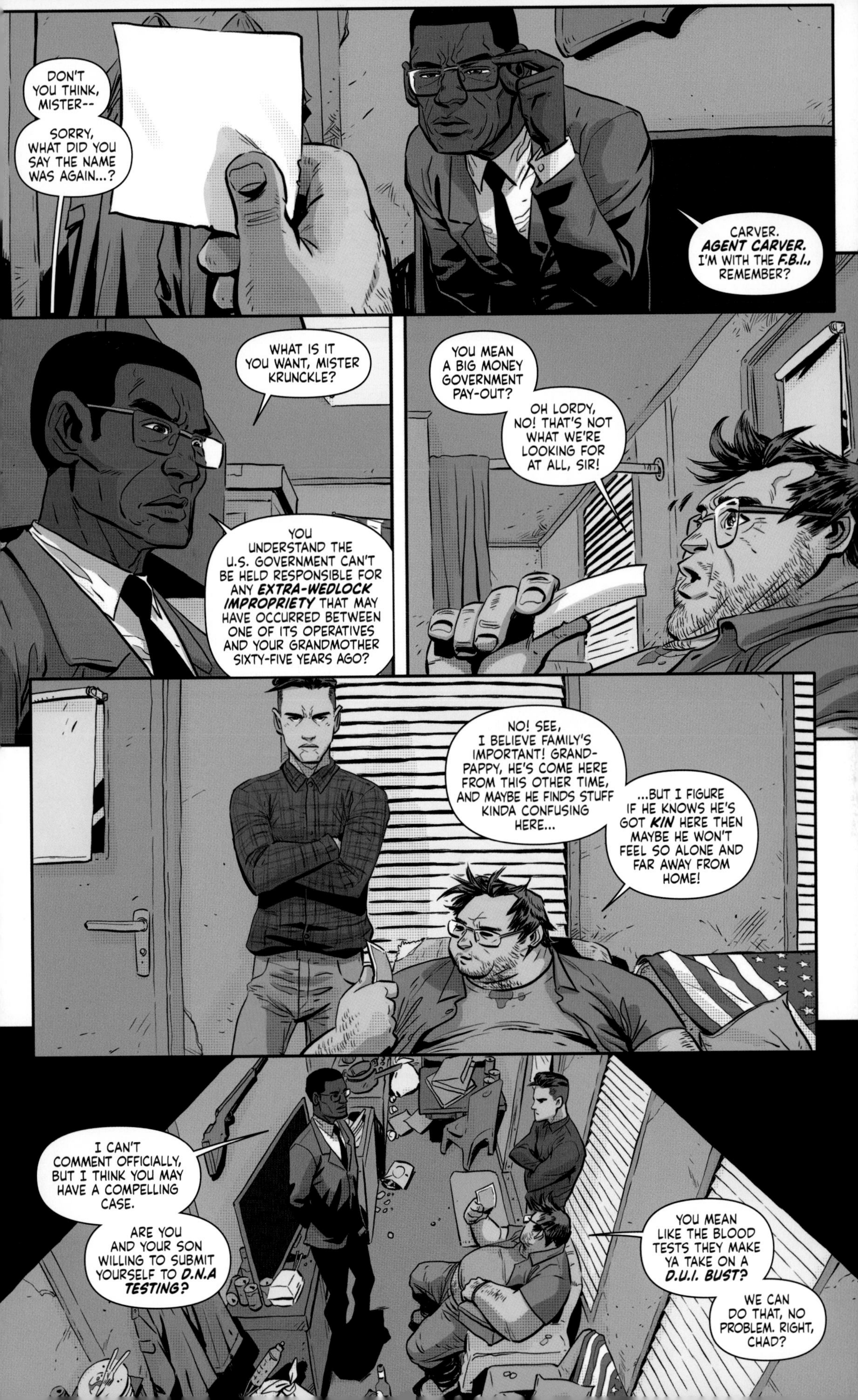
DON'T YOU THINK, MISTER--
SORRY, WHAT DID YOU SAY THE NAME WAS AGAIN...?
CARVER. AGENT CARVER. I'M WITH THE F.B.I., REMEMBER?
WHAT IS IT YOU WANT, MISTER KRUNCKLE?
YOU UNDERSTAND THE U.S. GOVERNMENT CAN'T BE HELD RESPONSIBLE FOR ANY EXTRA-WEDLOCK IMPROPRIETY THAT MAY HAVE OCCURRED BETWEEN ONE OF ITS OPERATIVES AND YOUR GRANDMOTHER SIXTY-FIVE YEARS AGO?
YOU MEAN A BIG MONEY GOVERNMENT PAY-OUT?
OH LORDY, NO! THAT'S NOT WHAT WE'RE LOOKING FOR AT ALL, SIR!
NO! SEE, I BELIEVE FAMILY'S IMPORTANT! GRAND-PAPPY, HE'S COME HERE FROM THIS OTHER TIME, AND MAYBE HE FINDS STUFF KINDA CONFUSING HERE...
...BUT I FIGURE IF HE KNOWS HE'S GOT KIN HERE THEN MAYBE HE WON'T FEEL SO ALONE AND FAR AWAY FROM HOME!
I CAN'T COMMENT OFFICIALLY, BUT I THINK YOU MAY HAVE A COMPELLING CASE.
ARE YOU AND YOUR SON WILLING TO SUBMIT YOURSELF TO D.N.A TESTING?
YOU MEAN LIKE THE BLOOD TESTS THEY MAKE YA TAKE ON A D.U.I. BUST?
WE CAN DO THAT, NO PROBLEM. RIGHT, CHAD?

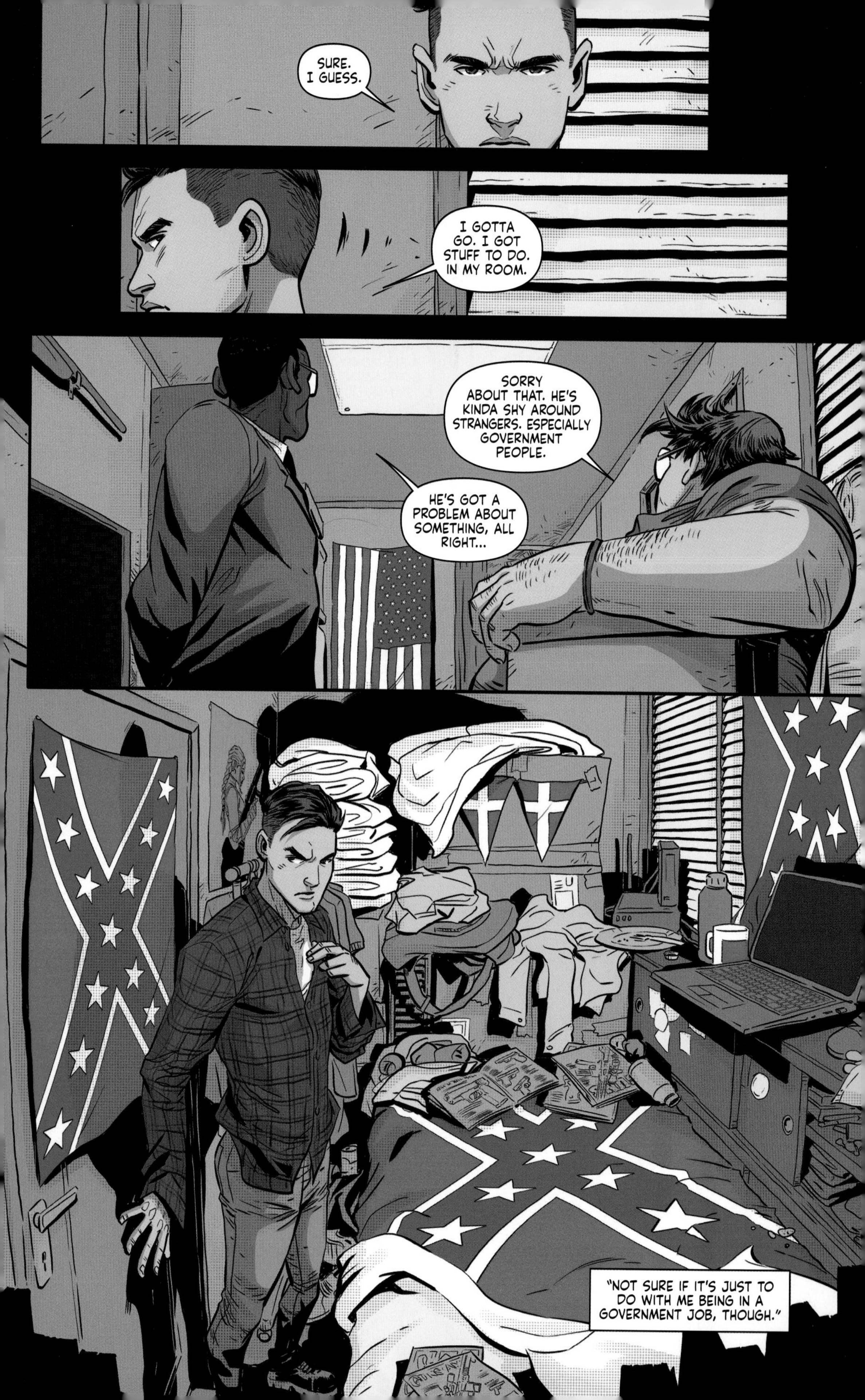
SURE. I GUESS.
I GOTTA GO. I GOT STUFF TO DO. IN MY ROOM.
SORRY ABOUT THAT. HE'S KINDA SHY AROUND STRANGERS. ESPECIALLY GOVERNMENT PEOPLE.
HE'S GOT A PROBLEM ABOUT SOMETHING, ALL RIGHT...
"NOT SURE IF IT'S JUST TO DO WITH ME BEING IN A GOVERNMENT JOB, THOUGH."

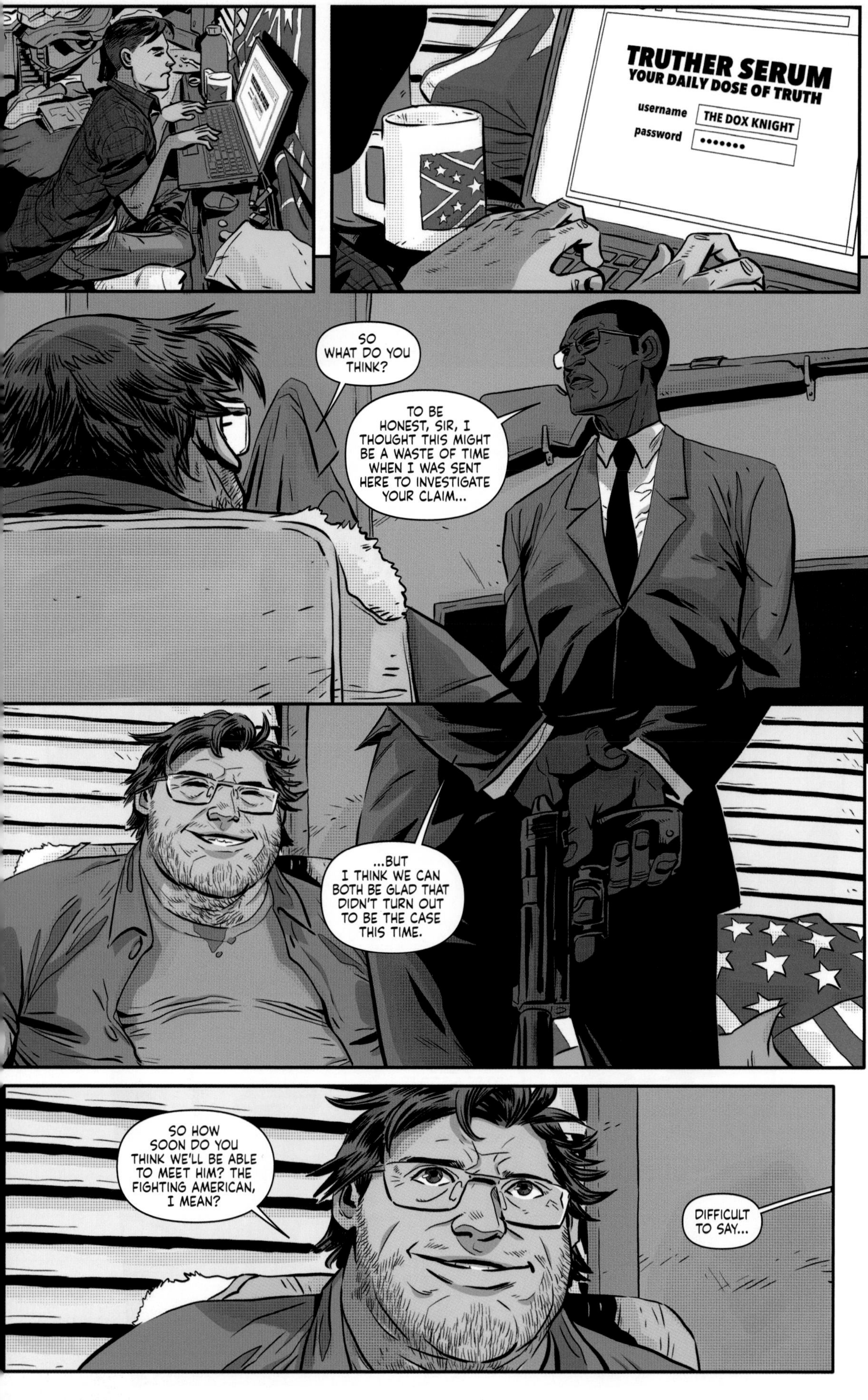
TRUTHER SERUM
YOUR DAILY DOSE OF TRUTH
username
THE DOX KNIGHT
password
•••••••
SO WHAT DO YOU THINK?
TO BE HONEST, SIR, I THOUGHT THIS MIGHT BE A WASTE OF TIME WHEN I WAS SENT HERE TO INVESTIGATE YOUR CLAIM...
...BUT I THINK WE CAN BOTH BE GLAD THAT DIDN'T TURN OUT TO BE THE CASE THIS TIME.
SO HOW SOON DO YOU THINK WE'LL BE ABLE TO MEET HIM? THE FIGHTING AMERICAN, I MEAN?
DIFFICULT TO SAY...

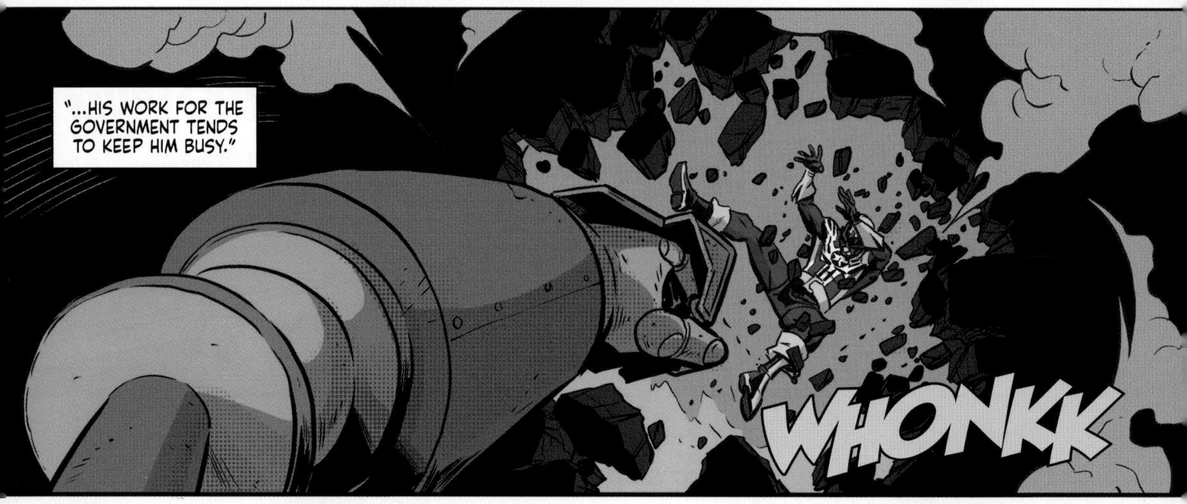
"...HIS WORK FOR THE GOVERNMENT TENDS TO KEEP HIM BUSY."
WHONKK

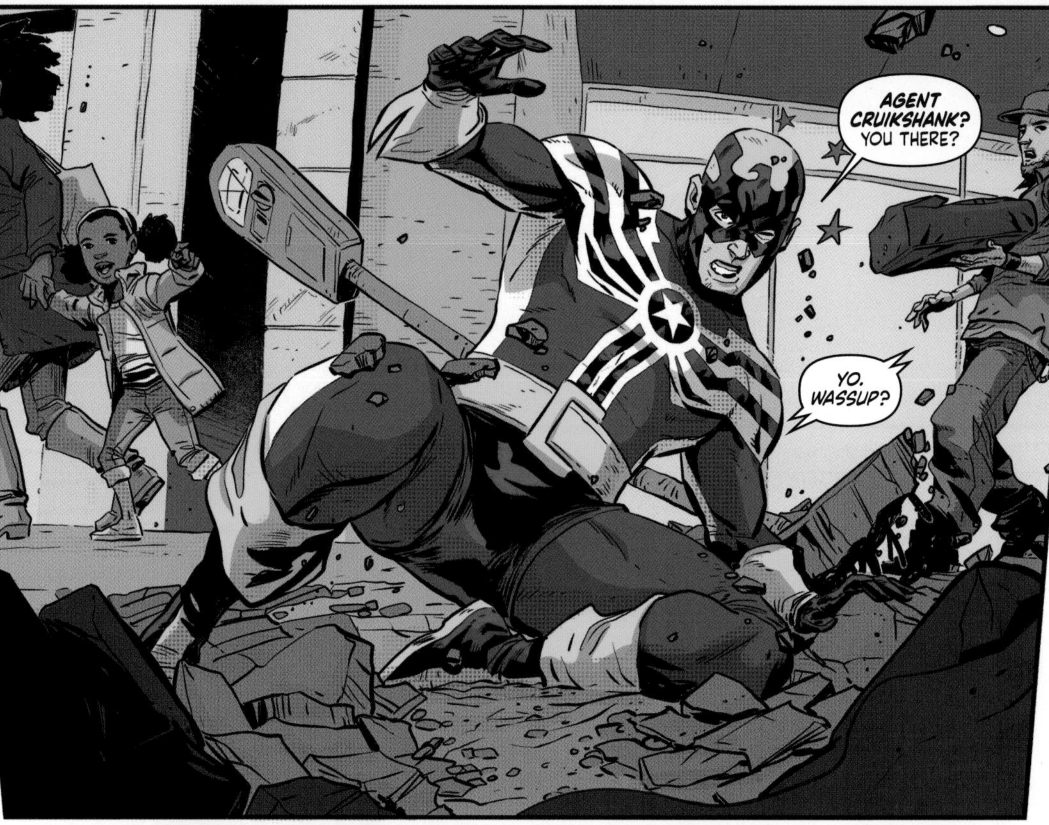
AGENT CRUIKSHANK? YOU THERE?
YO. WASSUP?

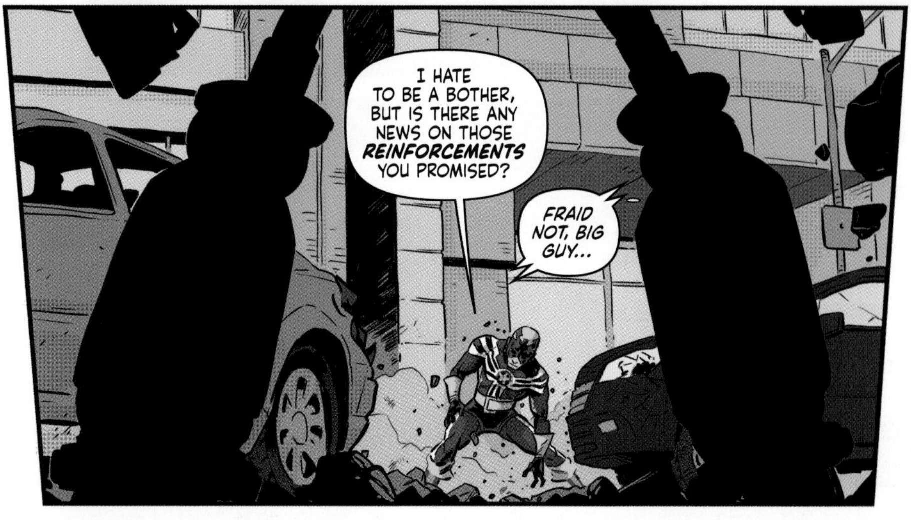
I HATE TO BE A BOTHER, BUT IS THERE ANY NEWS ON THOSE REINFORCEMENTS YOU PROMISED?
FRAID NOT, BIG GUY...

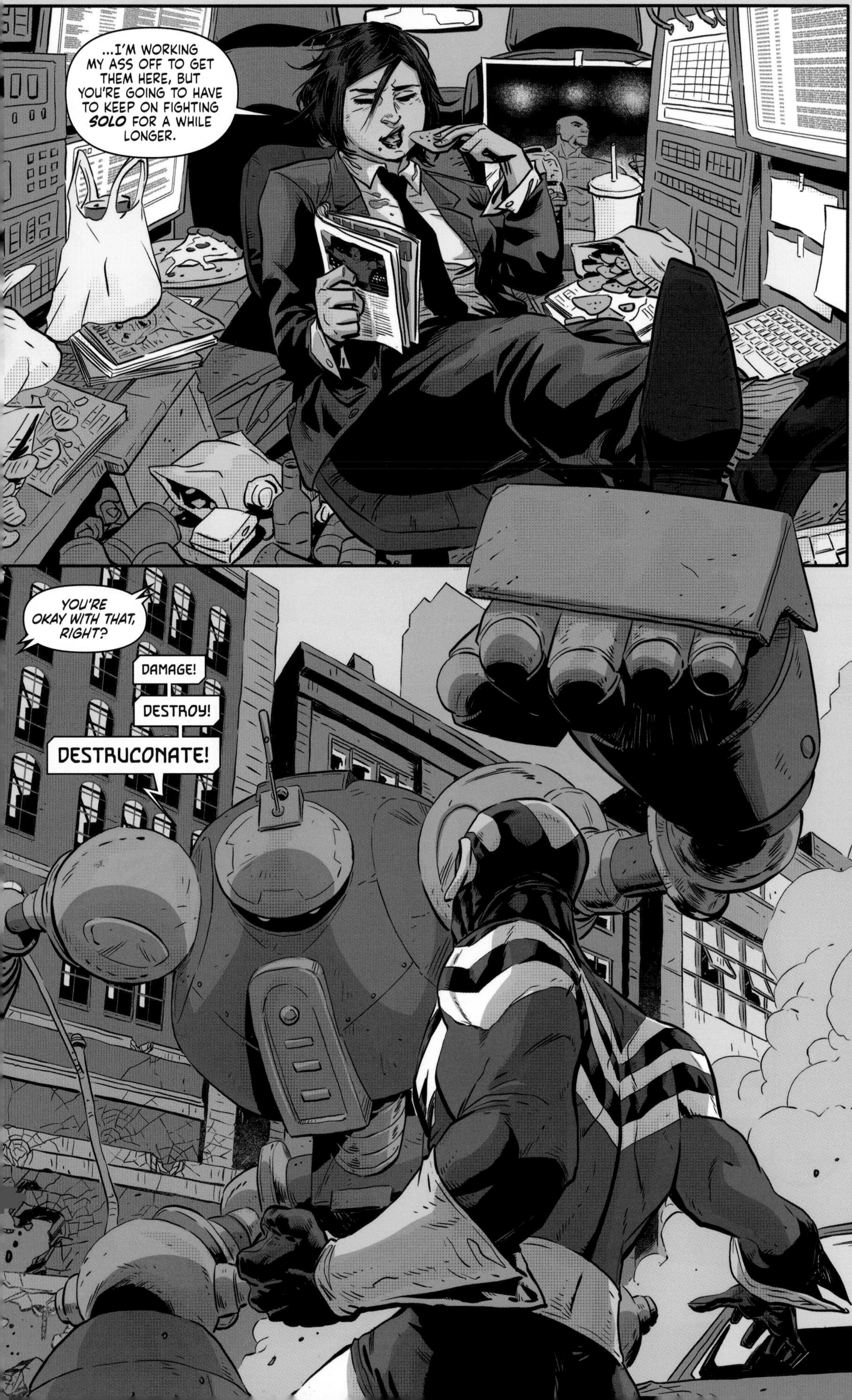
...I'M WORKING MY ASS OFF TO GET THEM HERE, BUT YOU'RE GOING TO HAVE TO KEEP ON FIGHTING SOLO FOR A WHILE LONGER.
YOU'RE OKAY WITH THAT, RIGHT?
DAMAGE!
DESTROY!
DESTRUCONATE!

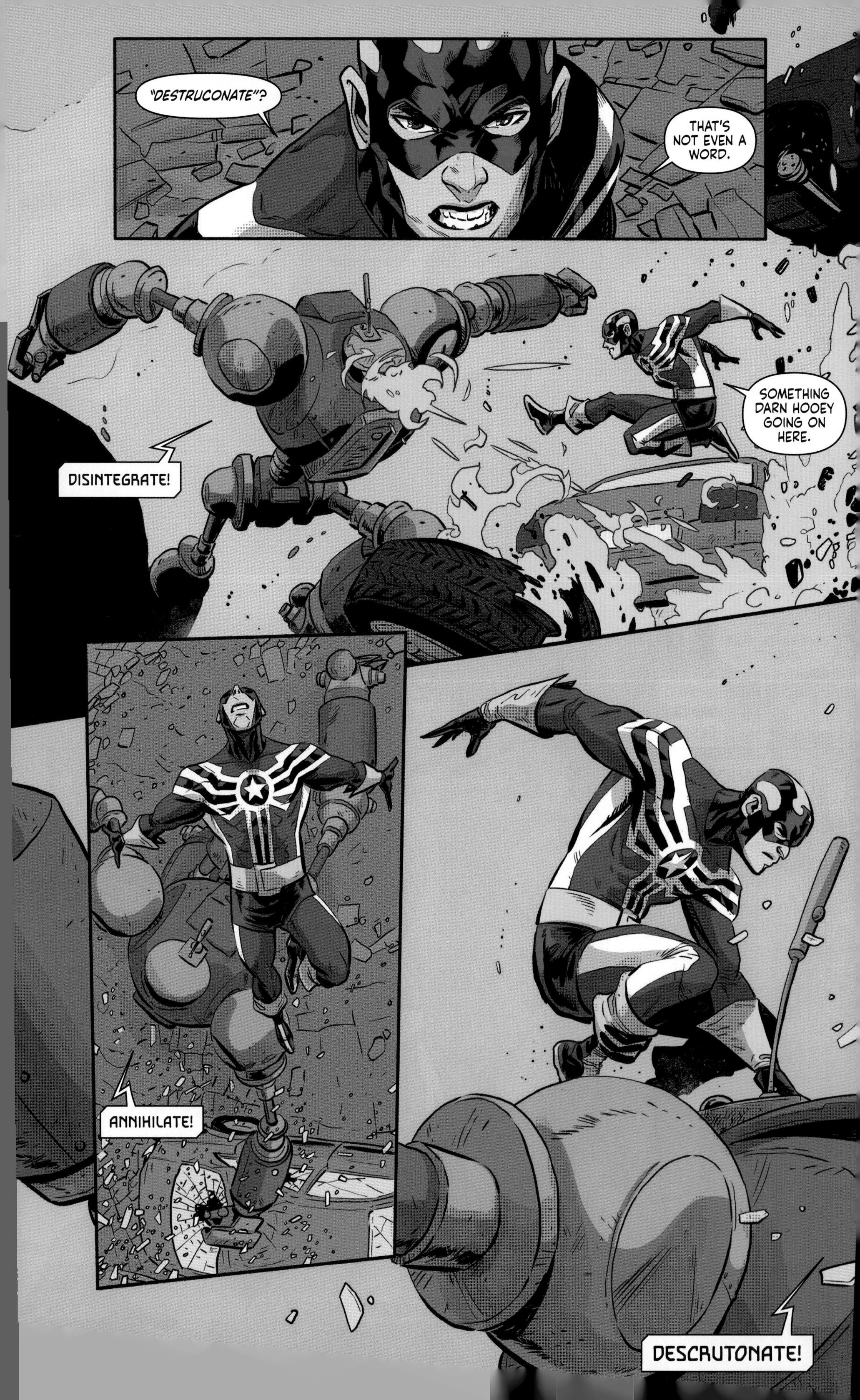
"DESTRUCONATE"?
THAT'S NOT EVEN A WORD.
DISINTEGRATE!
SOMETHING DARN HOOEY GOING ON HERE.
ANNIHILATE!
DESCRUTONATE!

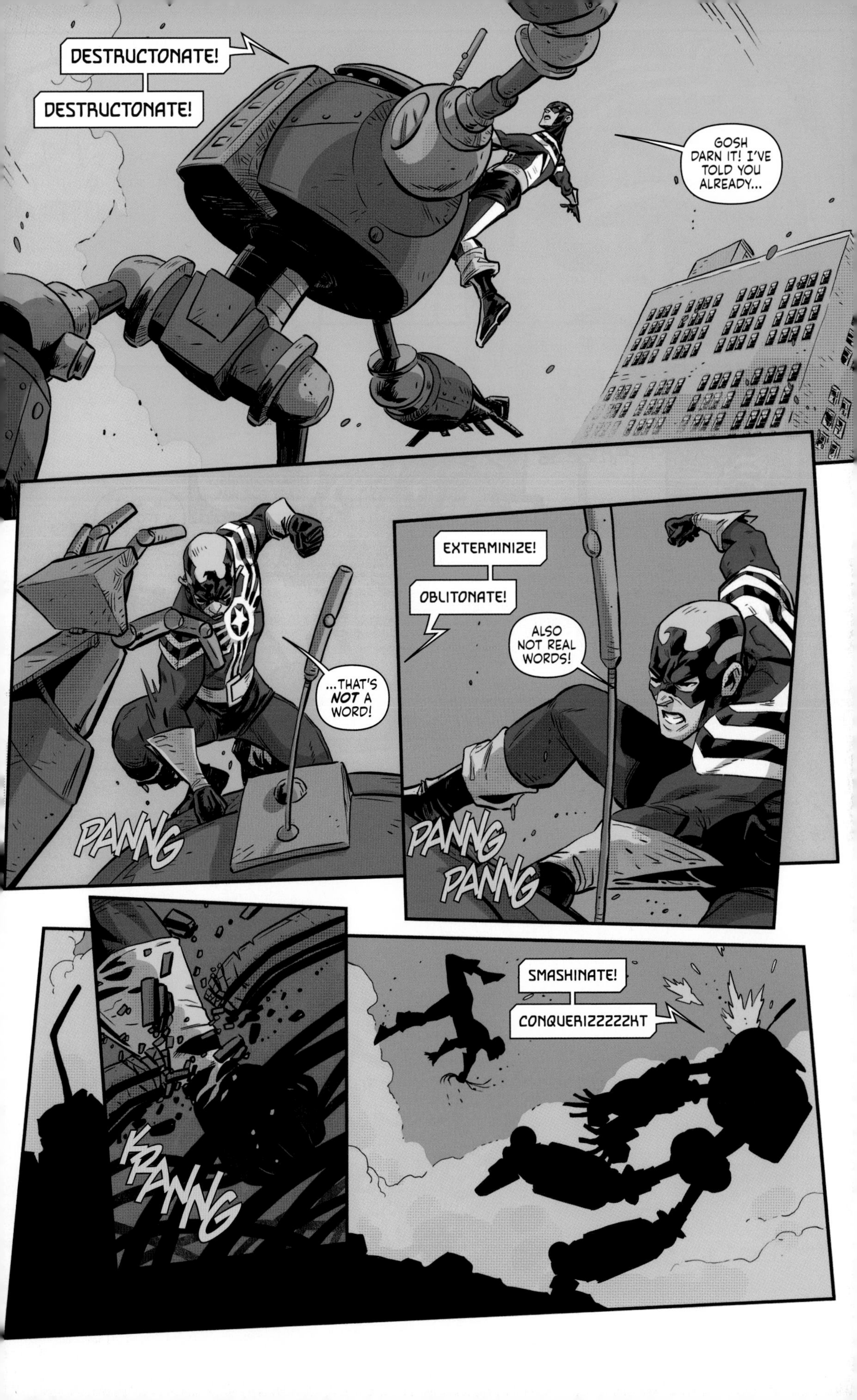
DESTRUCTONATE!
DESTRUCTONATE!
GOSH DARN IT! I'VE TOLD YOU ALREADY...
...THAT'S NOT A WORD!
PANNG
EXTERMINIZE!
OBLITONATE!
ALSO NOT REAL WORDS!
PANNG
PANNG
KRANNG
SMASHINATE!
CONQUERIZZZZZKT

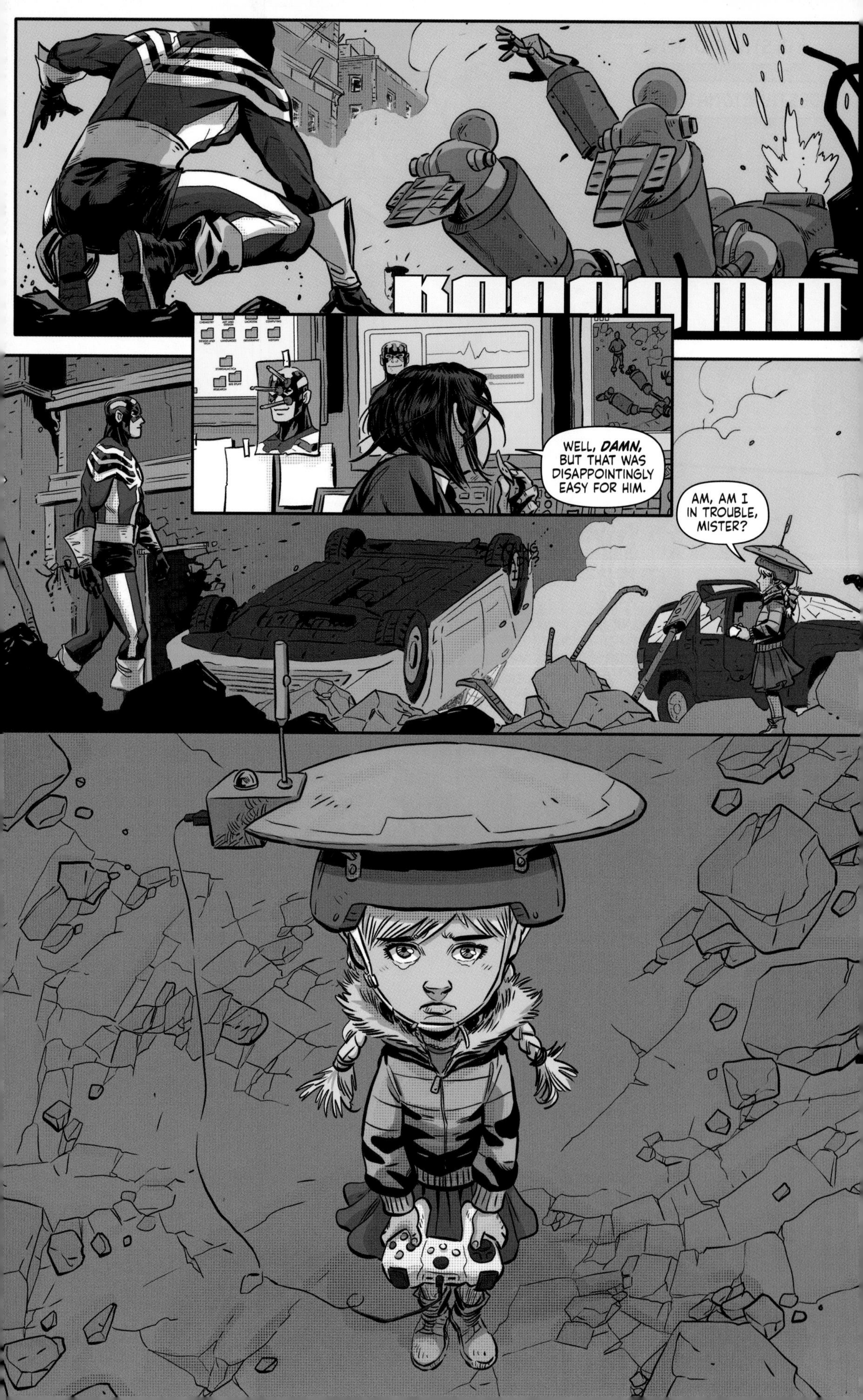
KOOOOMM
WELL, DAMN, BUT THAT WAS DISAPPOINTINGLY EASY FOR HIM.
AM, AM I IN TROUBLE, MISTER?

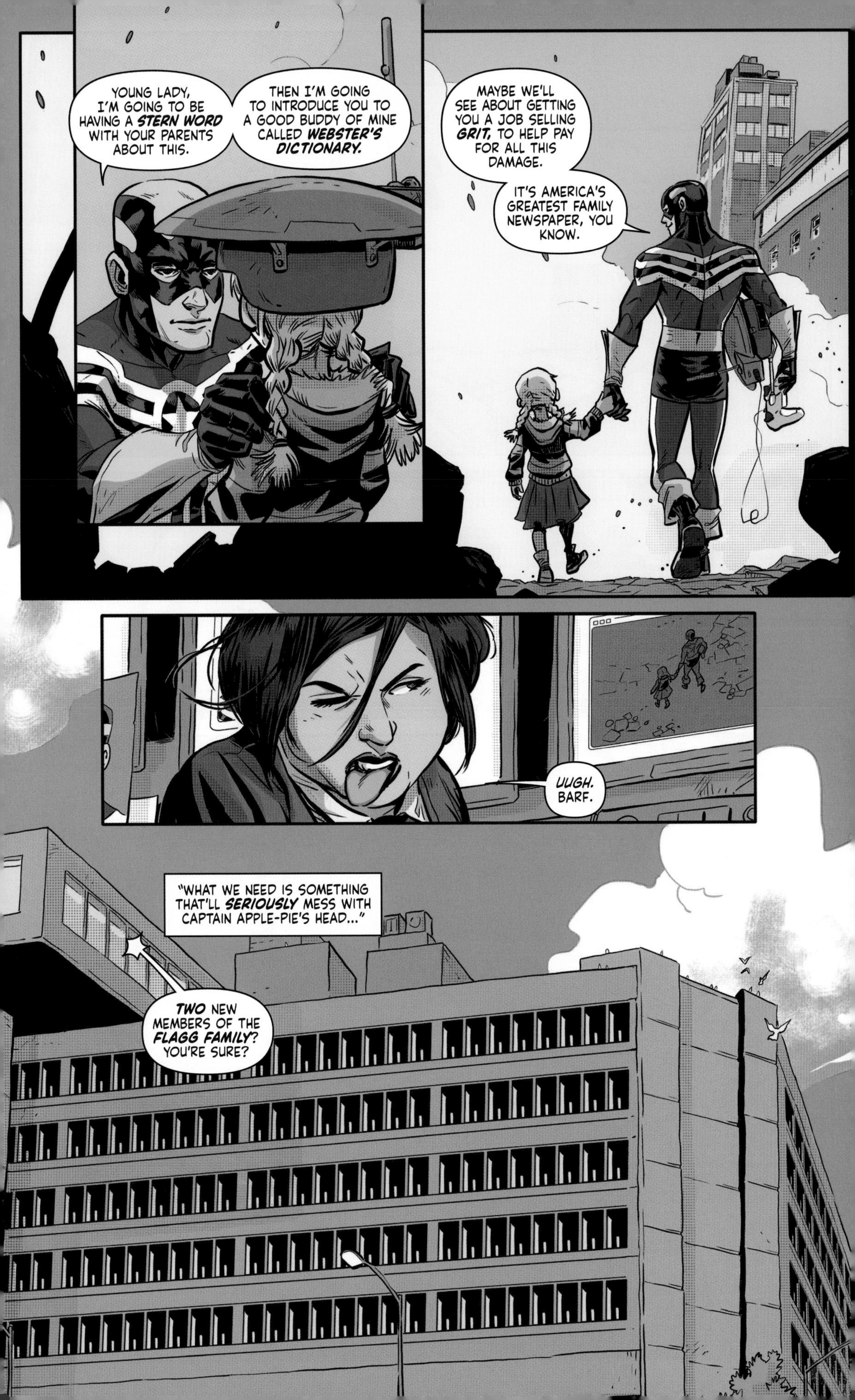
YOUNG LADY, I'M GOING TO BE HAVING A STERN WORD WITH YOUR PARENTS ABOUT THIS.
THEN I'M GOING TO INTRODUCE YOU TO A GOOD BUDDY OF MINE CALLED WEBSTER'S DICTIONARY.
MAYBE WE'LL SEE ABOUT GETTING YOU A JOB SELLING GRIT, TO HELP PAY FOR ALL THIS DAMAGE.
IT'S AMERICA'S GREATEST FAMILY NEWSPAPER, YOU KNOW.
UUGH. BARF.
"WHAT WE NEED IS SOMETHING THAT'LL SERIOUSLY MESS WITH CAPTAIN APPLE-PIE'S HEAD..."
TWO NEW MEMBERS OF THE FLAGG FAMILY? YOU'RE SURE?

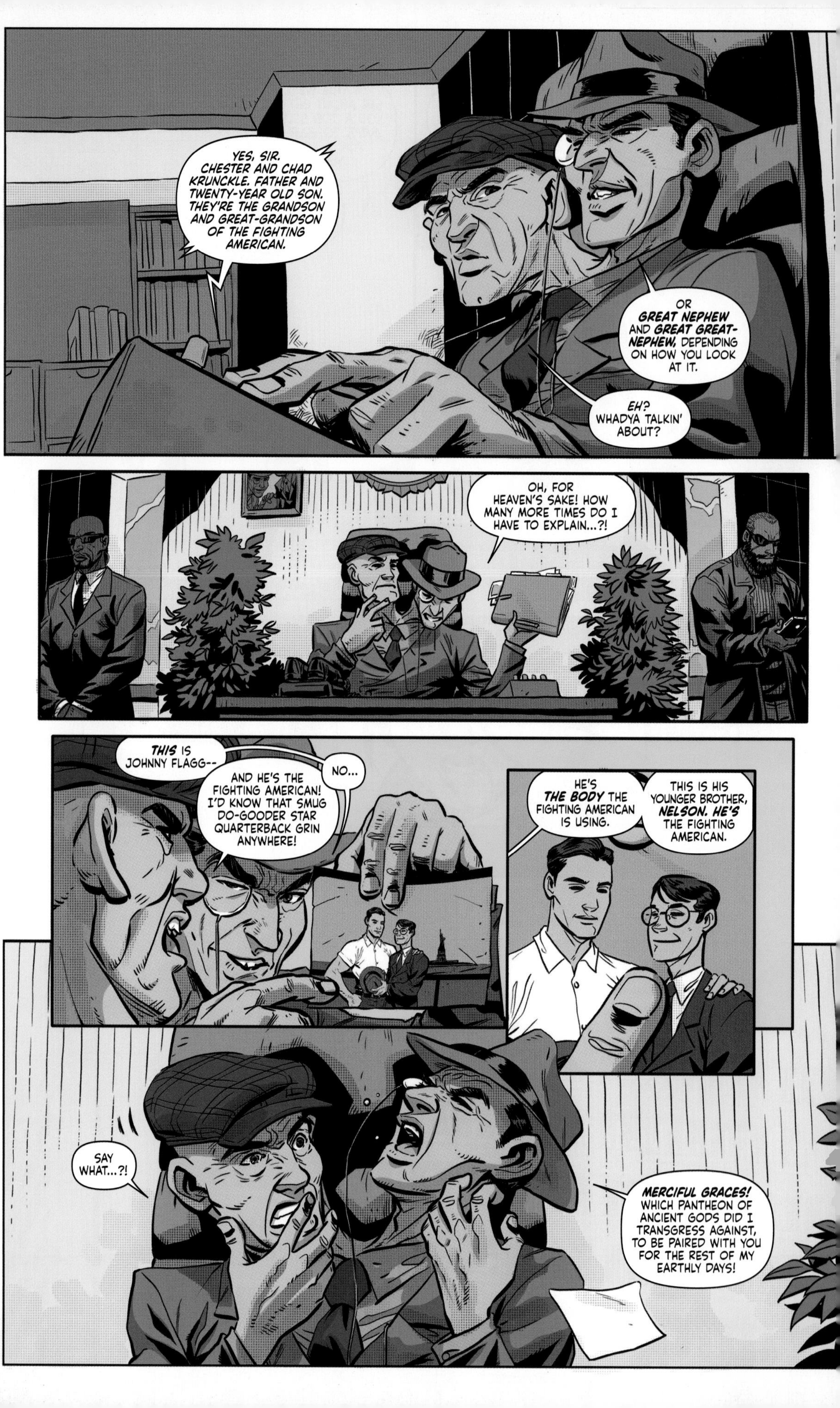

YES, SIR. CHESTER AND CHAD KRUNCKLE. FATHER AND TWENTY-YEAR OLD SON. THEY'RE THE GRANDSON AND GREAT-GRANDSON OF THE FIGHTING AMERICAN.
OR GREAT NEPHEW AND GREAT GREAT-NEPHEW, DEPENDING ON HOW YOU LOOK AT IT.
EH? WHADYA TALKIN' ABOUT?
OH, FOR HEAVEN'S SAKE! HOW MANY MORE TIMES DO I HAVE TO EXPLAIN...?!
THIS IS JOHNNY FLAGG--
AND HE'S THE FIGHTING AMERICAN! I'D KNOW THAT SMUG DO-GOODER STAR QUARTERBACK GRIN ANYWHERE!
NO...
HE'S THE BODY THE FIGHTING AMERICAN IS USING.
THIS IS HIS YOUNGER BROTHER, NELSON. HE'S THE FIGHTING AMERICAN.
SAY WHAT...?!
MERCIFUL GRACES! WHICH PANTHEON OF ANCIENT GODS DID I TRANSGRESS AGAINST, TO BE PAIRED WITH YOU FOR THE REST OF MY EARTHLY DAYS!

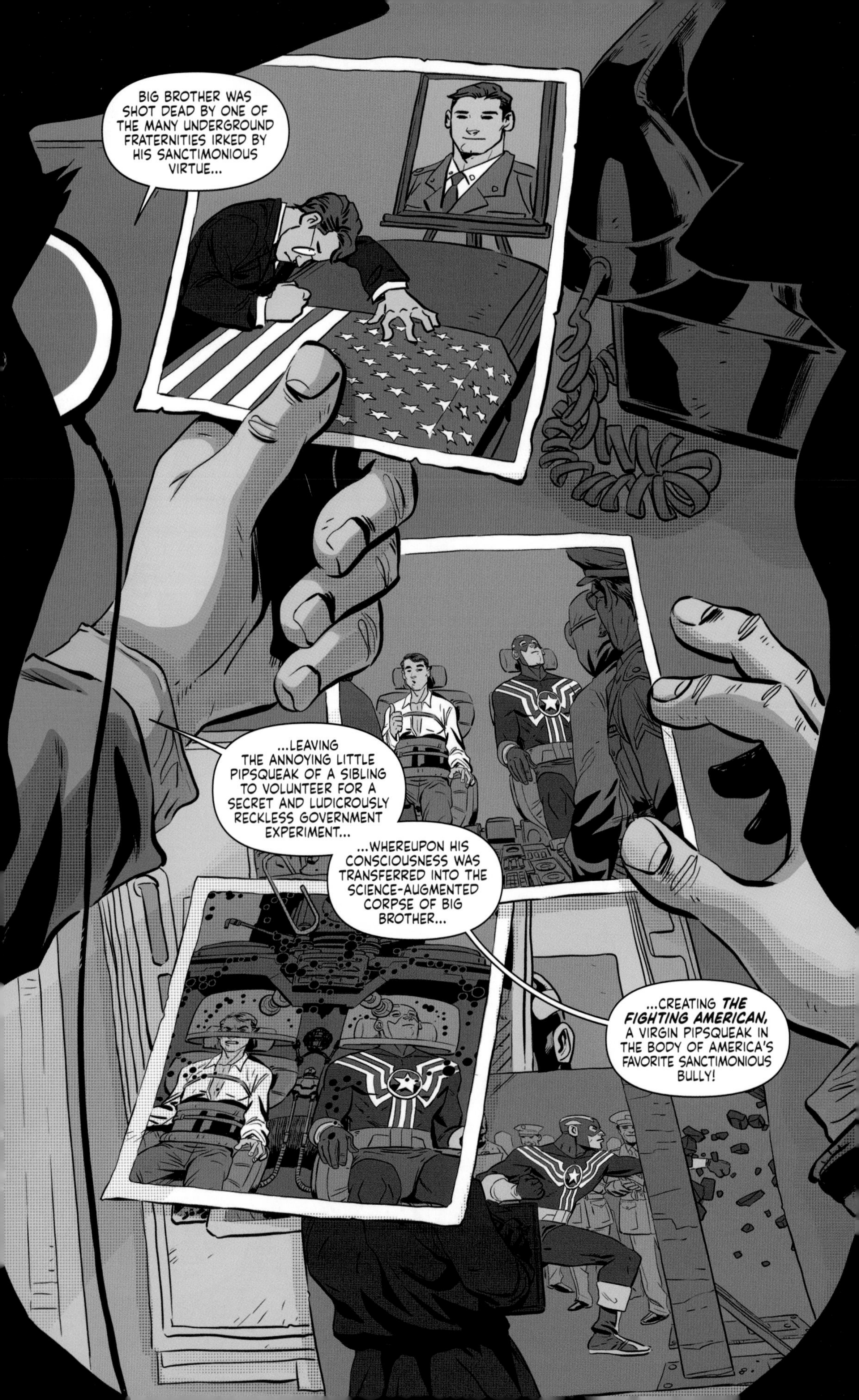
BIG BROTHER WAS SHOT DEAD BY ONE OF THE MANY UNDERGROUND FRATERNITIES IRKED BY HIS SANCTIMONIOUS VIRTUE...
...LEAVING THE ANNOYING LITTLE PIPSQUEAK OF A SIBLING TO VOLUNTEER FOR A SECRET AND LUDICROUSLY RECKLESS GOVERNMENT EXPERIMENT...
...WHEREUPON HIS CONSCIOUSNESS WAS TRANSFERRED INTO THE SCIENCE-AUGMENTED CORPSE OF BIG BROTHER...
...CREATING ***THE FIGHTING AMERICAN,*** A VIRGIN PIPSQUEAK IN THE BODY OF AMERICA'S FAVORITE SANCTIMONIOUS BULLY!

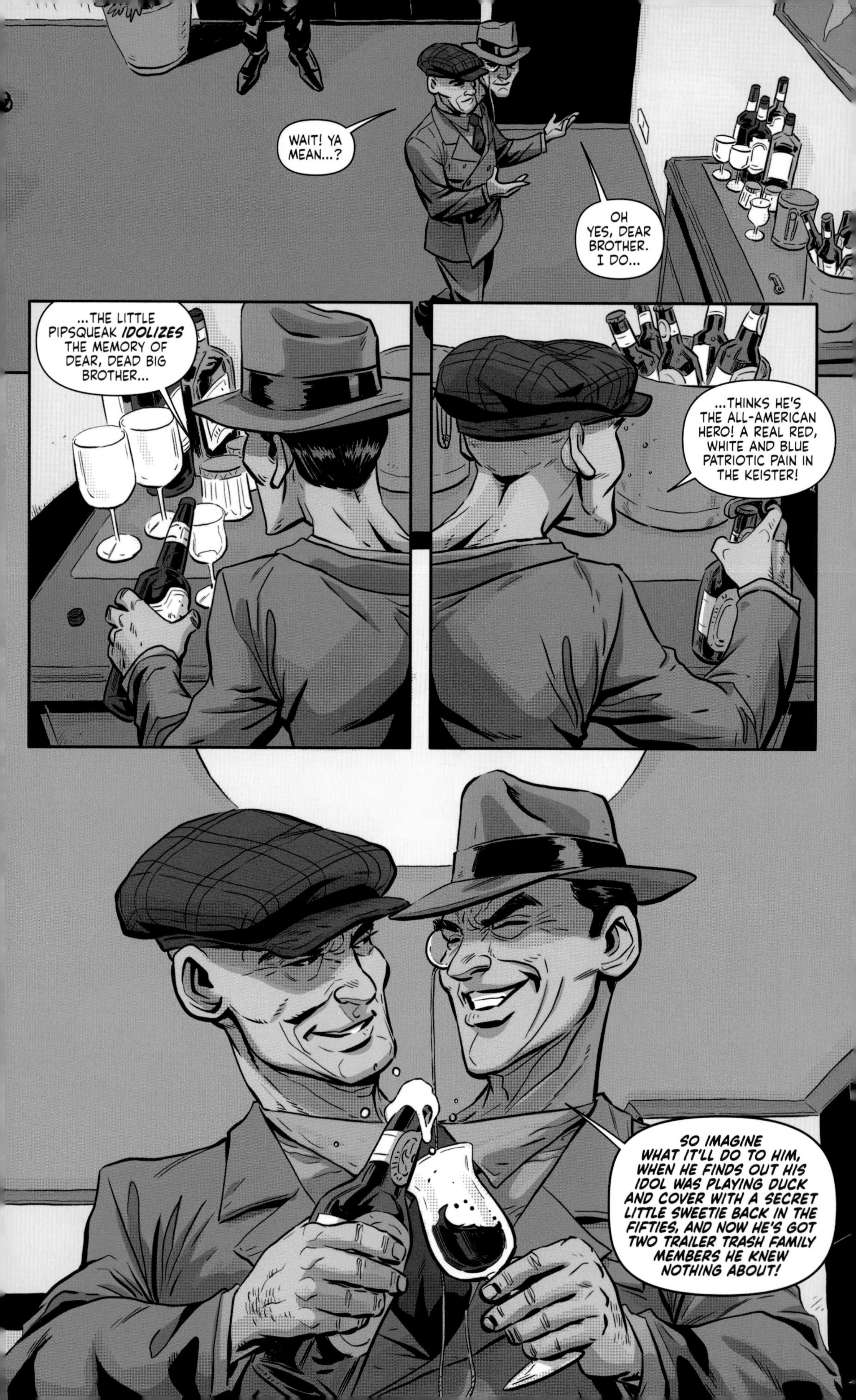
WAIT! YA MEAN...?
OH YES, DEAR BROTHER. I DO...
...THE LITTLE PIPSQUEAK IDOLIZES THE MEMORY OF DEAR, DEAD BIG BROTHER...
...THINKS HE'S THE ALL-AMERICAN HERO! A REAL RED, WHITE AND BLUE PATRIOTIC PAIN IN THE KEISTER!
SO IMAGINE WHAT IT'LL DO TO HIM, WHEN HE FINDS OUT HIS IDOL WAS PLAYING DUCK AND COVER WITH A SECRET LITTLE SWEETIE BACK IN THE FIFTIES, AND NOW HE'S GOT TWO TRAILER TRASH FAMILY MEMBERS HE KNEW NOTHING ABOUT!

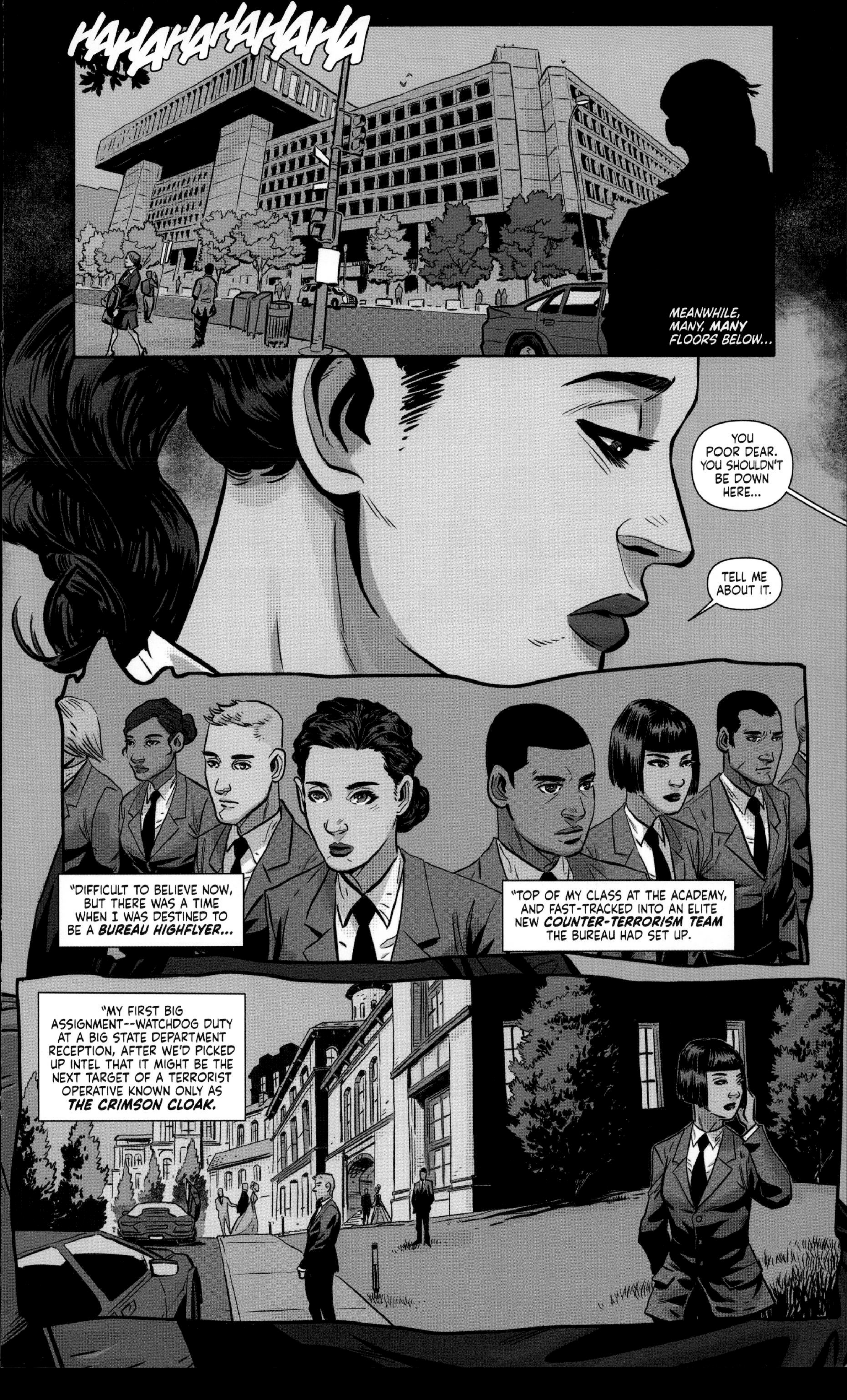
HAHAHAHAHAHAHA
MEANWHILE, MANY, MANY FLOORS BELOW...
YOU POOR DEAR. YOU SHOULDN'T BE DOWN HERE...
TELL ME ABOUT IT.
"DIFFICULT TO BELIEVE NOW, BUT THERE WAS A TIME WHEN I WAS DESTINED TO BE A BUREAU HIGHFLYER...
"TOP OF MY CLASS AT THE ACADEMY, AND FAST-TRACKED INTO AN ELITE NEW COUNTER-TERRORISM TEAM THE BUREAU HAD SET UP.
"MY FIRST BIG ASSIGNMENT--WATCHDOG DUTY AT A BIG STATE DEPARTMENT RECEPTION, AFTER WE'D PICKED UP INTEL THAT IT MIGHT BE THE NEXT TARGET OF A TERRORIST OPERATIVE KNOWN ONLY AS THE CRIMSON CLOAK.

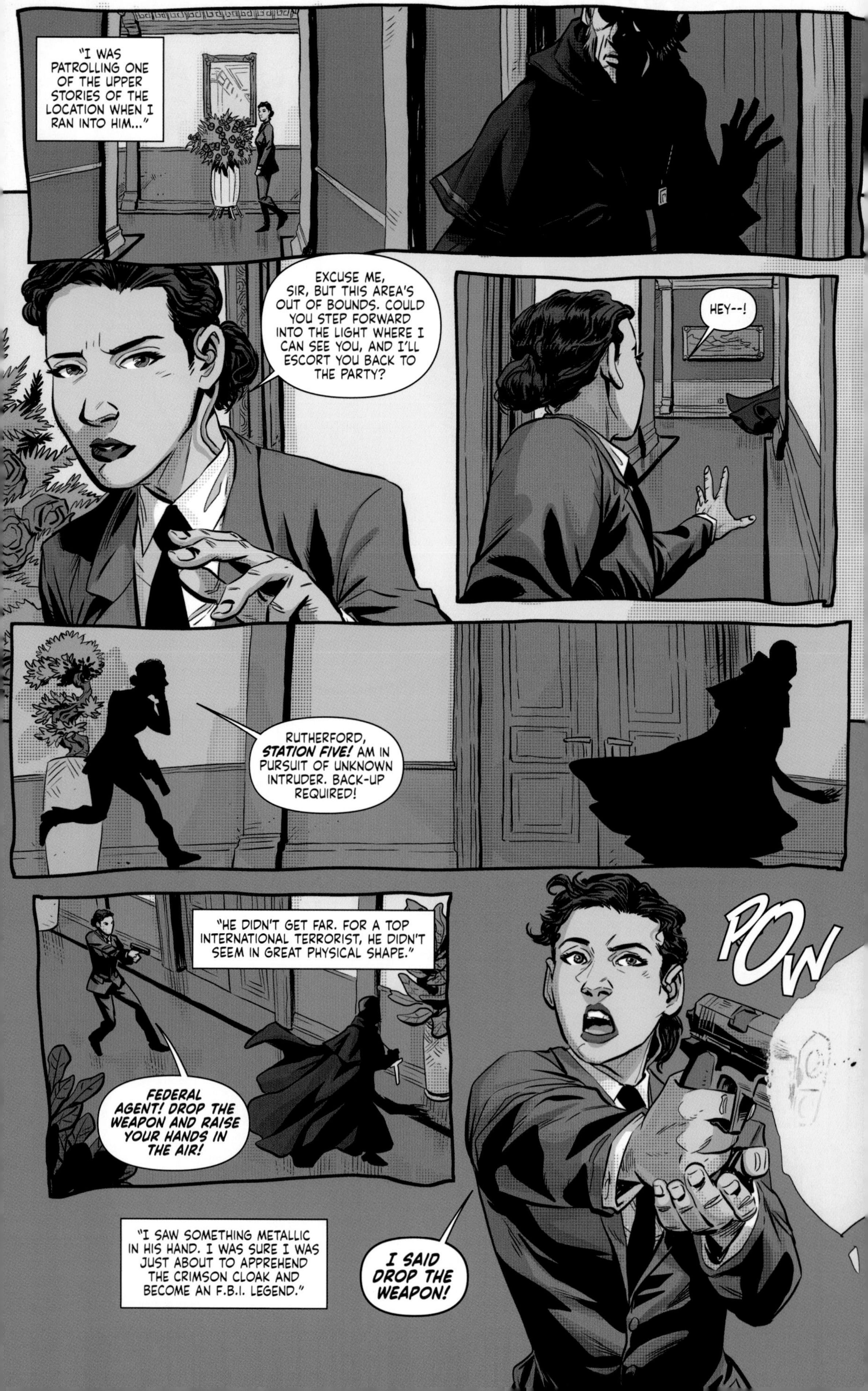
"I WAS PATROLLING ONE OF THE UPPER STORIES OF THE LOCATION WHEN I RAN INTO HIM..."
EXCUSE ME, SIR, BUT THIS AREA'S OUT OF BOUNDS. COULD YOU STEP FORWARD INTO THE LIGHT WHERE I CAN SEE YOU, AND I'LL ESCORT YOU BACK TO THE PARTY?
HEY--!
RUTHERFORD, STATION FIVE! AM IN PURSUIT OF UNKNOWN INTRUDER. BACK-UP REQUIRED!
"HE DIDN'T GET FAR. FOR A TOP INTERNATIONAL TERRORIST, HE DIDN'T SEEM IN GREAT PHYSICAL SHAPE."
FEDERAL AGENT! DROP THE WEAPON AND RAISE YOUR HANDS IN THE AIR!
POW
"I SAW SOMETHING METALLIC IN HIS HAND. I WAS SURE I WAS JUST ABOUT TO APPREHEND THE CRIMSON CLOAK AND BECOME AN F.B.I. LEGEND."
I SAID DROP THE WEAPON!

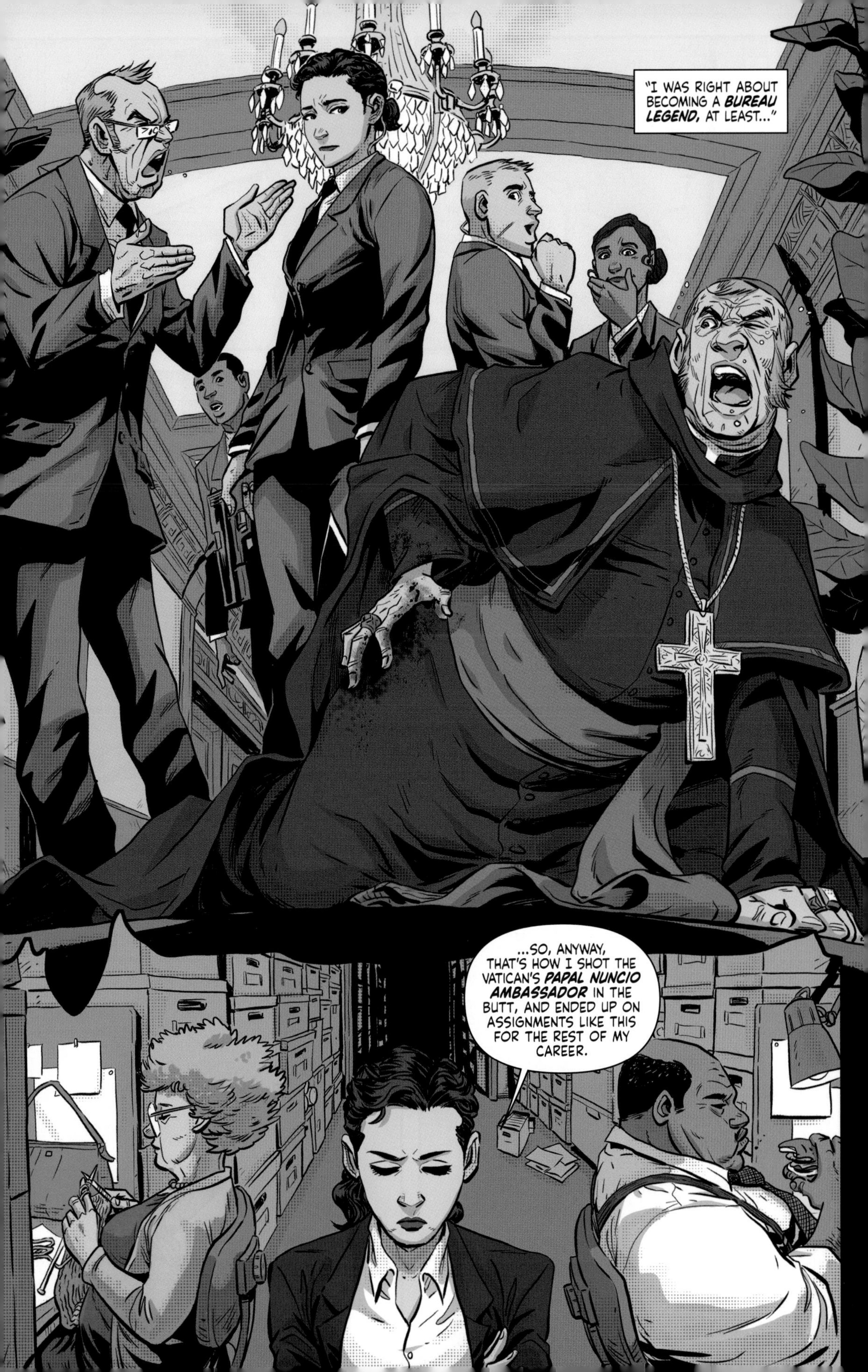
"I WAS RIGHT ABOUT BECOMING A BUREAU LEGEND, AT LEAST..."
...SO, ANYWAY, THAT'S HOW I SHOT THE VATICAN'S PAPAL NUNCIO AMBASSADOR IN THE BUTT, AND ENDED UP ON ASSIGNMENTS LIKE THIS FOR THE REST OF MY CAREER.

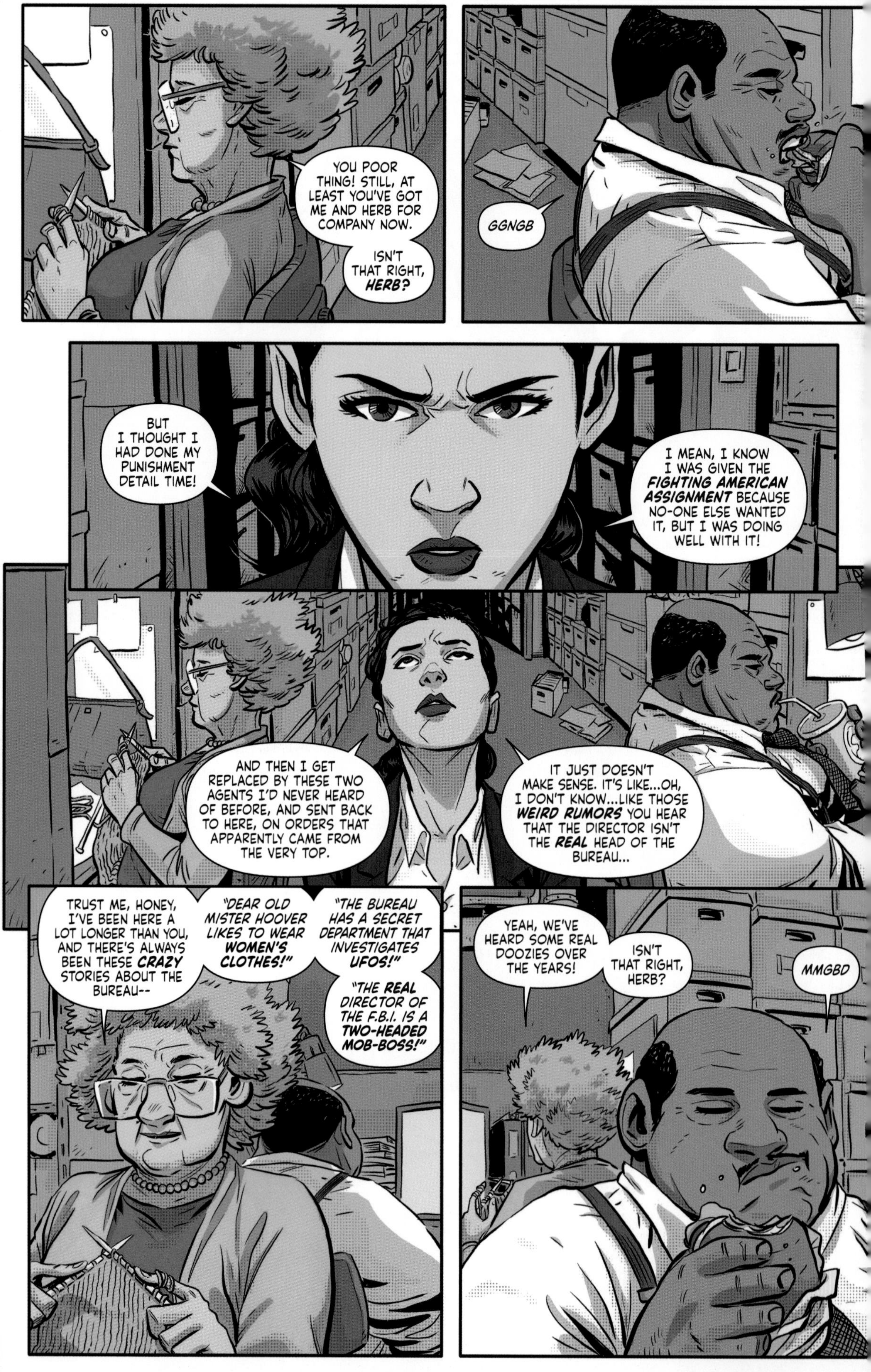
YOU POOR THING! STILL, AT LEAST YOU'VE GOT ME AND HERB FOR COMPANY NOW.
ISN'T THAT RIGHT, HERB?
GGNGB
BUT I THOUGHT I HAD DONE MY PUNISHMENT DETAIL TIME!
I MEAN, I KNOW I WAS GIVEN THE FIGHTING AMERICAN ASSIGNMENT BECAUSE NO-ONE ELSE WANTED IT, BUT I WAS DOING WELL WITH IT!
AND THEN I GET REPLACED BY THESE TWO AGENTS I'D NEVER HEARD OF BEFORE, AND SENT BACK TO HERE, ON ORDERS THAT APPARENTLY CAME FROM THE VERY TOP.
IT JUST DOESN'T MAKE SENSE. IT'S LIKE...OH, I DON'T KNOW...LIKE THOSE WEIRD RUMORS YOU HEAR THAT THE DIRECTOR ISN'T THE REAL HEAD OF THE BUREAU...
TRUST ME, HONEY, I'VE BEEN HERE A LOT LONGER THAN YOU, AND THERE'S ALWAYS BEEN THESE CRAZY STORIES ABOUT THE BUREAU--
"DEAR OLD MISTER HOOVER LIKES TO WEAR WOMEN'S CLOTHES!"
"THE BUREAU HAS A SECRET DEPARTMENT THAT INVESTIGATES UFOS!"
"THE REAL DIRECTOR OF THE F.B.I. IS A TWO-HEADED MOB-BOSS!"
YEAH, WE'VE HEARD SOME REAL DOOZIES OVER THE YEARS!
ISN'T THAT RIGHT, HERB?
MMGBD

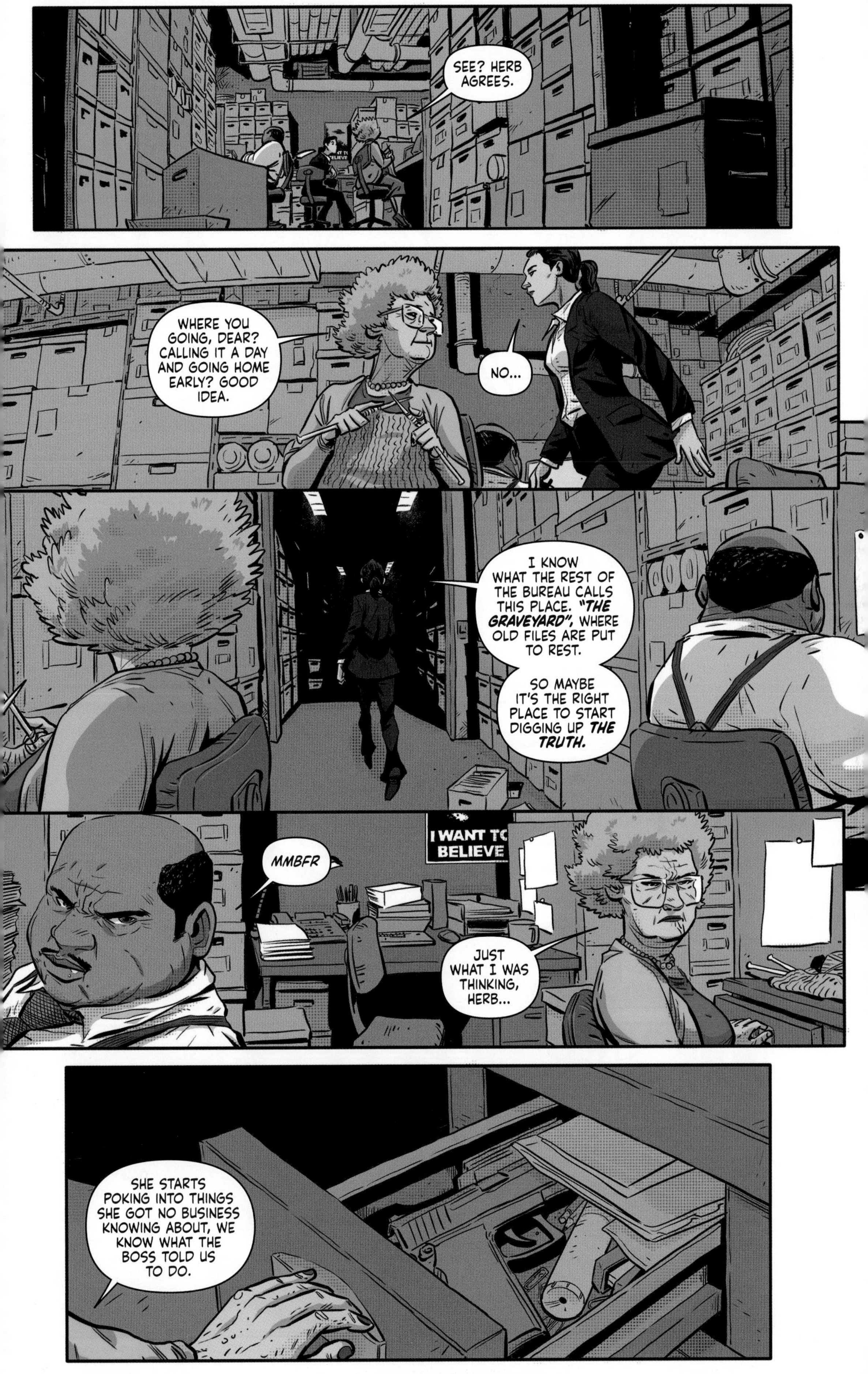
SEE? HERB AGREES.
I WANT TO BELIEVE
WHERE YOU GOING, DEAR? CALLING IT A DAY AND GOING HOME EARLY? GOOD IDEA.
NO...
I KNOW WHAT THE REST OF THE BUREAU CALLS THIS PLACE. "THE GRAVEYARD", WHERE OLD FILES ARE PUT TO REST.
SO MAYBE IT'S THE RIGHT PLACE TO START DIGGING UP THE TRUTH.
I WANT TO BELIEVE
MMBFR
JUST WHAT I WAS THINKING, HERB...
SHE STARTS POKING INTO THINGS SHE GOT NO BUSINESS KNOWING ABOUT, WE KNOW WHAT THE BOSS TOLD US TO DO.

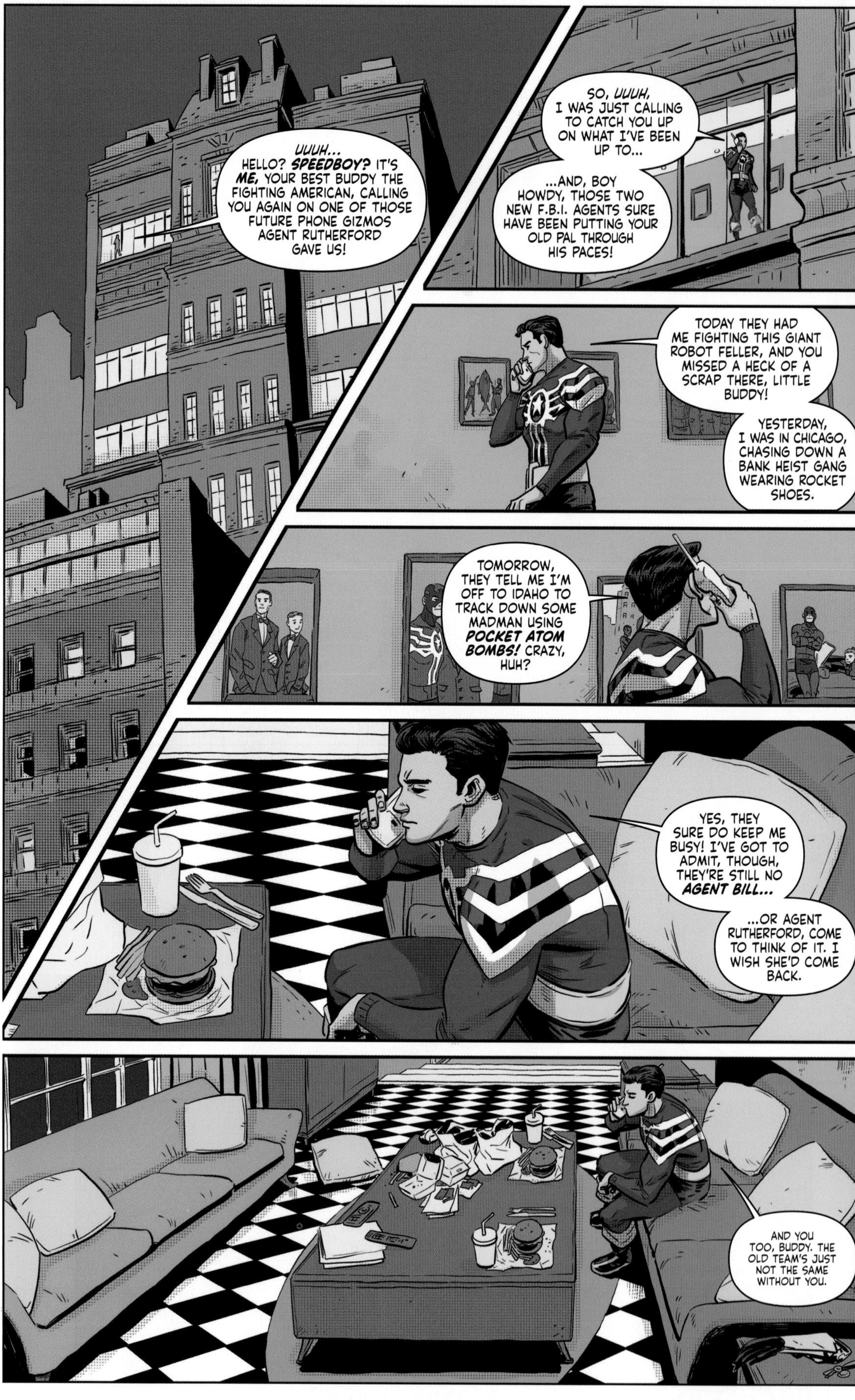
UUUH... HELLO? SPEEDBOY? IT'S ME, YOUR BEST BUDDY THE FIGHTING AMERICAN, CALLING YOU AGAIN ON ONE OF THOSE FUTURE PHONE GIZMOS AGENT RUTHERFORD GAVE US!
SO, UUUH, I WAS JUST CALLING TO CATCH YOU UP ON WHAT I'VE BEEN UP TO...
...AND, BOY HOWDY, THOSE TWO NEW F.B.I. AGENTS SURE HAVE BEEN PUTTING YOUR OLD PAL THROUGH HIS PACES!
TODAY THEY HAD ME FIGHTING THIS GIANT ROBOT FELLER, AND YOU MISSED A HECK OF A SCRAP THERE, LITTLE BUDDY!
YESTERDAY, I WAS IN CHICAGO, CHASING DOWN A BANK HEIST GANG WEARING ROCKET SHOES.
TOMORROW, THEY TELL ME I'M OFF TO IDAHO TO TRACK DOWN SOME MADMAN USING POCKET ATOM BOMBS! CRAZY, HUH?
YES, THEY SURE DO KEEP ME BUSY! I'VE GOT TO ADMIT, THOUGH, THEY'RE STILL NO AGENT BILL...
...OR AGENT RUTHERFORD, COME TO THINK OF IT. I WISH SHE'D COME BACK.
AND YOU TOO, BUDDY. THE OLD TEAM'S JUST NOT THE SAME WITHOUT YOU.

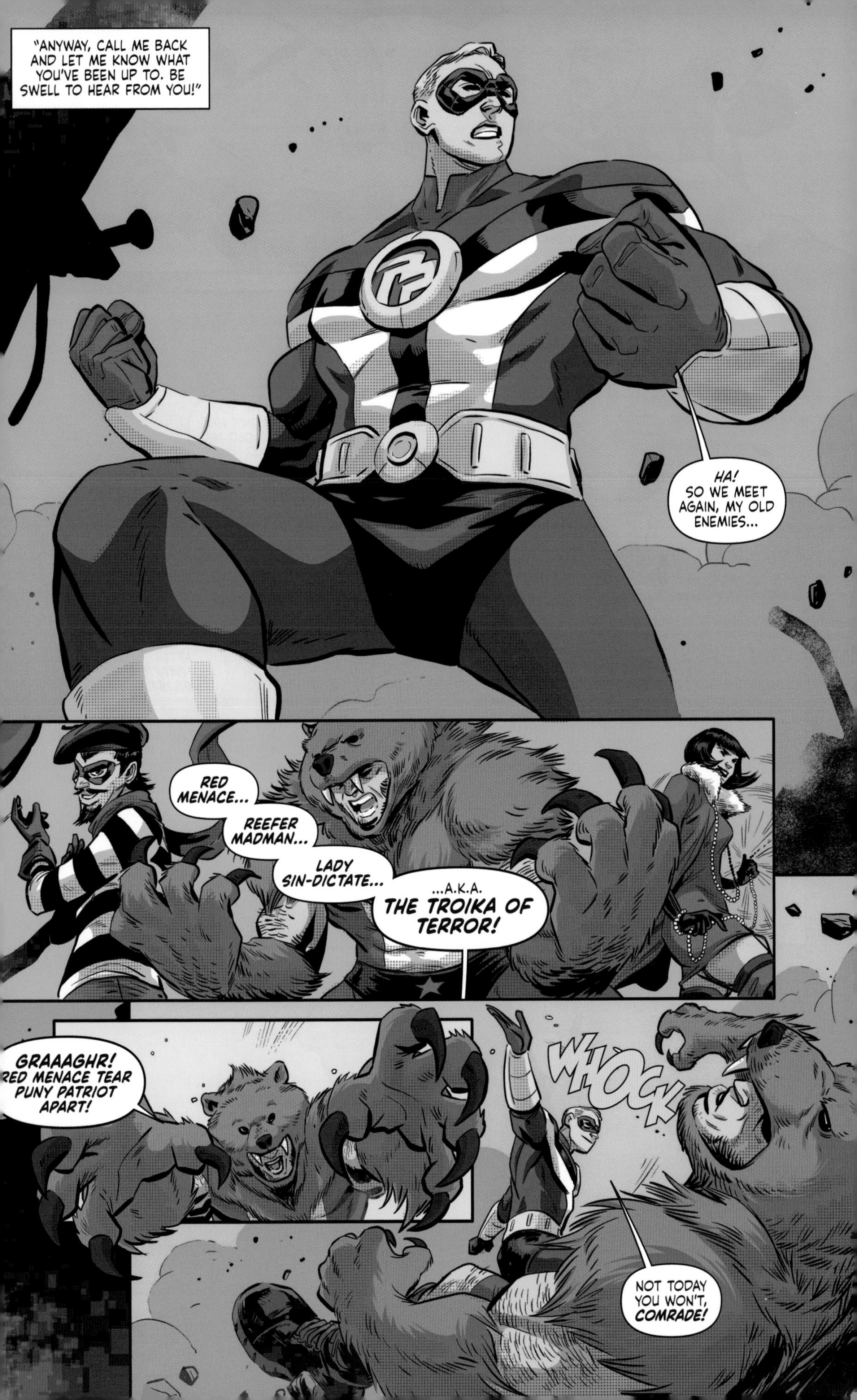
"ANYWAY, CALL ME BACK AND LET ME KNOW WHAT YOU'VE BEEN UP TO. BE SWELL TO HEAR FROM YOU!"
HA! SO WE MEET AGAIN, MY OLD ENEMIES...
RED MENACE...
REEFER MADMAN...
LADY SIN-DICTATE...
...A.K.A. THE TROIKA OF TERROR!
GRAAAGHR! RED MENACE TEAR PUNY PATRIOT APART!
WHOCK
NOT TODAY YOU WON'T, COMRADE!

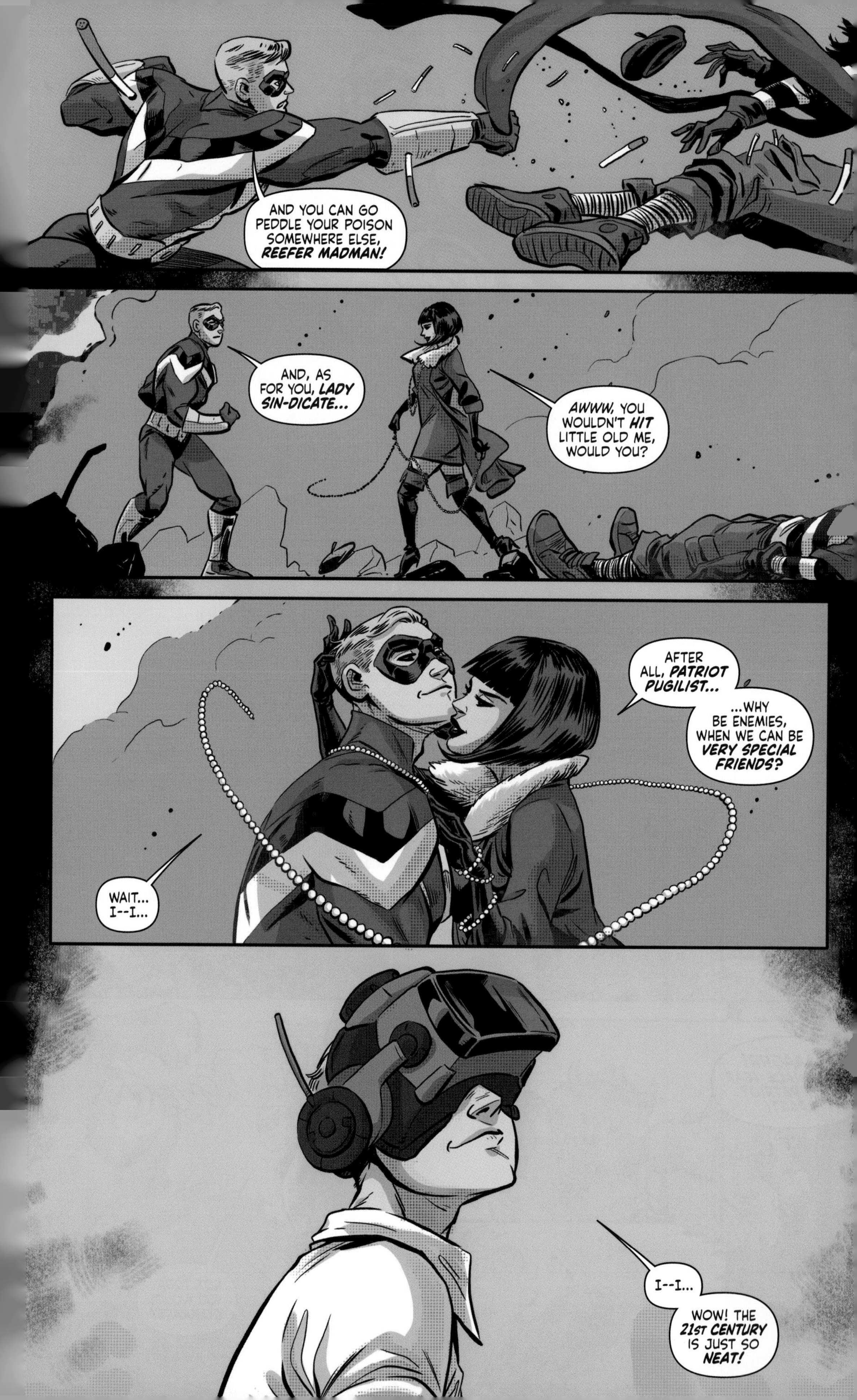
AND YOU CAN GO PEDDLE YOUR POISON SOMEWHERE ELSE, REEFER MADMAN!
AND, AS FOR YOU, LADY SIN-DICATE...
AWWW, YOU WOULDN'T HIT LITTLE OLD ME, WOULD YOU?
AFTER ALL, PATRIOT PUGILIST...
...WHY BE ENEMIES, WHEN WE CAN BE VERY SPECIAL FRIENDS?
WAIT... I--I...
I--I...
WOW! THE 21ST CENTURY IS JUST SO NEAT!

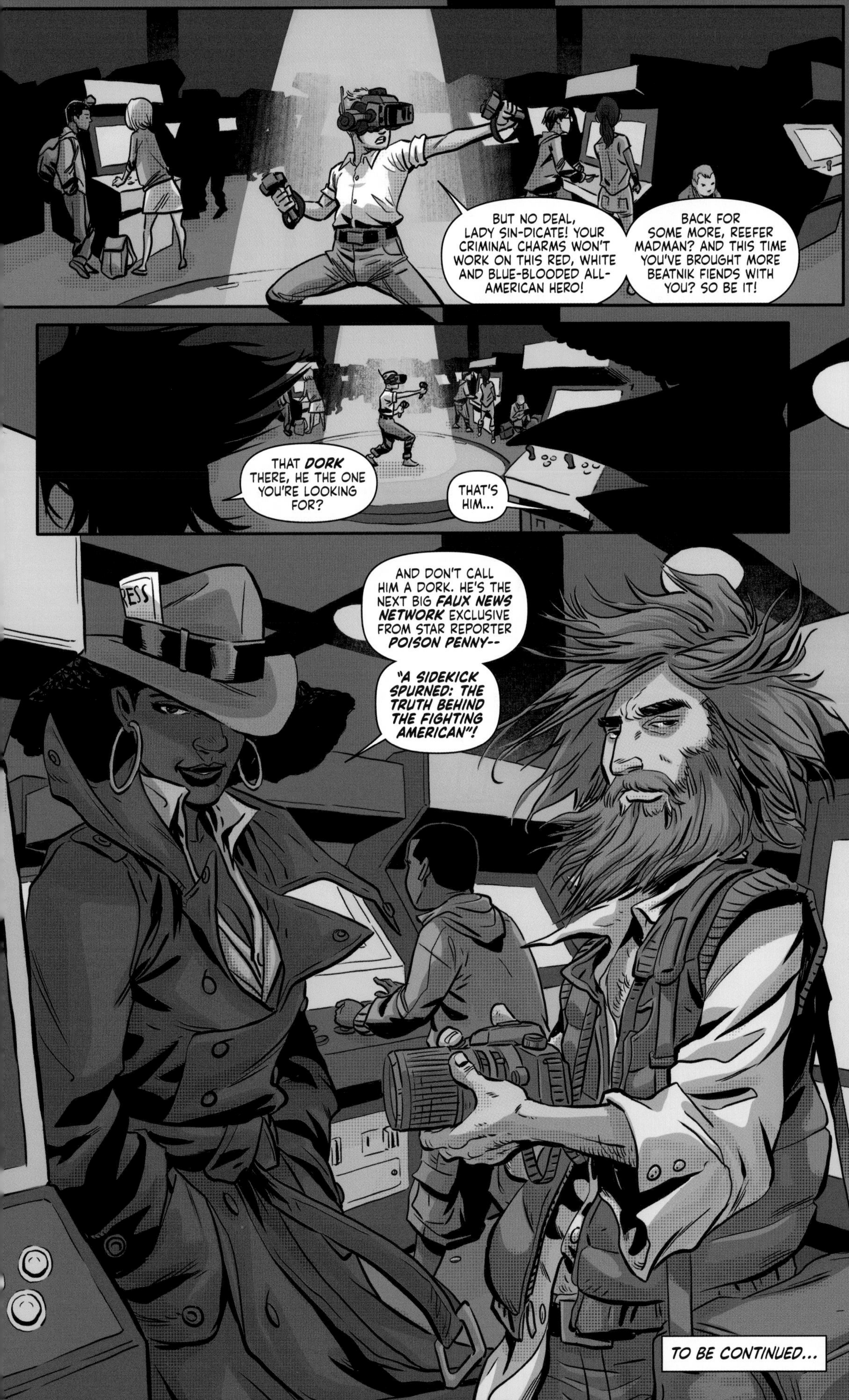
BUT NO DEAL, LADY SIN-DICATE! YOUR CRIMINAL CHARMS WON'T WORK ON THIS RED, WHITE AND BLUE-BLOODED ALL-AMERICAN HERO!
BACK FOR SOME MORE, REEFER MADMAN? AND THIS TIME YOU'VE BROUGHT MORE BEATNIK FIENDS WITH YOU? SO BE IT!
THAT DORK THERE, HE THE ONE YOU'RE LOOKING FOR?
THAT'S HIM...
AND DON'T CALL HIM A DORK. HE'S THE NEXT BIG FAUX NEWS NETWORK EXCLUSIVE FROM STAR REPORTER POISON PENNY--
"A SIDEKICK SPURNED: THE TRUTH BEHIND THE FIGHTING AMERICAN"!
TO BE CONTINUED...

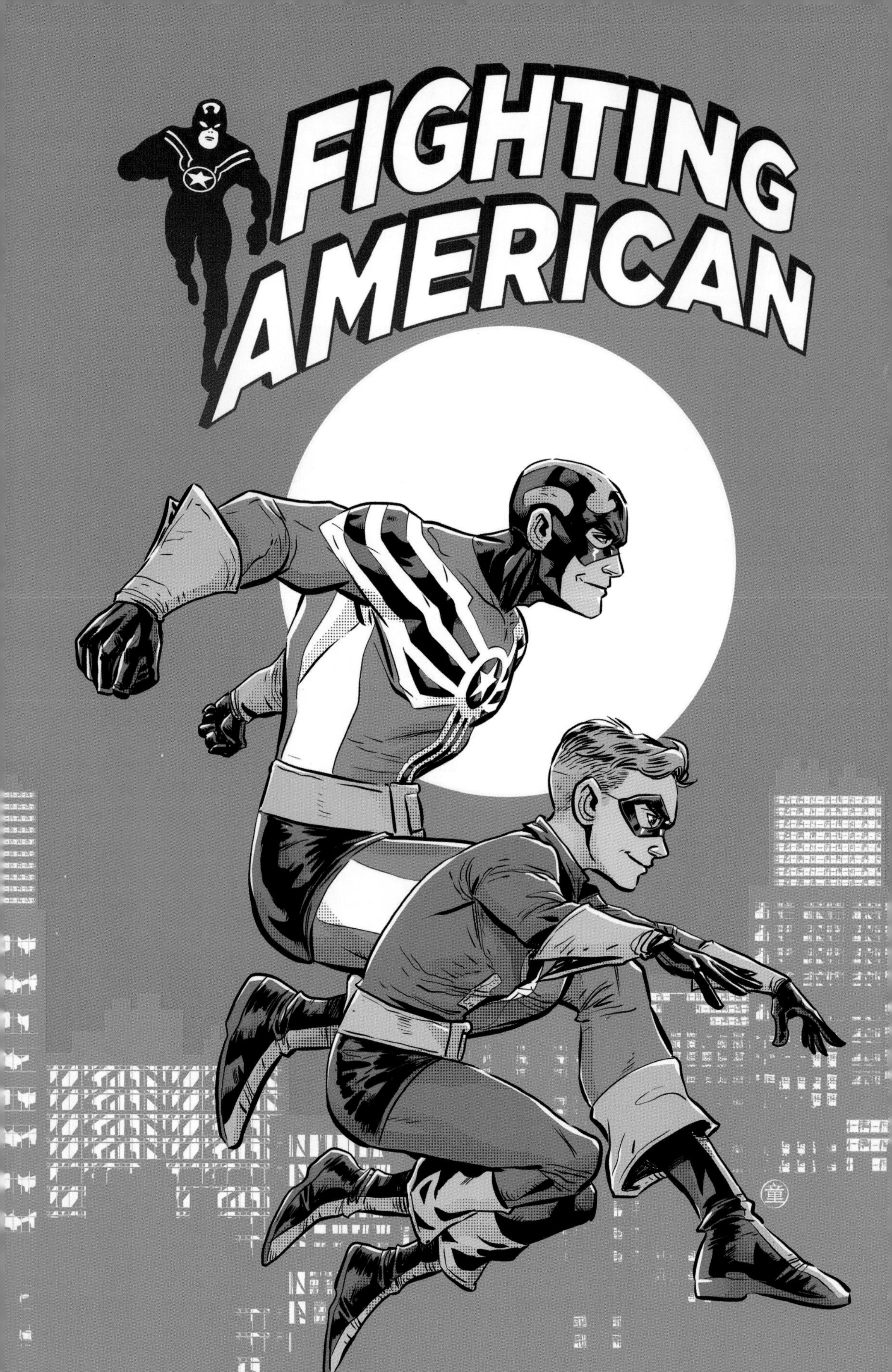
FIGHTING
AMERICAN

CHAPTER THREE COVER 3A ART
BY ANDIE TONG

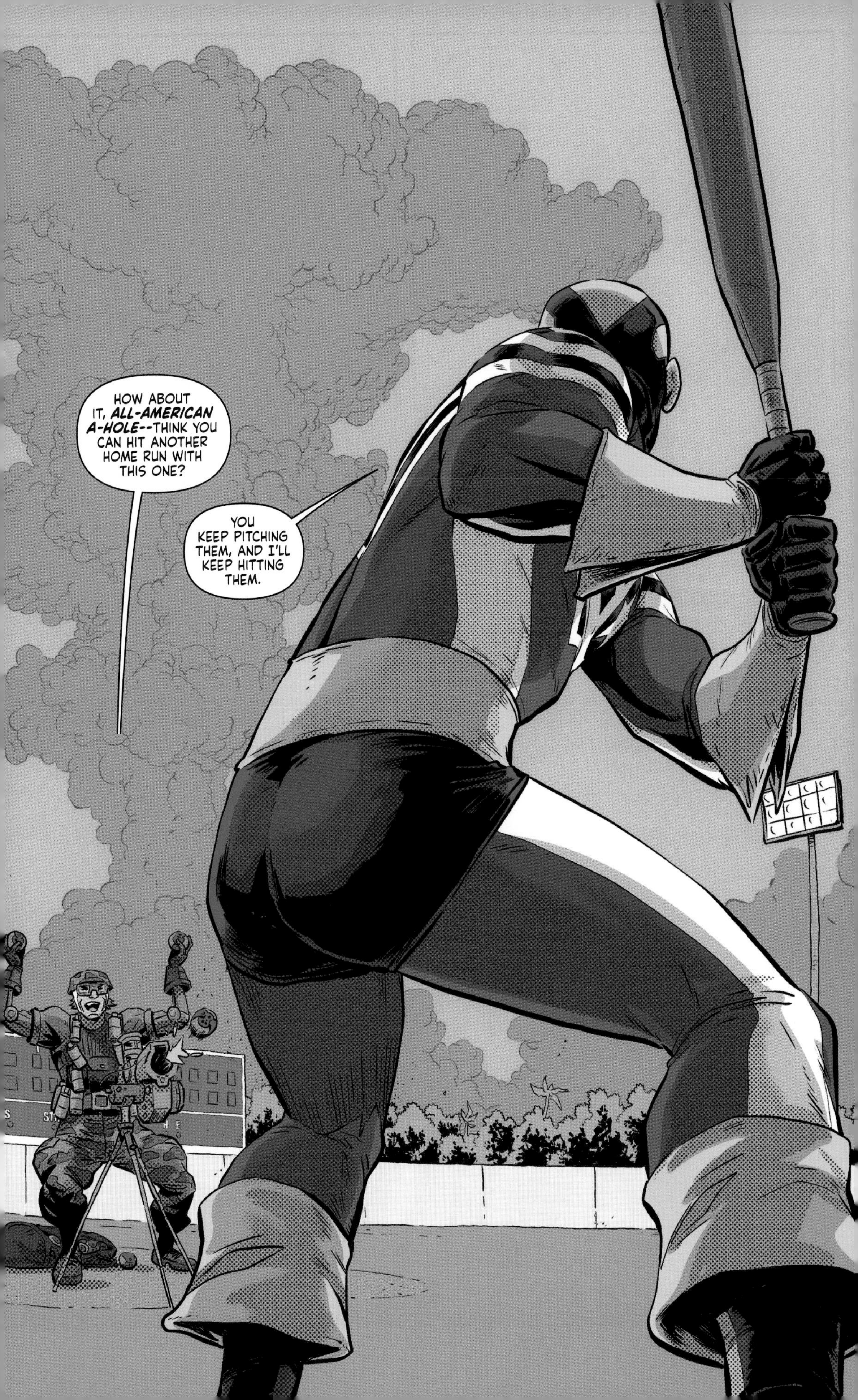

HOW ABOUT IT, ALL-AMERICAN A-HOLE--THINK YOU CAN HIT ANOTHER HOME RUN WITH THIS ONE?
YOU KEEP PITCHING THEM, AND I'LL KEEP HITTING THEM.

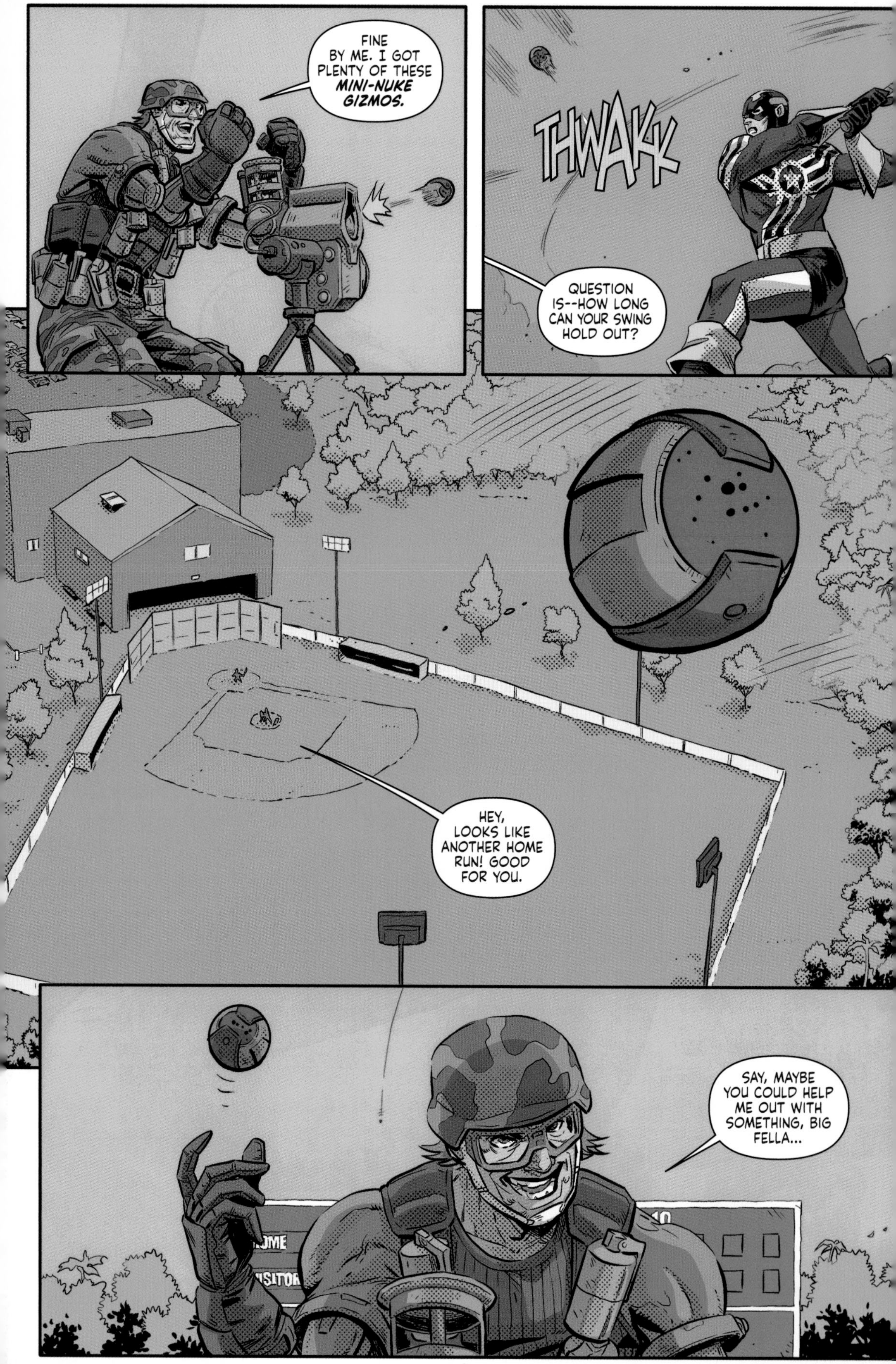
FINE BY ME. I GOT PLENTY OF THESE *MINI-NUKE GIZMOS.*
THWAKK
QUESTION IS--HOW LONG CAN YOUR SWING HOLD OUT?
HEY, LOOKS LIKE ANOTHER HOME RUN! GOOD FOR YOU.
SAY, MAYBE YOU COULD HELP ME OUT WITH SOMETHING, BIG FELLA...

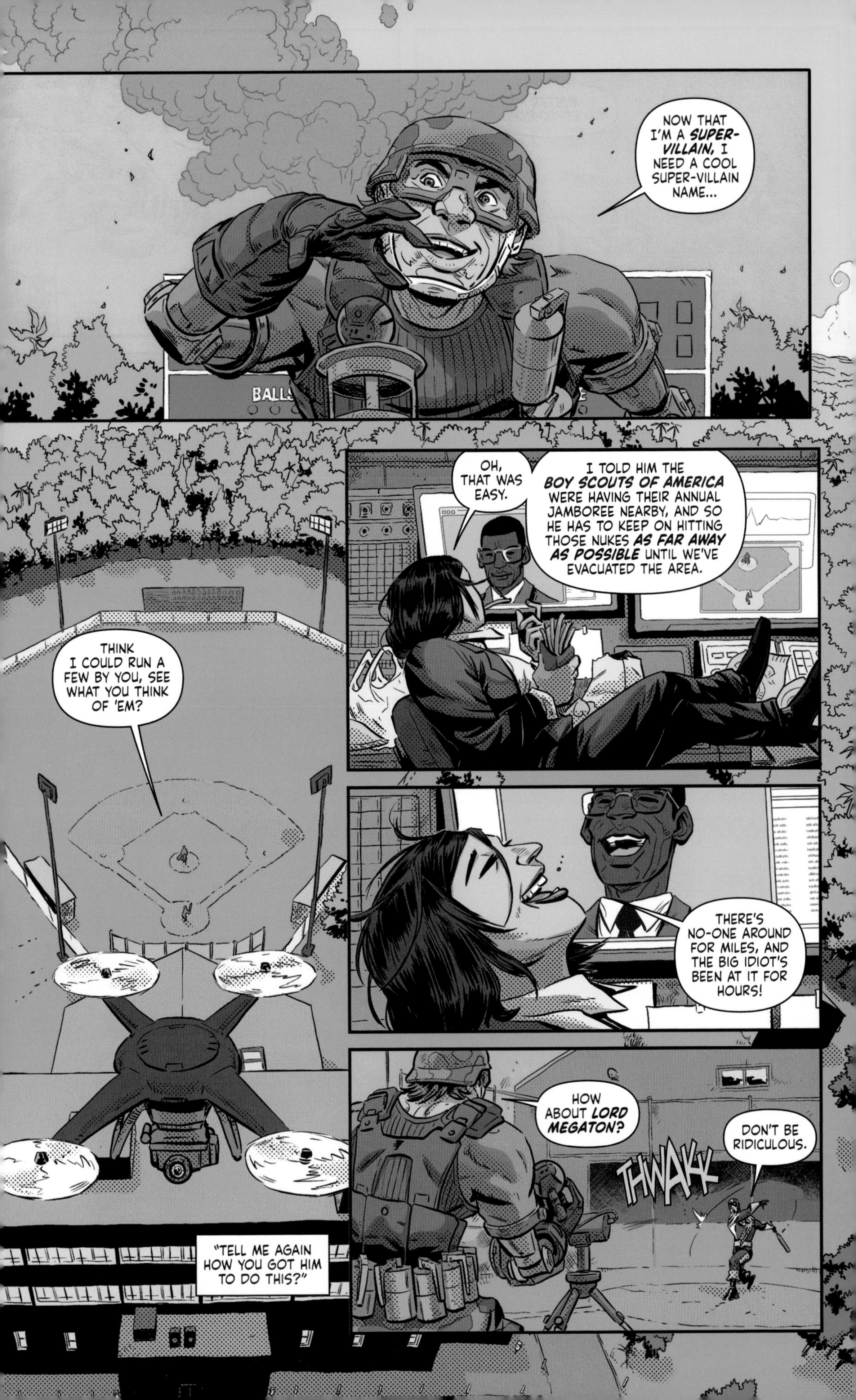
NOW THAT I'M A SUPER-VILLAIN, I NEED A COOL SUPER-VILLAIN NAME...
THINK I COULD RUN A FEW BY YOU, SEE WHAT YOU THINK OF 'EM?
"TELL ME AGAIN HOW YOU GOT HIM TO DO THIS?"
OH, THAT WAS EASY.
I TOLD HIM THE BOY SCOUTS OF AMERICA WERE HAVING THEIR ANNUAL JAMBOREE NEARBY, AND SO HE HAS TO KEEP ON HITTING THOSE NUKES AS FAR AWAY AS POSSIBLE UNTIL WE'VE EVACUATED THE AREA.
THERE'S NO-ONE AROUND FOR MILES, AND THE BIG IDIOT'S BEEN AT IT FOR HOURS!
HOW ABOUT LORD MEGATON?
THWAKK
DON'T BE RIDICULOUS.

MISTER NUKESPLOSION.
IS THAT EVEN ENGLISH?
THWAKK
KABOOM THE NUCLEAR GUY.
ABSOLUTELY NOT.
THWAKK
MELTDOWN MANIAC?
STILL NO.
THWAKK
CAPTAIN KABLAMAGEDDON?
I DON'T THINK SO.
THWAKK
ACTUALLY, I HAVE A SUGGESTION FOR YOU.

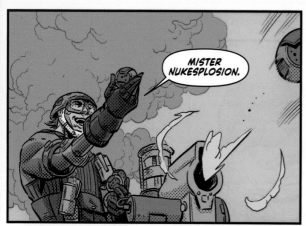

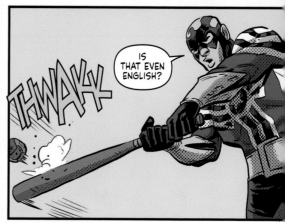

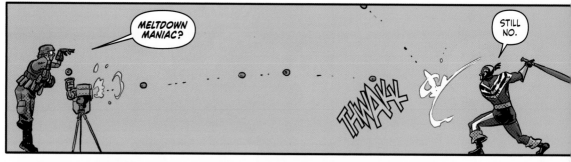

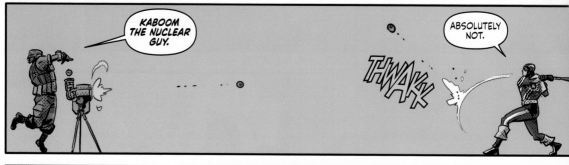

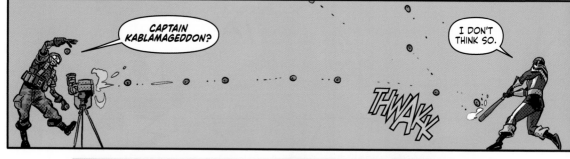

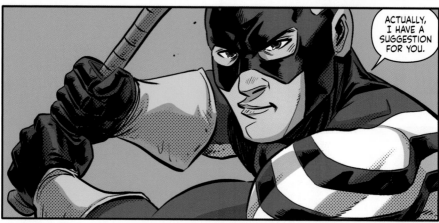

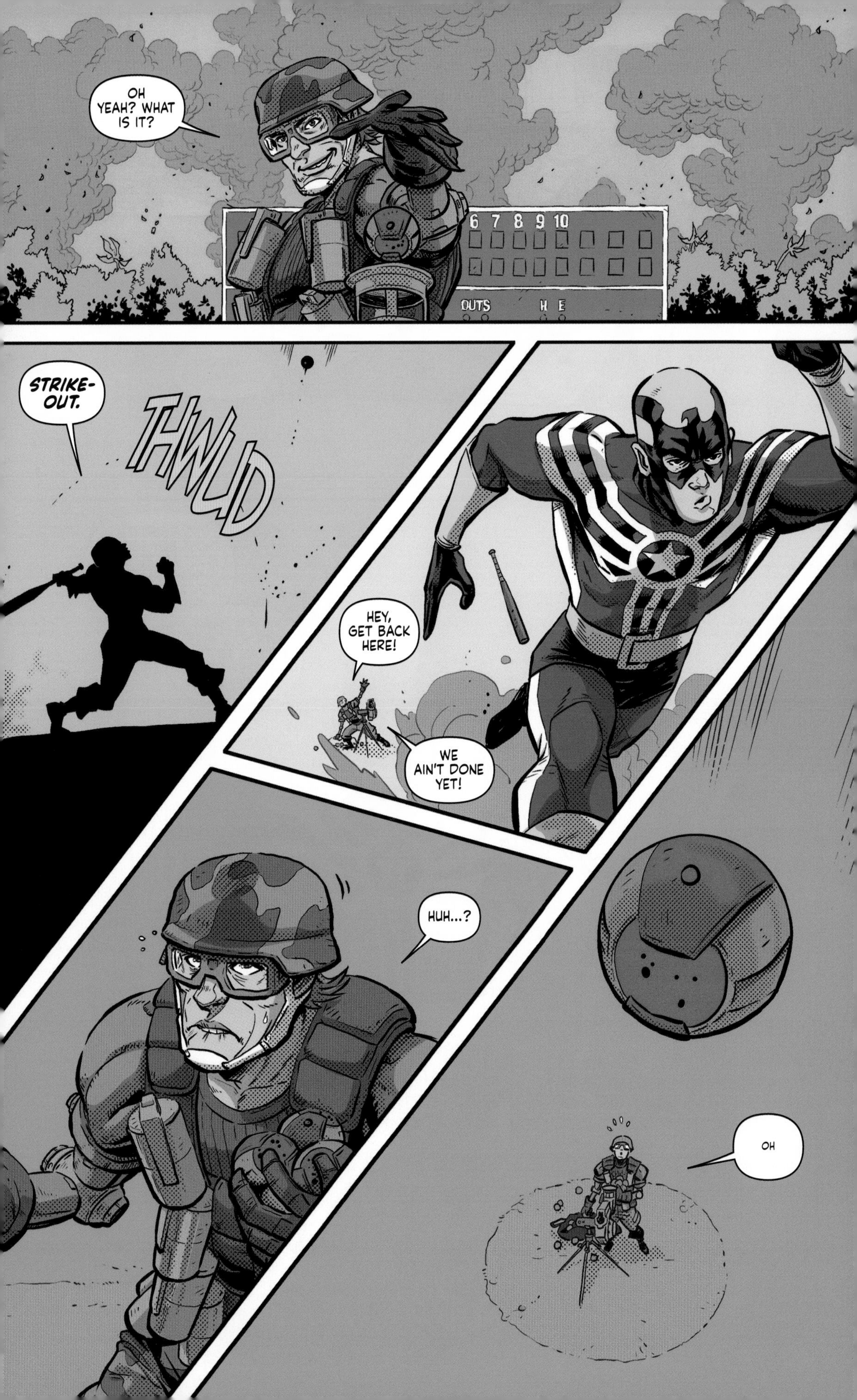
OH YEAH? WHAT IS IT?
6 7 8 9 10
OUTS H E
STRIKE-OUT.
THWUD
HEY, GET BACK HERE!
WE AIN'T DONE YET!
HUH...?
OH

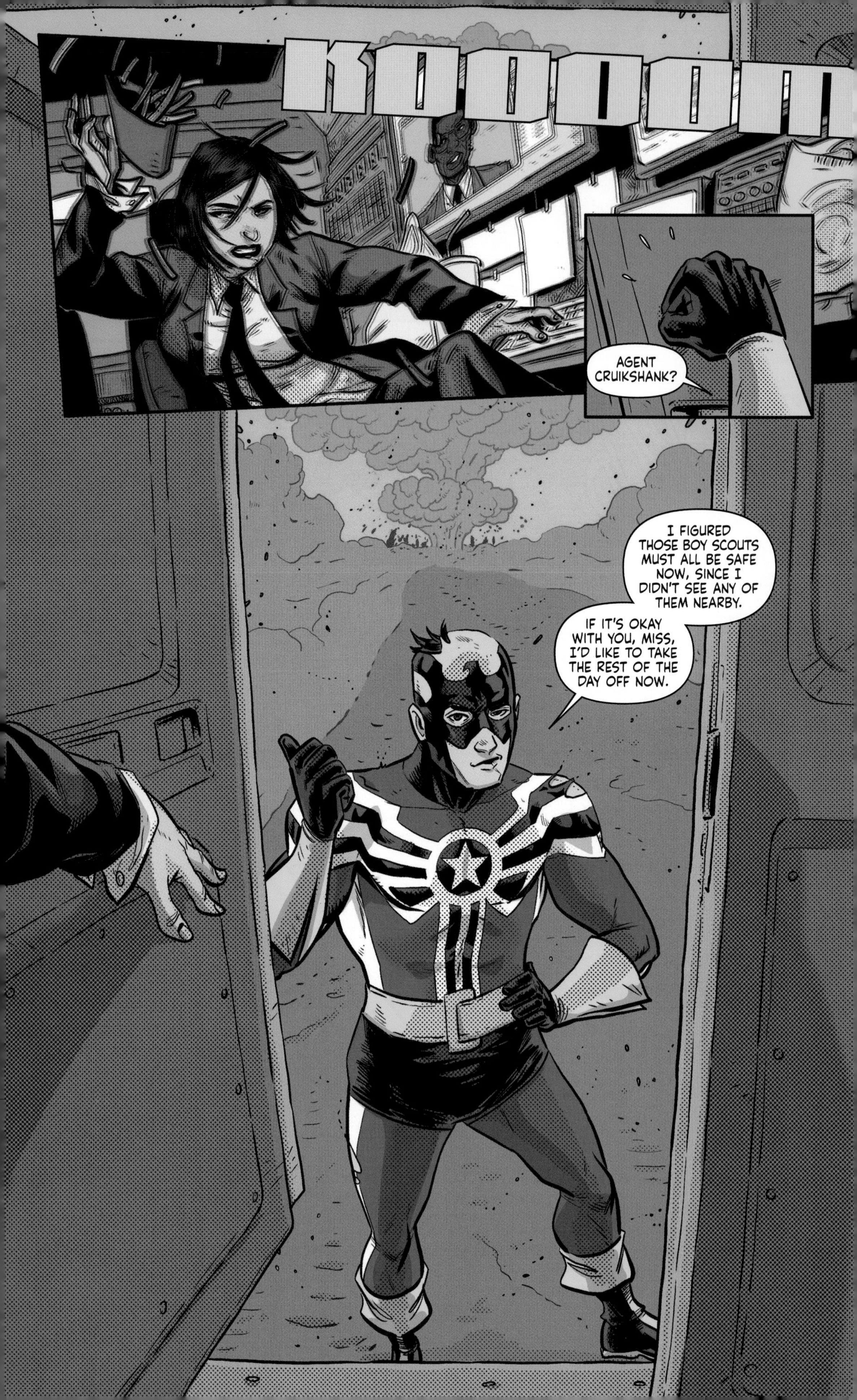
KOOOOM
AGENT CRUIKSHANK?
I FIGURED THOSE BOY SCOUTS MUST ALL BE SAFE NOW, SINCE I DIDN'T SEE ANY OF THEM NEARBY.
IF IT'S OKAY WITH YOU, MISS, I'D LIKE TO TAKE THE REST OF THE DAY OFF NOW.

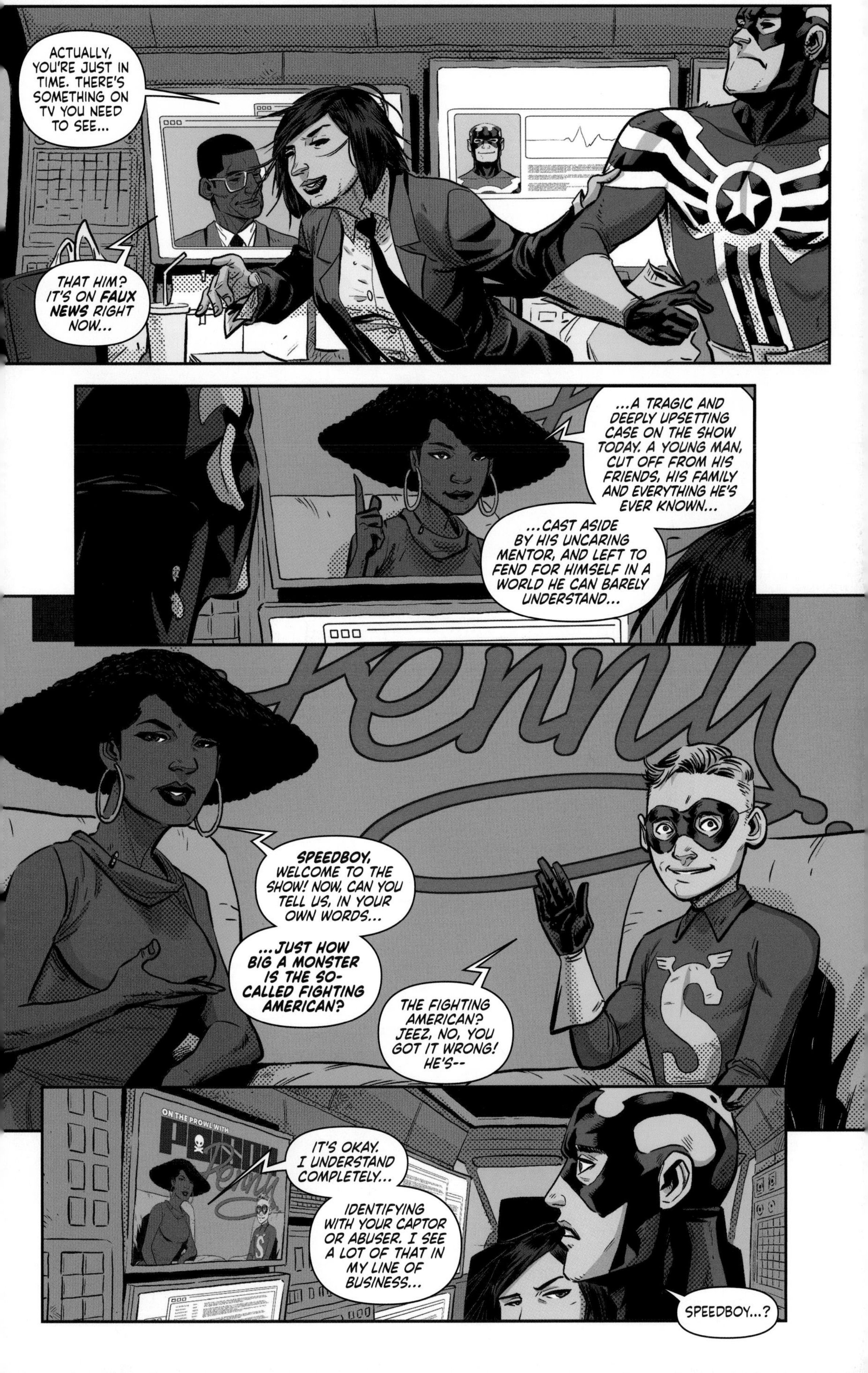
ACTUALLY, YOU'RE JUST IN TIME. THERE'S SOMETHING ON TV YOU NEED TO SEE...
THAT HIM? IT'S ON FAUX NEWS RIGHT NOW...
...A TRAGIC AND DEEPLY UPSETTING CASE ON THE SHOW TODAY. A YOUNG MAN, CUT OFF FROM HIS FRIENDS, HIS FAMILY AND EVERYTHING HE'S EVER KNOWN...
...CAST ASIDE BY HIS UNCARING MENTOR, AND LEFT TO FEND FOR HIMSELF IN A WORLD HE CAN BARELY UNDERSTAND...
SPEEDBOY, WELCOME TO THE SHOW! NOW, CAN YOU TELL US, IN YOUR OWN WORDS...
...JUST HOW BIG A MONSTER IS THE SO-CALLED FIGHTING AMERICAN?
THE FIGHTING AMERICAN? JEEZ, NO, YOU GOT IT WRONG! HE'S--
ON THE PROWL WITH
IT'S OKAY. I UNDERSTAND COMPLETELY...
IDENTIFYING WITH YOUR CAPTOR OR ABUSER. I SEE A LOT OF THAT IN MY LINE OF BUSINESS...
SPEEDBOY...?

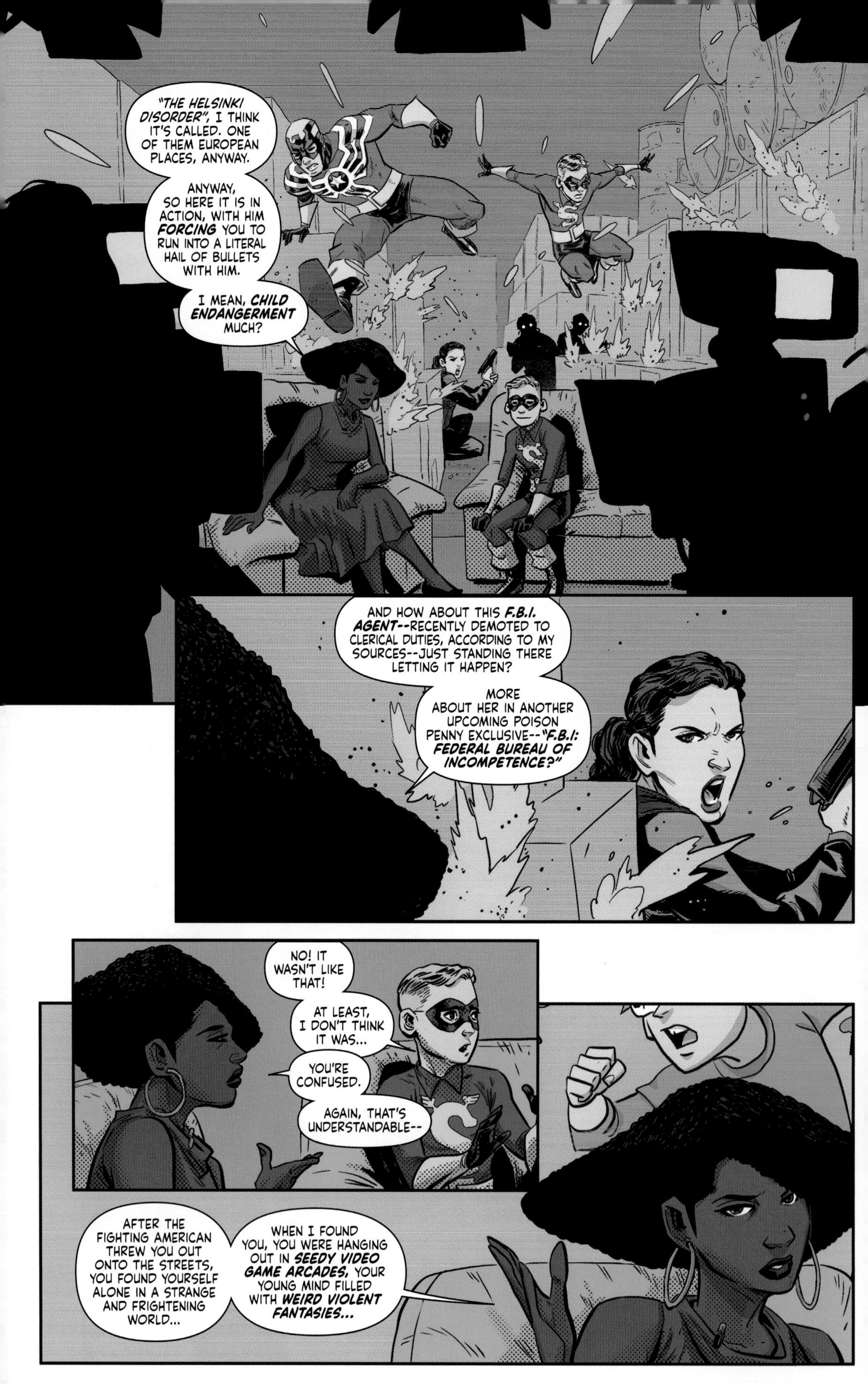
"THE HELSINKI DISORDER", I THINK IT'S CALLED. ONE OF THEM EUROPEAN PLACES, ANYWAY.
ANYWAY, SO HERE IT IS IN ACTION, WITH HIM FORCING YOU TO RUN INTO A LITERAL HAIL OF BULLETS WITH HIM.
I MEAN, CHILD ENDANGERMENT MUCH?
AND HOW ABOUT THIS F.B.I. AGENT--RECENTLY DEMOTED TO CLERICAL DUTIES, ACCORDING TO MY SOURCES--JUST STANDING THERE LETTING IT HAPPEN?
MORE ABOUT HER IN ANOTHER UPCOMING POISON PENNY EXCLUSIVE--"F.B.I: FEDERAL BUREAU OF INCOMPETENCE?"
NO! IT WASN'T LIKE THAT!
AT LEAST, I DON'T THINK IT WAS...
YOU'RE CONFUSED.
AGAIN, THAT'S UNDERSTANDABLE--
AFTER THE FIGHTING AMERICAN THREW YOU OUT ONTO THE STREETS, YOU FOUND YOURSELF ALONE IN A STRANGE AND FRIGHTENING WORLD...
WHEN I FOUND YOU, YOU WERE HANGING OUT IN SEEDY VIDEO GAME ARCADES, YOUR YOUNG MIND FILLED WITH WEIRD VIOLENT FANTASIES...

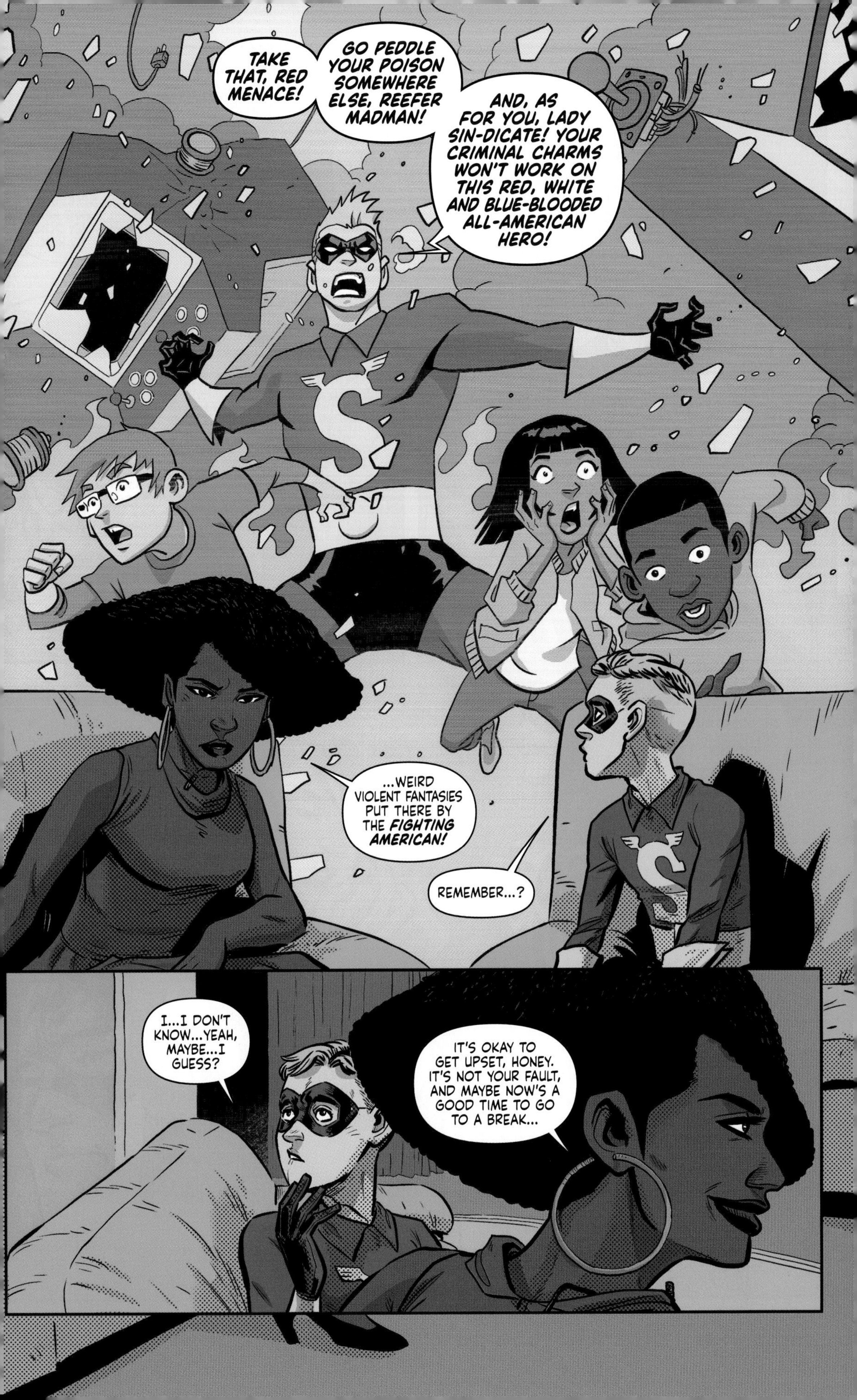
TAKE THAT, RED MENACE!
GO PEDDLE YOUR POISON SOMEWHERE ELSE, REEFER MADMAN!
AND, AS FOR YOU, LADY SIN-DICATE! YOUR CRIMINAL CHARMS WON'T WORK ON THIS RED, WHITE AND BLUE-BLOODED ALL-AMERICAN HERO!
...WEIRD VIOLENT FANTASIES PUT THERE BY THE *FIGHTING AMERICAN!*
REMEMBER...?
I...I DON'T KNOW...YEAH, MAYBE...I GUESS?
IT'S OKAY TO GET UPSET, HONEY. IT'S NOT YOUR FAULT, AND MAYBE NOW'S A GOOD TIME TO GO TO A BREAK...

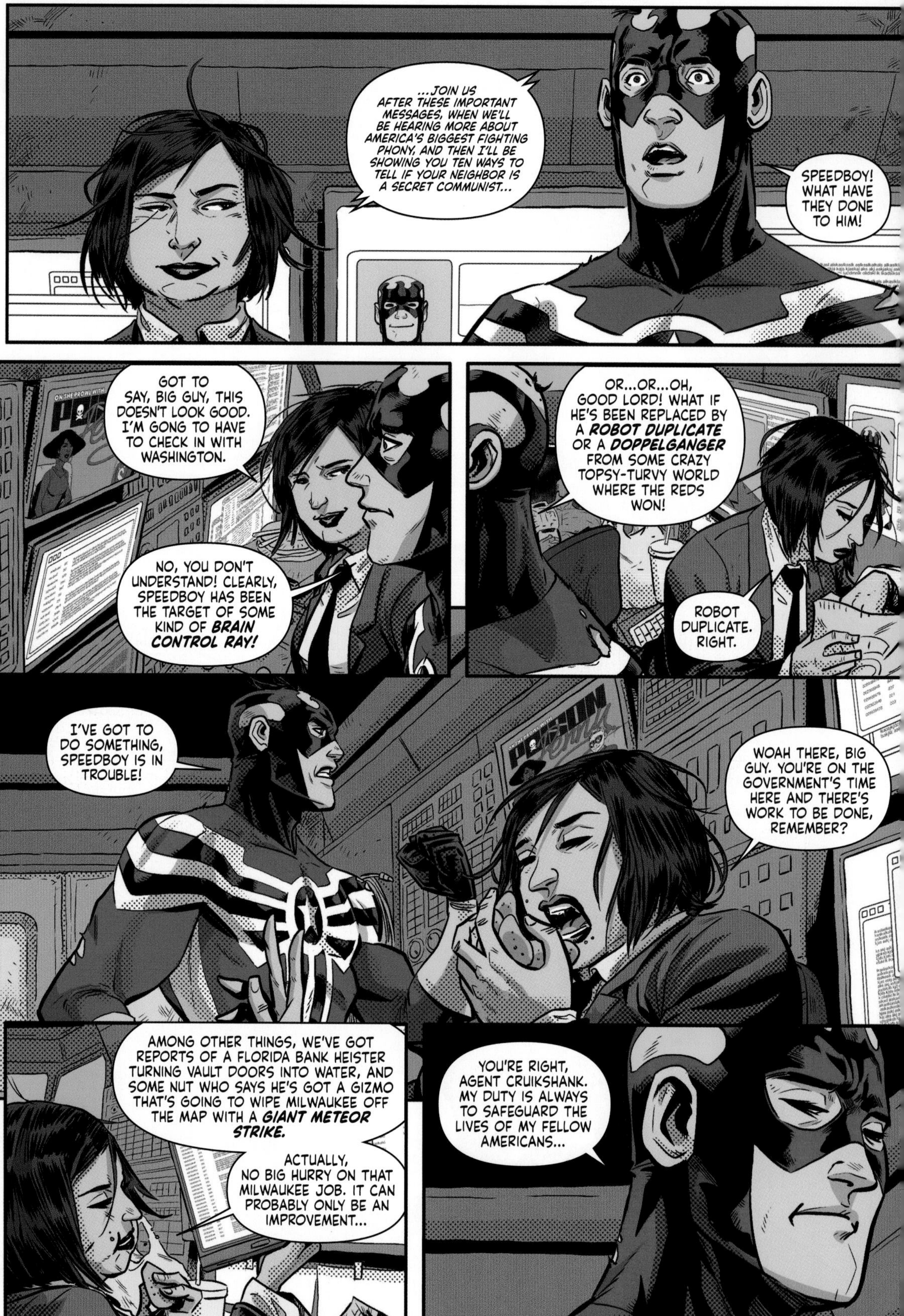
...JOIN US AFTER THESE IMPORTANT MESSAGES, WHEN WE'LL BE HEARING MORE ABOUT AMERICA'S BIGGEST FIGHTING PHONY, AND THEN I'LL BE SHOWING YOU TEN WAYS TO TELL IF YOUR NEIGHBOR IS A SECRET COMMUNIST...
SPEEDBOY! WHAT HAVE THEY DONE TO HIM!
GOT TO SAY, BIG GUY, THIS DOESN'T LOOK GOOD. I'M GONG TO HAVE TO CHECK IN WITH WASHINGTON.
NO, YOU DON'T UNDERSTAND! CLEARLY, SPEEDBOY HAS BEEN THE TARGET OF SOME KIND OF BRAIN CONTROL RAY!
OR...OR...OH, GOOD LORD! WHAT IF HE'S BEEN REPLACED BY A ROBOT DUPLICATE OR A DOPPELGANGER FROM SOME CRAZY TOPSY-TURVY WORLD WHERE THE REDS WON!
ROBOT DUPLICATE. RIGHT.
I'VE GOT TO DO SOMETHING, SPEEDBOY IS IN TROUBLE!
WOAH THERE, BIG GUY. YOU'RE ON THE GOVERNMENT'S TIME HERE AND THERE'S WORK TO BE DONE, REMEMBER?
AMONG OTHER THINGS, WE'VE GOT REPORTS OF A FLORIDA BANK HEISTER TURNING VAULT DOORS INTO WATER, AND SOME NUT WHO SAYS HE'S GOT A GIZMO THAT'S GOING TO WIPE MILWAUKEE OFF THE MAP WITH A GIANT METEOR STRIKE.
ACTUALLY, NO BIG HURRY ON THAT MILWAUKEE JOB. IT CAN PROBABLY ONLY BE AN IMPROVEMENT...
YOU'RE RIGHT, AGENT CRUIKSHANK. MY DUTY IS ALWAYS TO SAFEGUARD THE LIVES OF MY FELLOW AMERICANS...

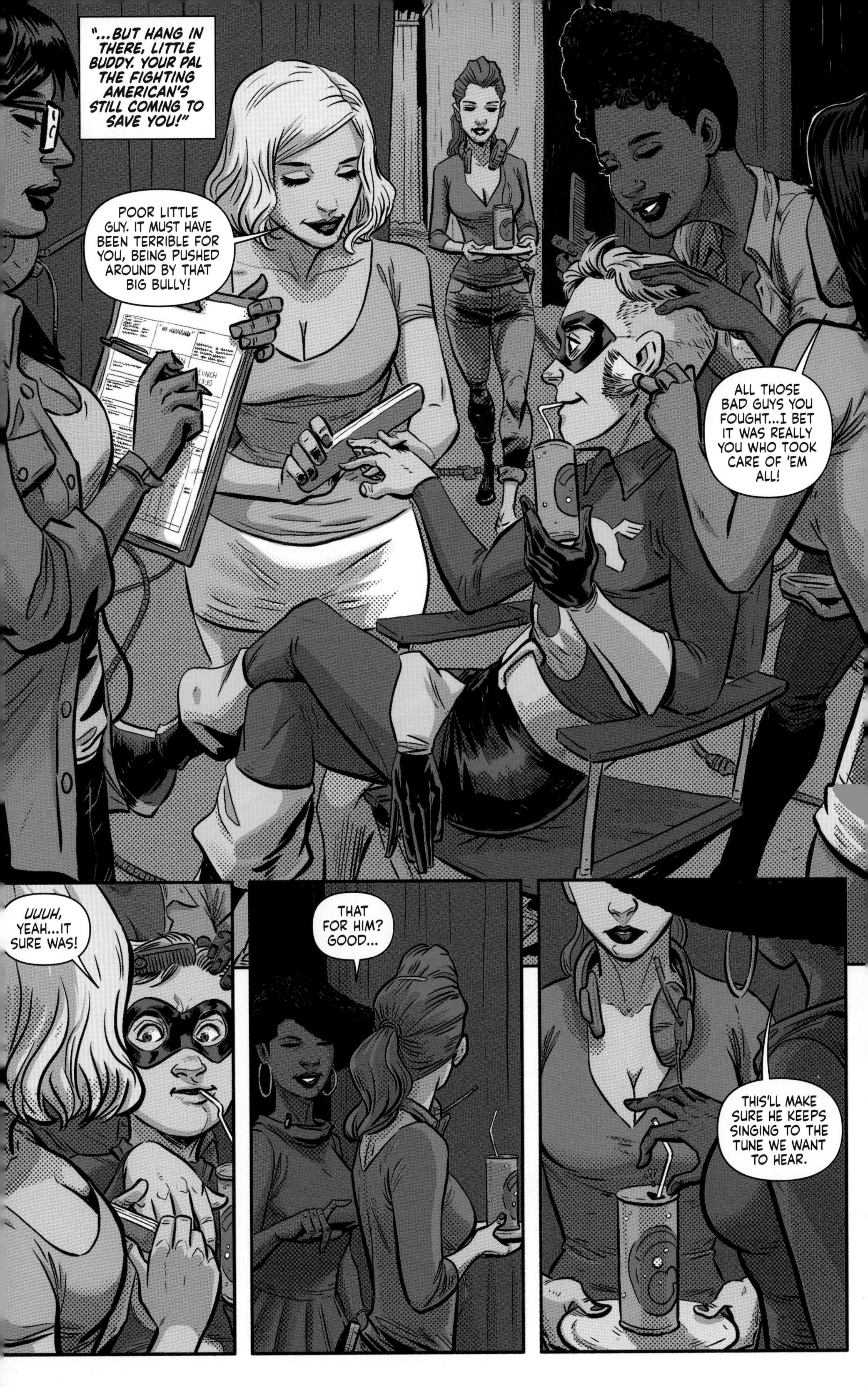
"...BUT HANG IN THERE, LITTLE BUDDY. YOUR PAL THE FIGHTING AMERICAN'S STILL COMING TO SAVE YOU!"
POOR LITTLE GUY. IT MUST HAVE BEEN TERRIBLE FOR YOU, BEING PUSHED AROUND BY THAT BIG BULLY!
ALL THOSE BAD GUYS YOU FOUGHT...I BET IT WAS REALLY YOU WHO TOOK CARE OF 'EM ALL!
UUUH, YEAH...IT SURE WAS!
THAT FOR HIM? GOOD...
THIS'LL MAKE SURE HE KEEPS SINGING TO THE TUNE WE WANT TO HEAR.

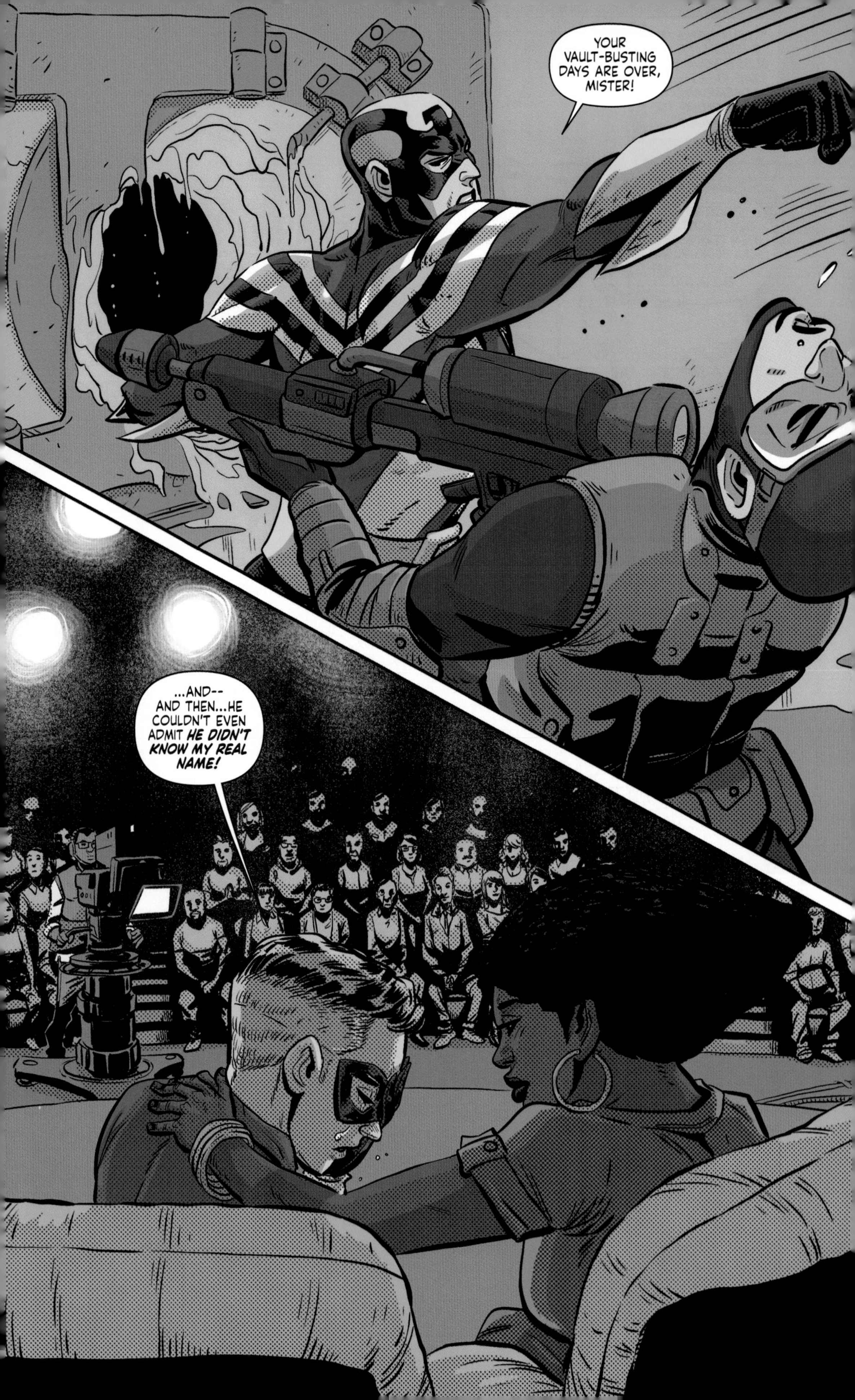
YOUR VAULT-BUSTING DAYS ARE OVER, MISTER!
...AND-- AND THEN...HE COULDN'T EVEN ADMIT HE DIDN'T KNOW MY REAL NAME!

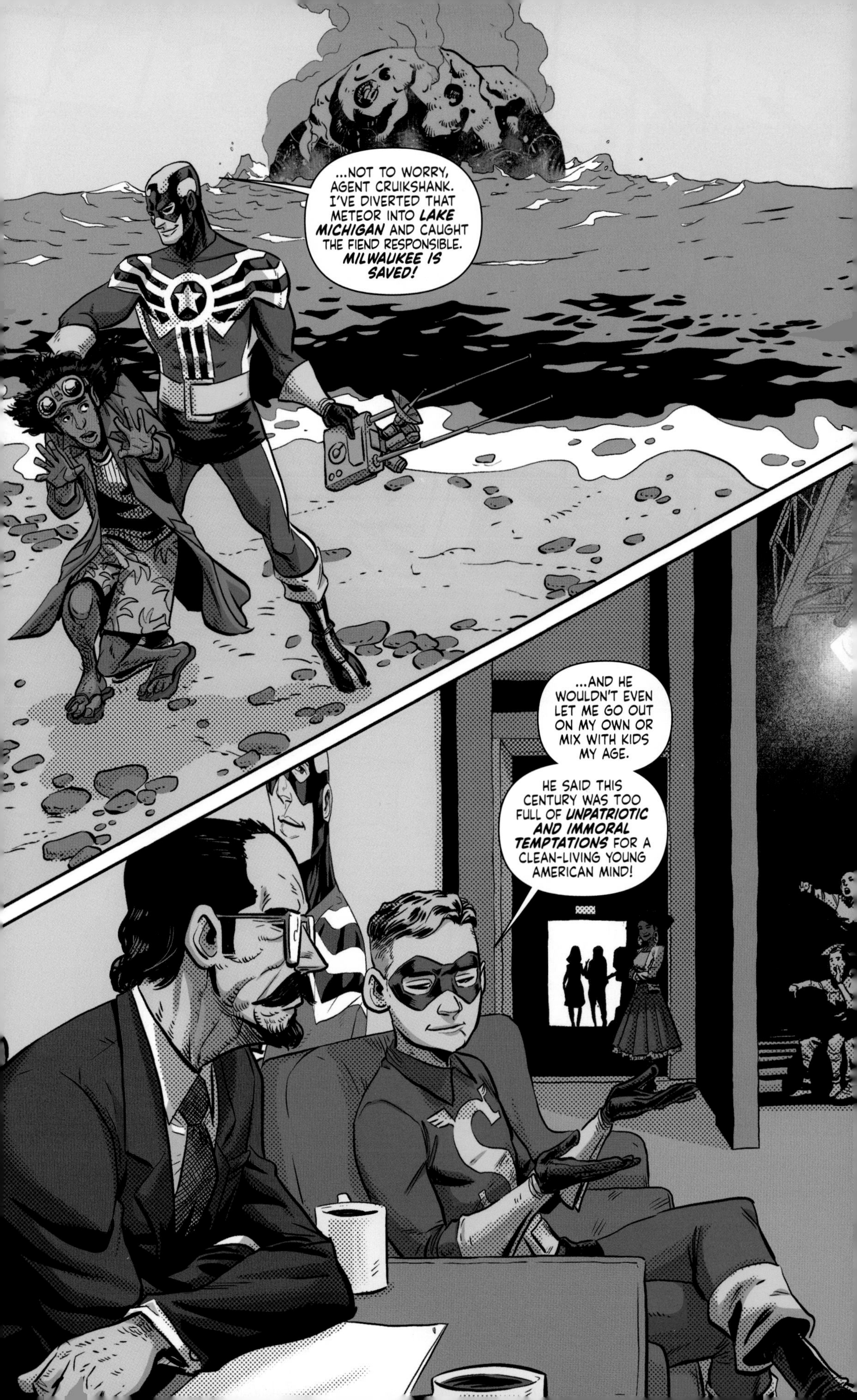
...NOT TO WORRY, AGENT CRUIKSHANK. I'VE DIVERTED THAT METEOR INTO LAKE MICHIGAN AND CAUGHT THE FIEND RESPONSIBLE. MILWAUKEE IS SAVED!
...AND HE WOULDN'T EVEN LET ME GO OUT ON MY OWN OR MIX WITH KIDS MY AGE.
HE SAID THIS CENTURY WAS TOO FULL OF UNPATRIOTIC AND IMMORAL TEMPTATIONS FOR A CLEAN-LIVING YOUNG AMERICAN MIND!

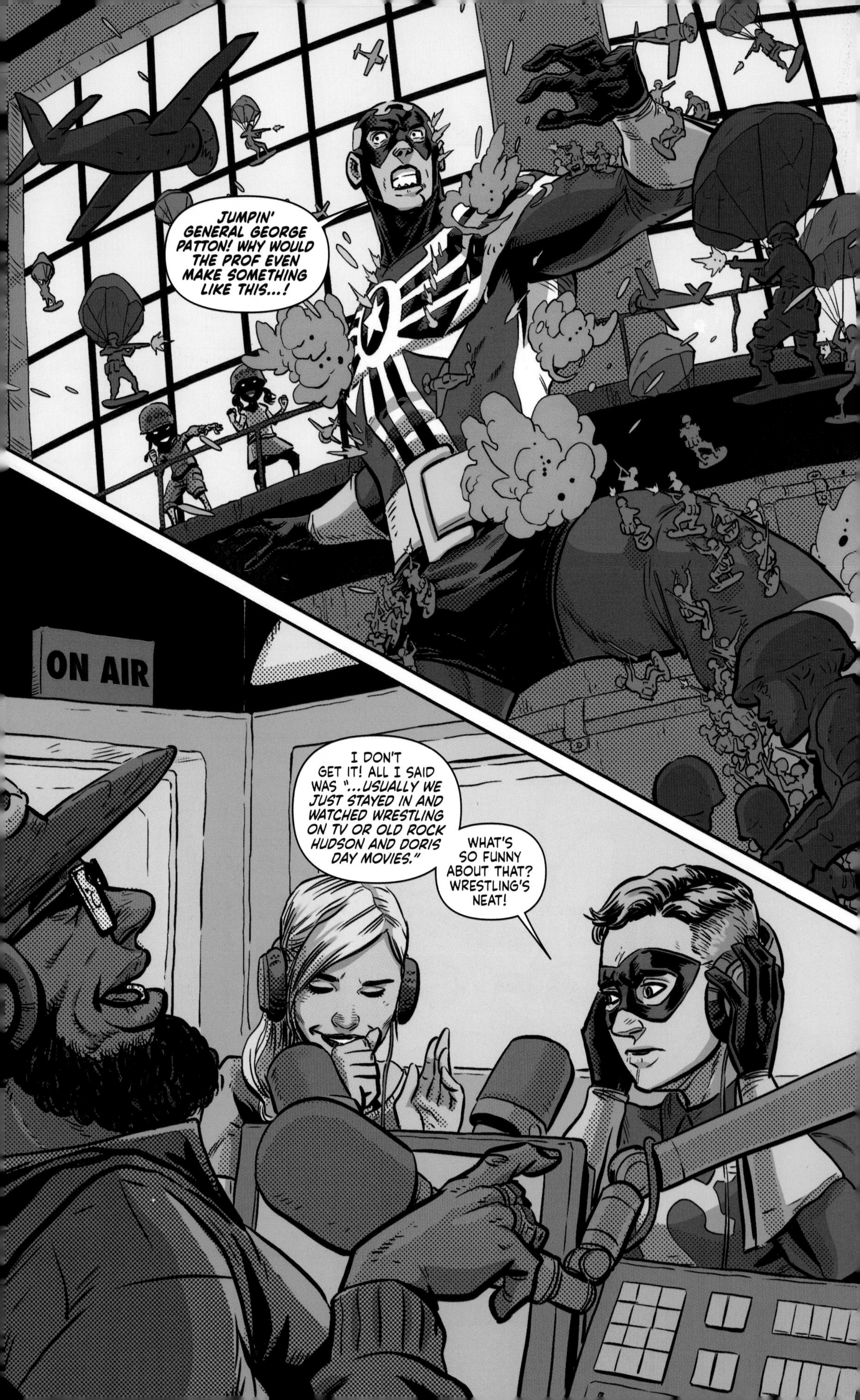
JUMPIN' GENERAL GEORGE PATTON! WHY WOULD THE PROF EVEN MAKE SOMETHING LIKE THIS...!
ON AIR
I DON'T GET IT! ALL I SAID WAS "...USUALLY WE JUST STAYED IN AND WATCHED WRESTLING ON TV OR OLD ROCK HUDSON AND DORIS DAY MOVIES."
WHAT'S SO FUNNY ABOUT THAT? WRESTLING'S NEAT!

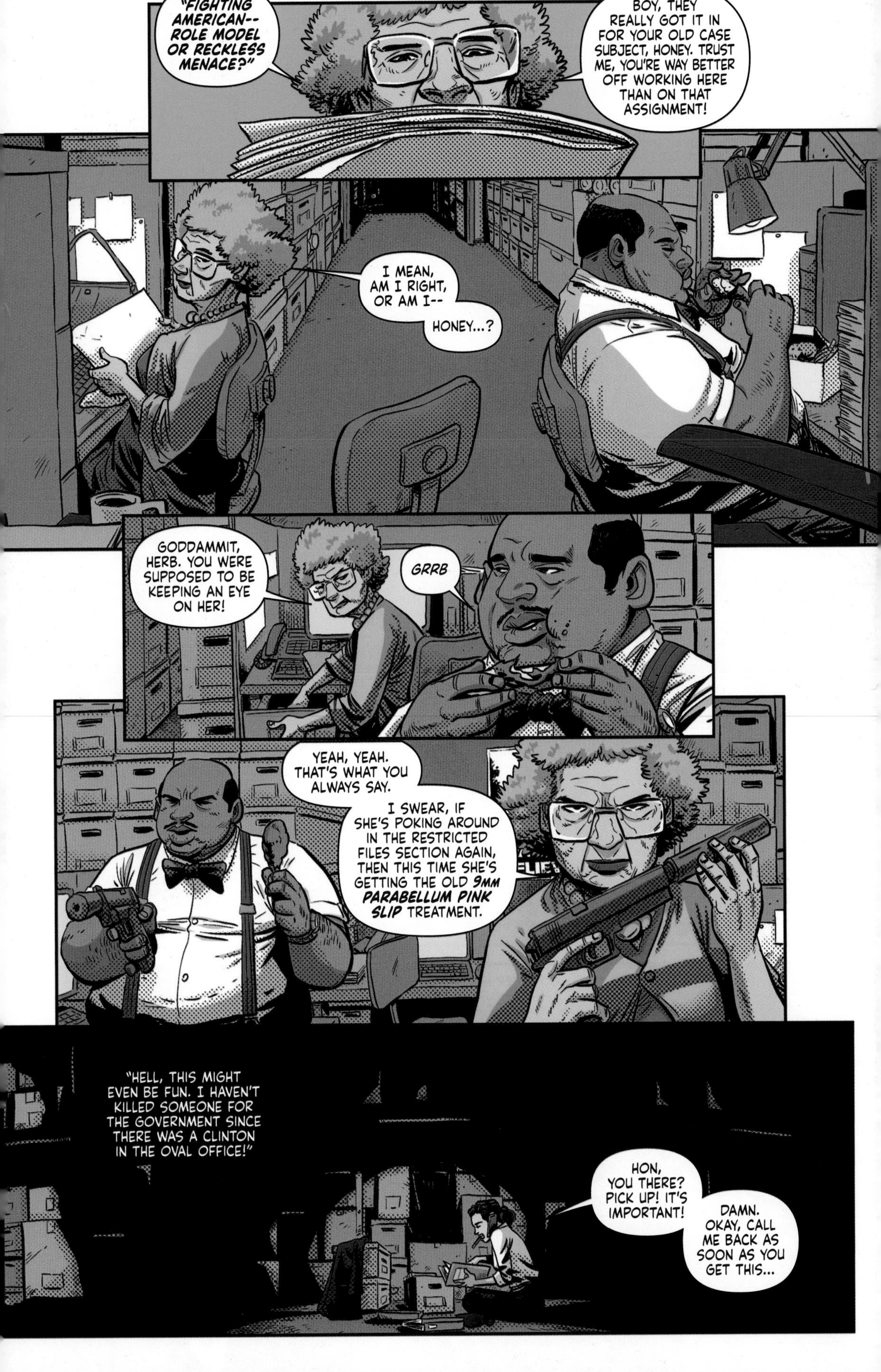
"FIGHTING AMERICAN-- ROLE MODEL OR RECKLESS MENACE?"
BOY, THEY REALLY GOT IT IN FOR YOUR OLD CASE SUBJECT, HONEY. TRUST ME, YOU'RE WAY BETTER OFF WORKING HERE THAN ON THAT ASSIGNMENT!
I MEAN, AM I RIGHT, OR AM I--
HONEY...?
GODDAMMIT, HERB. YOU WERE SUPPOSED TO BE KEEPING AN EYE ON HER!
GRRB
YEAH, YEAH. THAT'S WHAT YOU ALWAYS SAY.
I SWEAR, IF SHE'S POKING AROUND IN THE RESTRICTED FILES SECTION AGAIN, THEN THIS TIME SHE'S GETTING THE OLD 9MM PARABELLUM PINK SLIP TREATMENT.
"HELL, THIS MIGHT EVEN BE FUN. I HAVEN'T KILLED SOMEONE FOR THE GOVERNMENT SINCE THERE WAS A CLINTON IN THE OVAL OFFICE!"
HON, YOU THERE? PICK UP! IT'S IMPORTANT!
DAMN. OKAY, CALL ME BACK AS SOON AS YOU GET THIS...

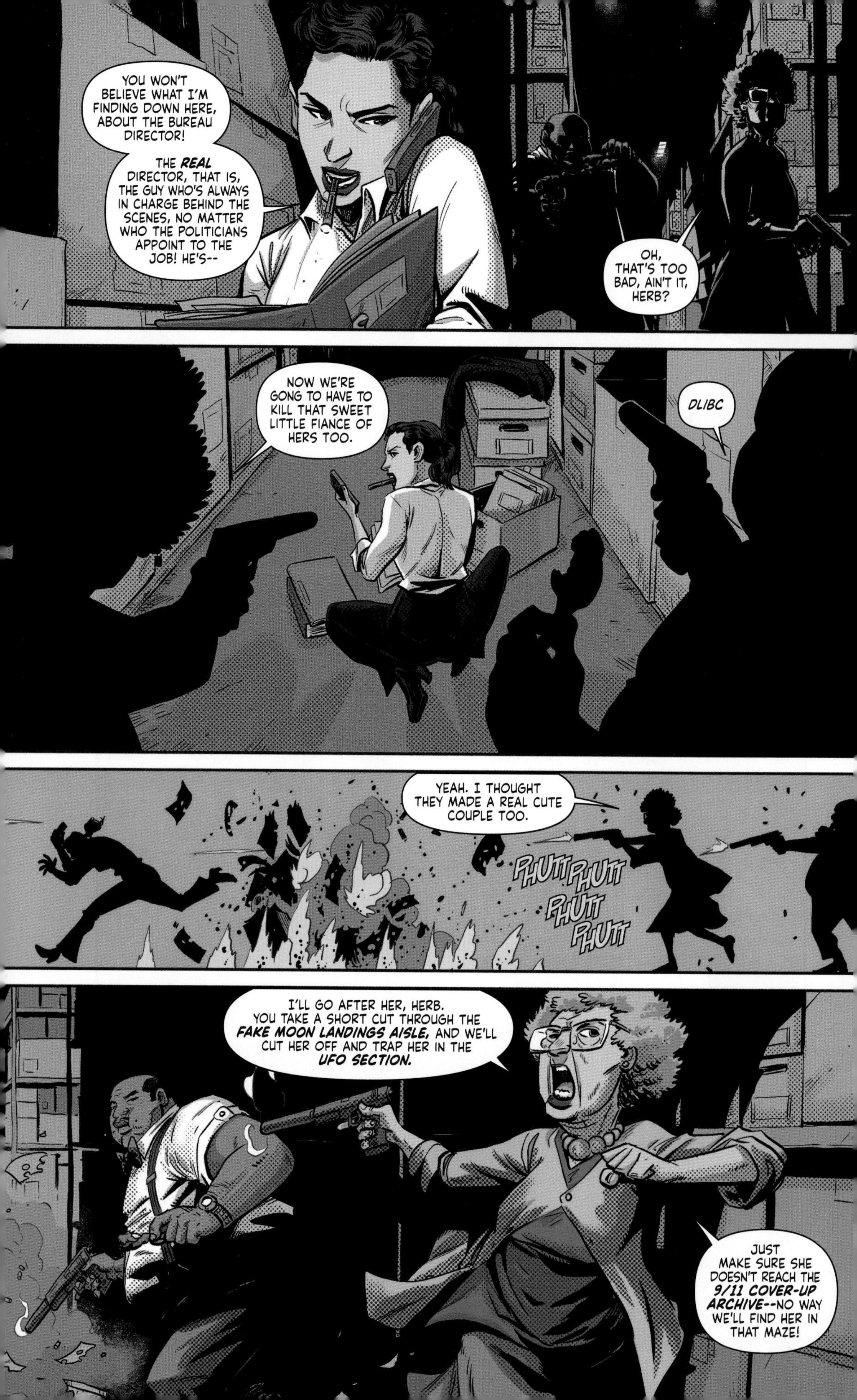
YOU WON'T BELIEVE WHAT I'M FINDING DOWN HERE, ABOUT THE BUREAU DIRECTOR!
THE REAL DIRECTOR, THAT IS, THE GUY WHO'S ALWAYS IN CHARGE BEHIND THE SCENES, NO MATTER WHO THE POLITICIANS APPOINT TO THE JOB! HE'S--
OH, THAT'S TOO BAD, AIN'T IT, HERB?
NOW WE'RE GONG TO HAVE TO KILL THAT SWEET LITTLE FIANCE OF HERS TOO.
DLIBC
YEAH. I THOUGHT THEY MADE A REAL CUTE COUPLE TOO.
PHUTT PHUTT PHUTT PHUTT
I'LL GO AFTER HER, HERB. YOU TAKE A SHORT CUT THROUGH THE FAKE MOON LANDINGS AISLE, AND WE'LL CUT HER OFF AND TRAP HER IN THE UFO SECTION.
JUST MAKE SURE SHE DOESN'T REACH THE 9/11 COVER-UP ARCHIVE--NO WAY WE'LL FIND HER IN THAT MAZE!

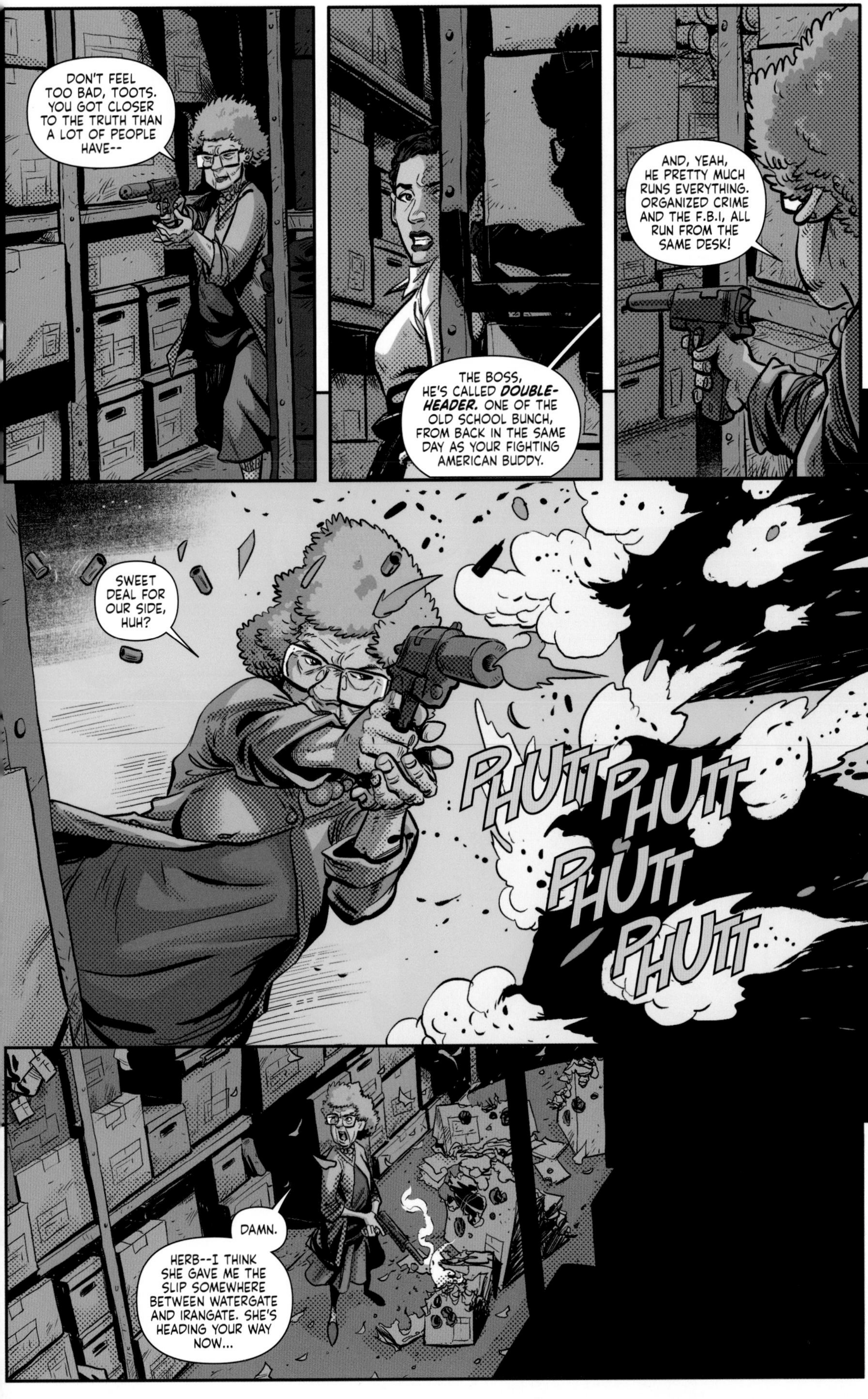
DON'T FEEL TOO BAD, TOOTS. YOU GOT CLOSER TO THE TRUTH THAN A LOT OF PEOPLE HAVE--
THE BOSS, HE'S CALLED DOUBLE-HEADER. ONE OF THE OLD SCHOOL BUNCH, FROM BACK IN THE SAME DAY AS YOUR FIGHTING AMERICAN BUDDY.
AND, YEAH, HE PRETTY MUCH RUNS EVERYTHING. ORGANIZED CRIME AND THE F.B.I, ALL RUN FROM THE SAME DESK!
SWEET DEAL FOR OUR SIDE, HUH?
PHUTT PHUTT PHUTT PHUTT...
DAMN.
HERB--I THINK SHE GAVE ME THE SLIP SOMEWHERE BETWEEN WATERGATE AND IRANGATE. SHE'S HEADING YOUR WAY NOW...

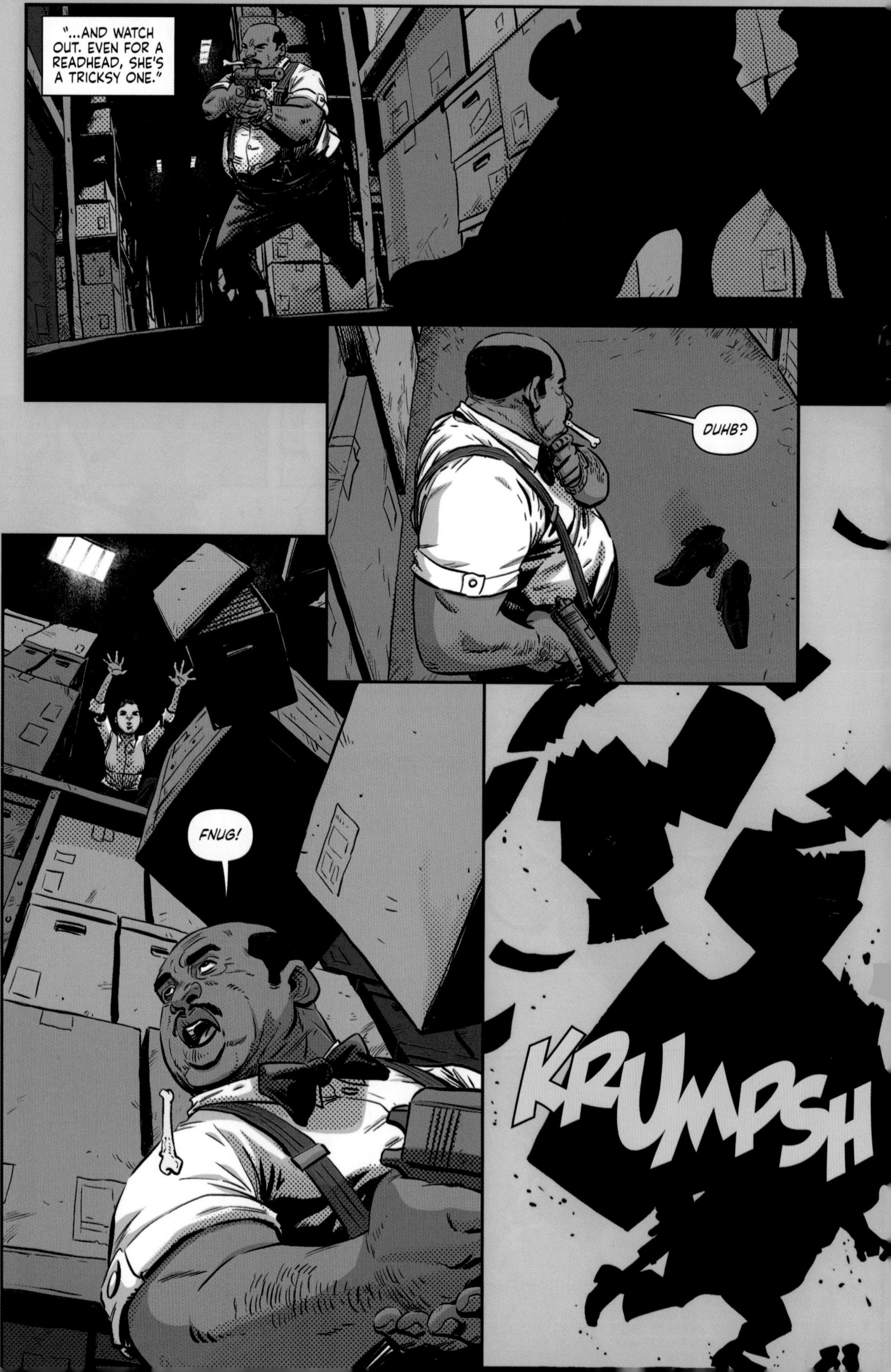
"...AND WATCH OUT. EVEN FOR A READHEAD, SHE'S A TRICKSY ONE."
DUHB?
FNUG!
KRUMPSH

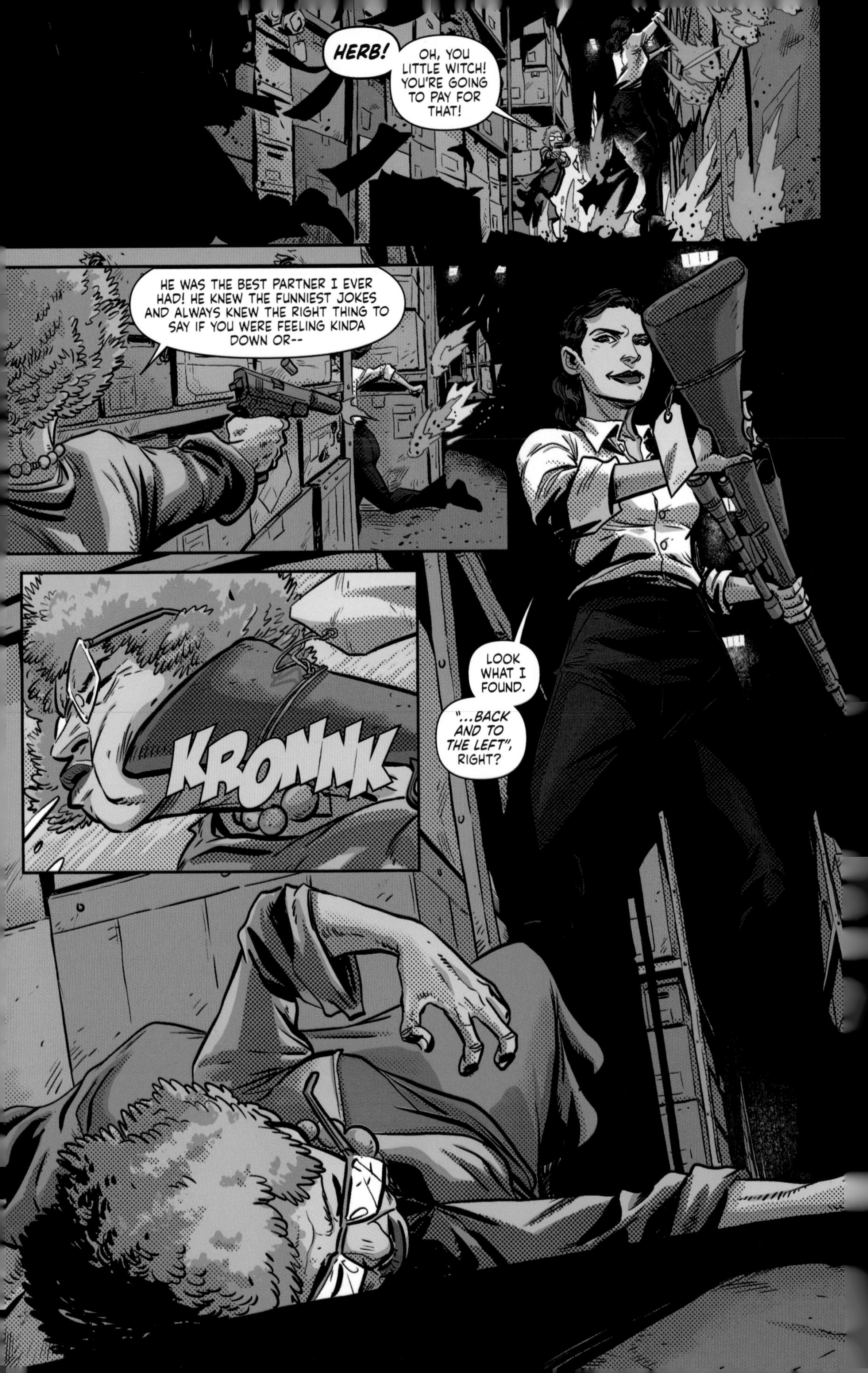
HERB!
OH, YOU LITTLE WITCH! YOU'RE GOING TO PAY FOR THAT!
HE WAS THE BEST PARTNER I EVER HAD! HE KNEW THE FUNNIEST JOKES AND ALWAYS KNEW THE RIGHT THING TO SAY IF YOU WERE FEELING KINDA DOWN OR--
KRONNK
LOOK WHAT I FOUND.
"...BACK AND TO THE LEFT", RIGHT?

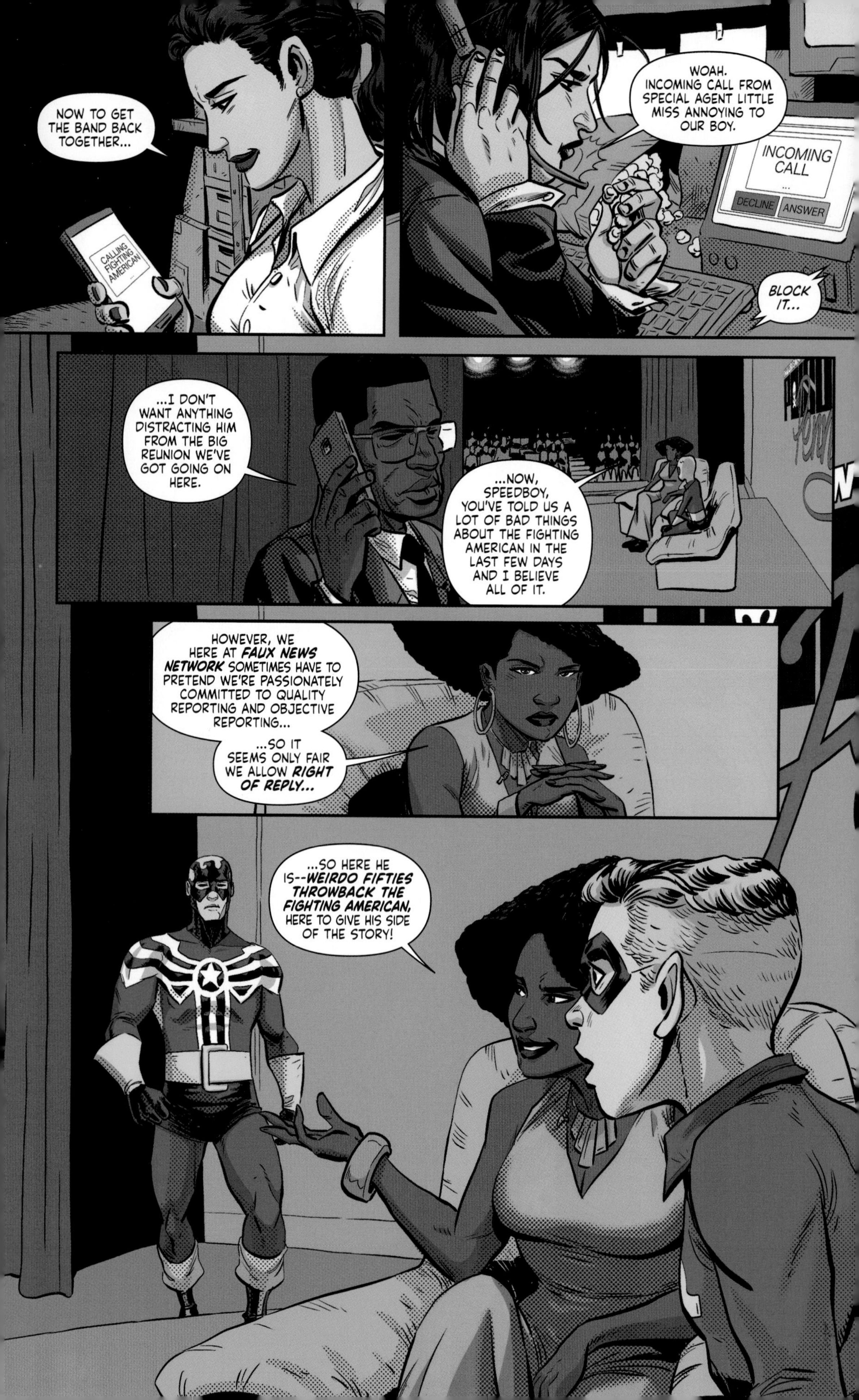
NOW TO GET THE BAND BACK TOGETHER...
CALLING FIGHTING AMERICAN
WOAH. INCOMING CALL FROM SPECIAL AGENT LITTLE MISS ANNOYING TO OUR BOY.
INCOMING CALL
DECLINE
ANSWER
BLOCK IT...
...I DON'T WANT ANYTHING DISTRACTING HIM FROM THE BIG REUNION WE'VE GOT GOING ON HERE.
...NOW, SPEEDBOY, YOU'VE TOLD US A LOT OF BAD THINGS ABOUT THE FIGHTING AMERICAN IN THE LAST FEW DAYS AND I BELIEVE ALL OF IT.
HOWEVER, WE HERE AT FAUX NEWS NETWORK SOMETIMES HAVE TO PRETEND WE'RE PASSIONATELY COMMITTED TO QUALITY REPORTING AND OBJECTIVE REPORTING...
...SO IT SEEMS ONLY FAIR WE ALLOW RIGHT OF REPLY...
...SO HERE HE IS--WEIRDO FIFTIES THROWBACK THE FIGHTING AMERICAN, HERE TO GIVE HIS SIDE OF THE STORY!

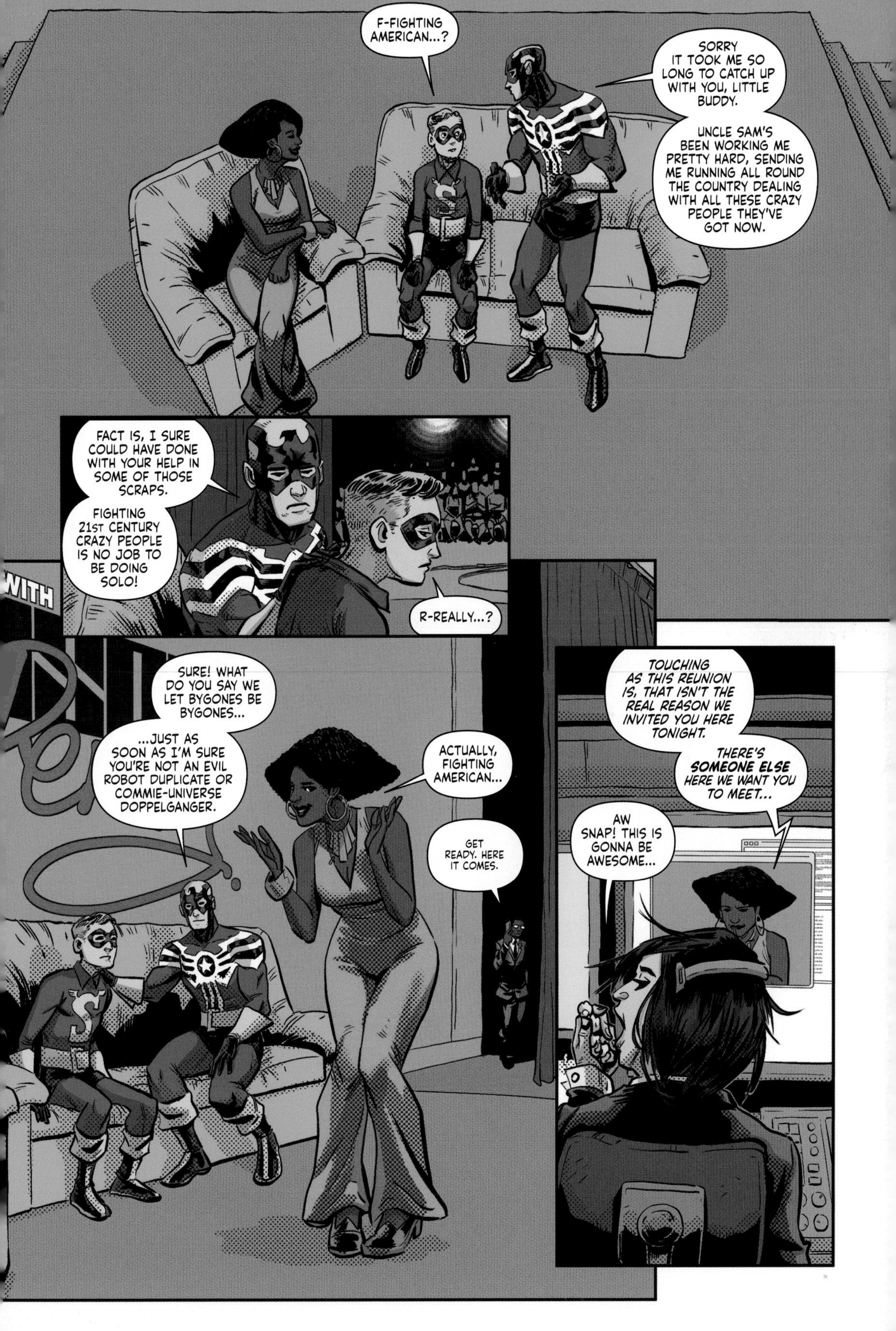
F-FIGHTING AMERICAN...?
SORRY IT TOOK ME SO LONG TO CATCH UP WITH YOU, LITTLE BUDDY.
UNCLE SAM'S BEEN WORKING ME PRETTY HARD, SENDING ME RUNNING ALL ROUND THE COUNTRY DEALING WITH ALL THESE CRAZY PEOPLE THEY'VE GOT NOW.
FACT IS, I SURE COULD HAVE DONE WITH YOUR HELP IN SOME OF THOSE SCRAPS.
FIGHTING 21ST CENTURY CRAZY PEOPLE IS NO JOB TO BE DOING SOLO!
R-REALLY...?
WITH
SURE! WHAT DO YOU SAY WE LET BYGONES BE BYGONES...
...JUST AS SOON AS I'M SURE YOU'RE NOT AN EVIL ROBOT DUPLICATE OR COMMIE-UNIVERSE DOPPELGANGER.
ACTUALLY, FIGHTING AMERICAN...
GET READY. HERE IT COMES.
TOUCHING AS THIS REUNION IS, THAT ISN'T THE REAL REASON WE INVITED YOU HERE TONIGHT.
THERE'S **SOMEONE ELSE** HERE WE WANT YOU TO MEET...
AW SNAP! THIS IS GONNA BE AWESOME...

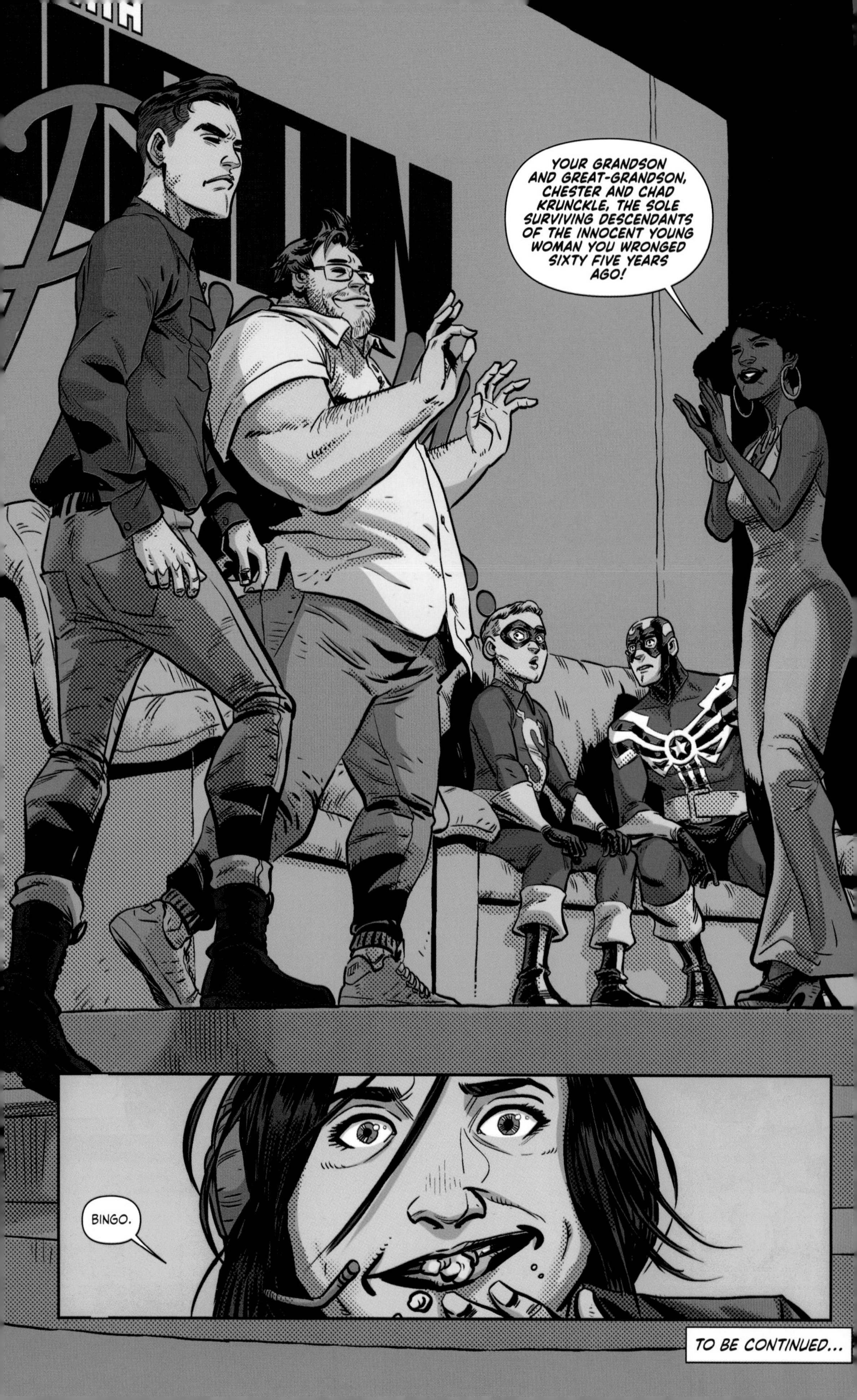
YOUR GRANDSON AND GREAT-GRANDSON, CHESTER AND CHAD KRUNCKLE, THE SOLE SURVIVING DESCENDANTS OF THE INNOCENT YOUNG WOMAN YOU WRONGED SIXTY FIVE YEARS AGO!
BINGO.
TO BE CONTINUED...

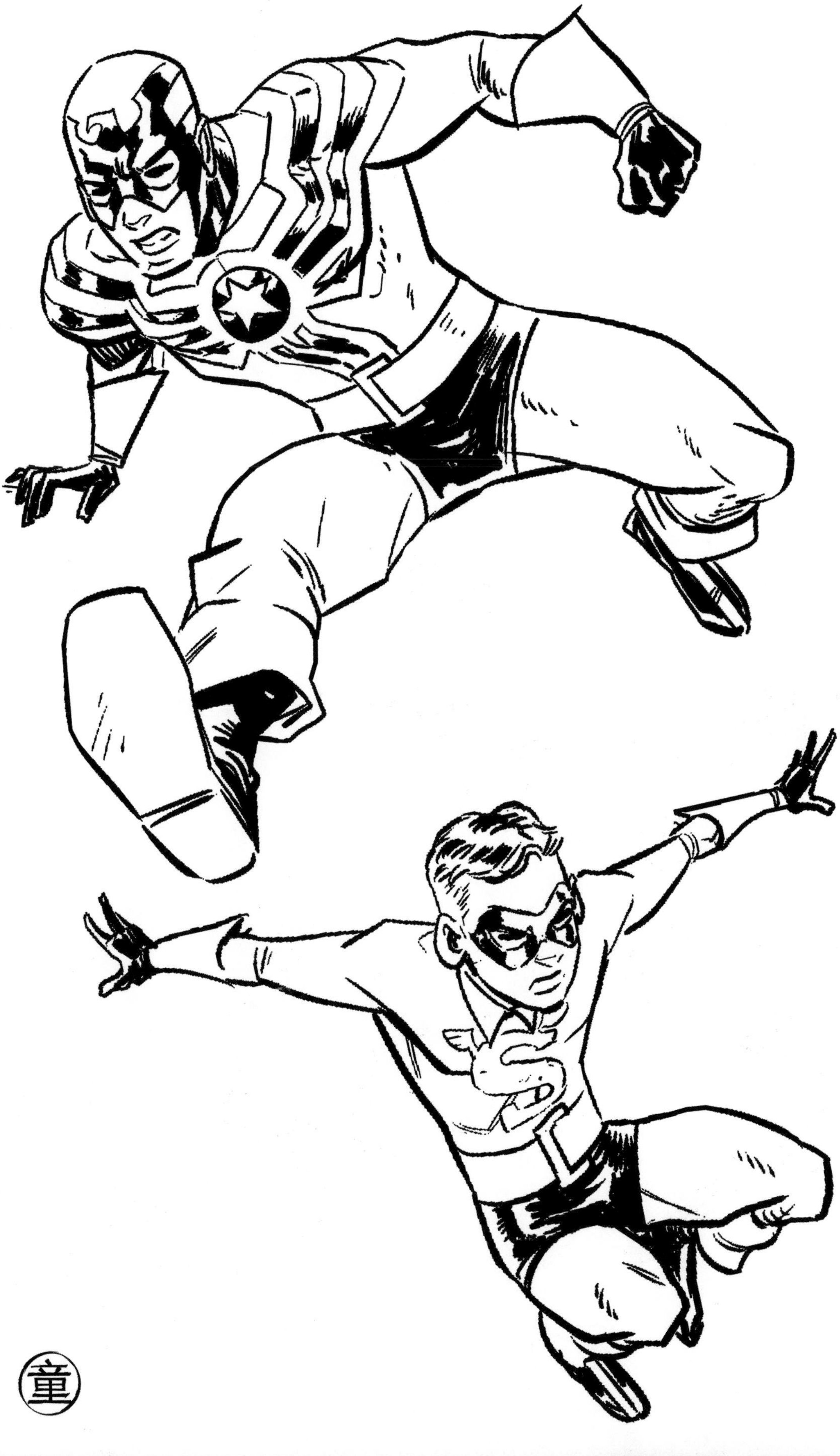

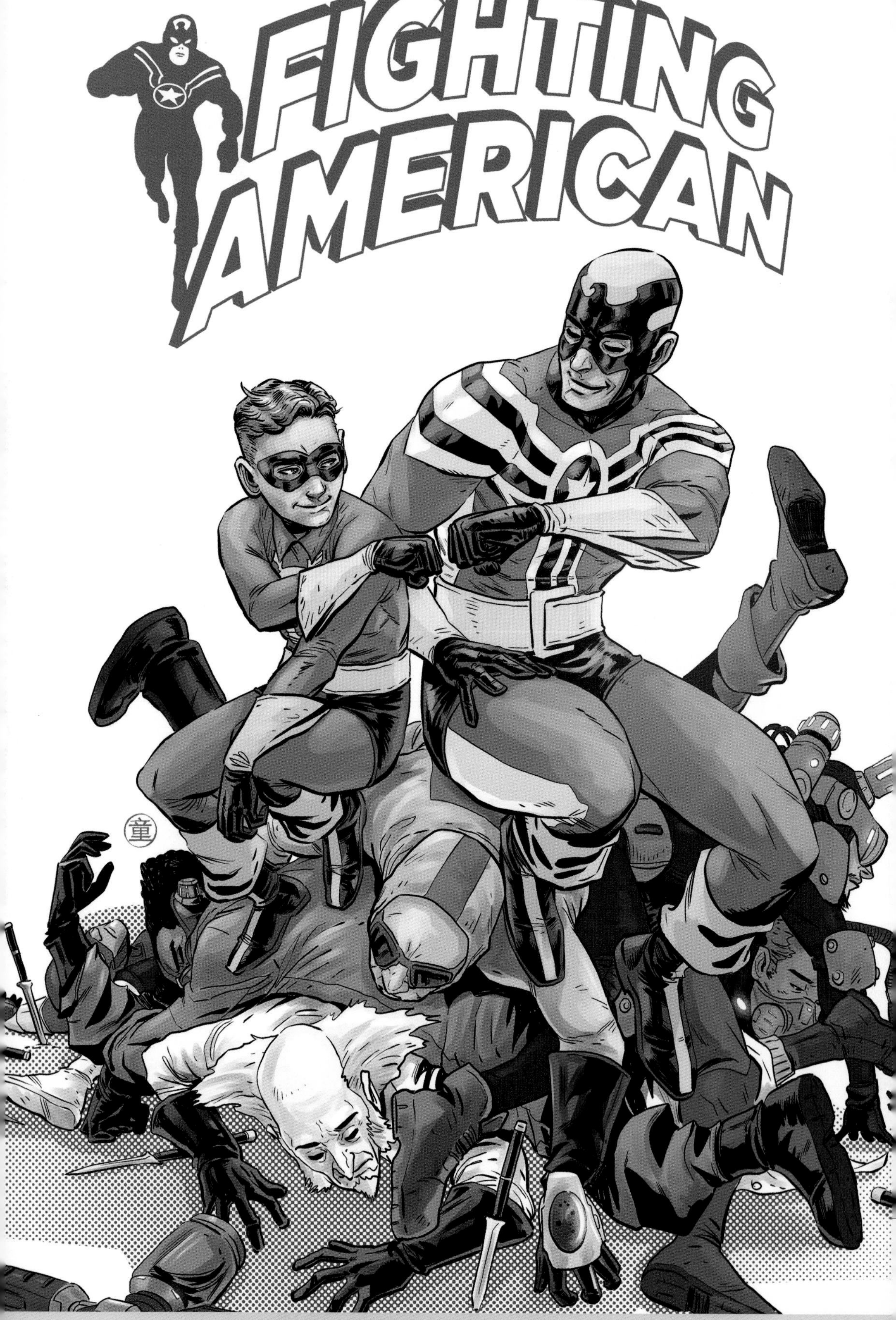
FIGHTING AMERICAN

CHAPTER FOUR

COVER 4A ART
BY ANDIE TONG

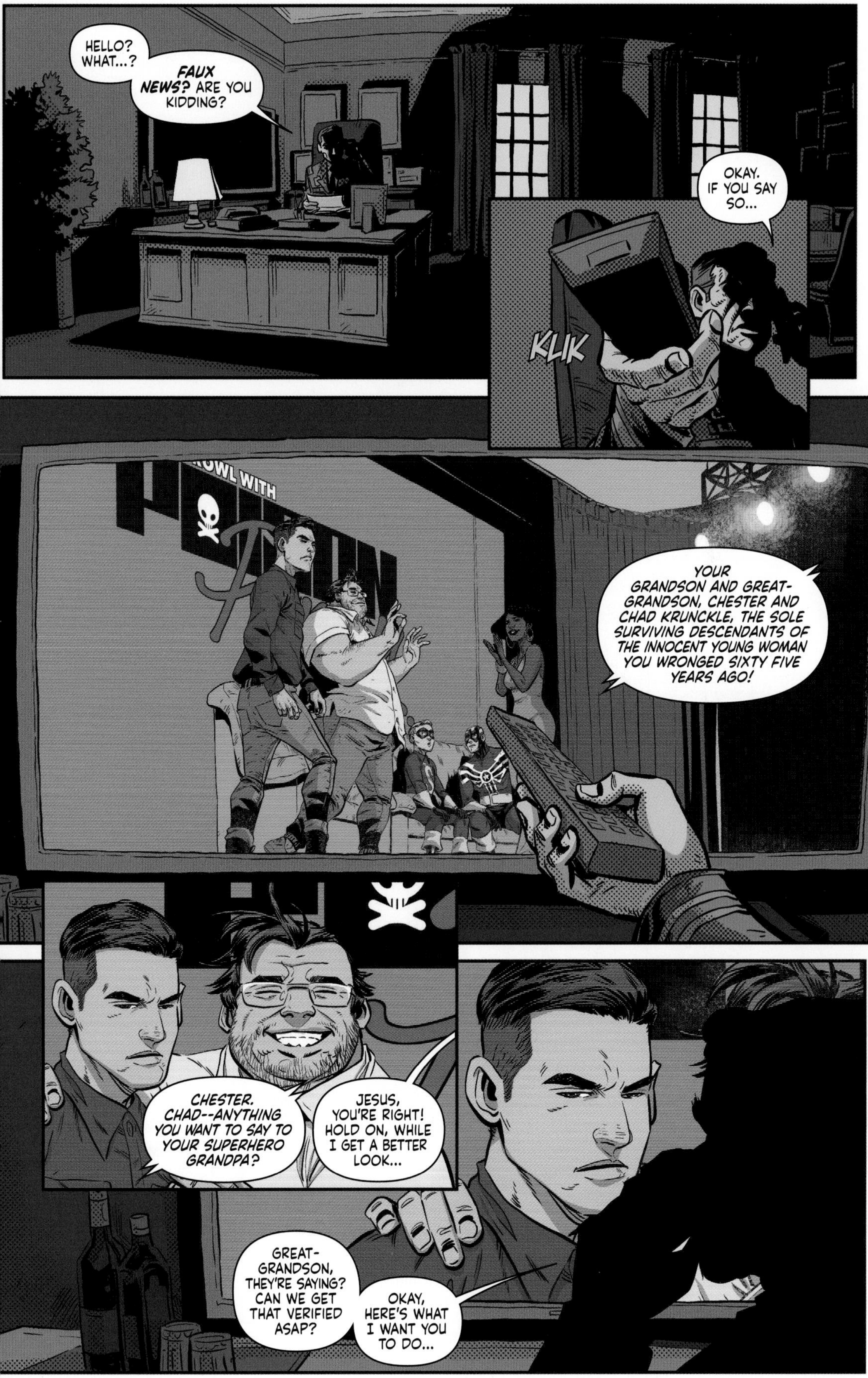
HELLO? WHAT...?
FAUX NEWS? ARE YOU KIDDING?
OKAY. IF YOU SAY SO...
KLIK
ROWL WITH
YOUR GRANDSON AND GREAT-GRANDSON, CHESTER AND CHAD KRUNCKLE, THE SOLE SURVIVING DESCENDANTS OF THE INNOCENT YOUNG WOMAN YOU WRONGED SIXTY FIVE YEARS AGO!
CHESTER. CHAD--ANYTHING YOU WANT TO SAY TO YOUR SUPERHERO GRANDPA?
JESUS, YOU'RE RIGHT! HOLD ON, WHILE I GET A BETTER LOOK...
GREAT-GRANDSON, THEY'RE SAYING? CAN WE GET THAT VERIFIED ASAP?
OKAY, HERE'S WHAT I WANT YOU TO DO...

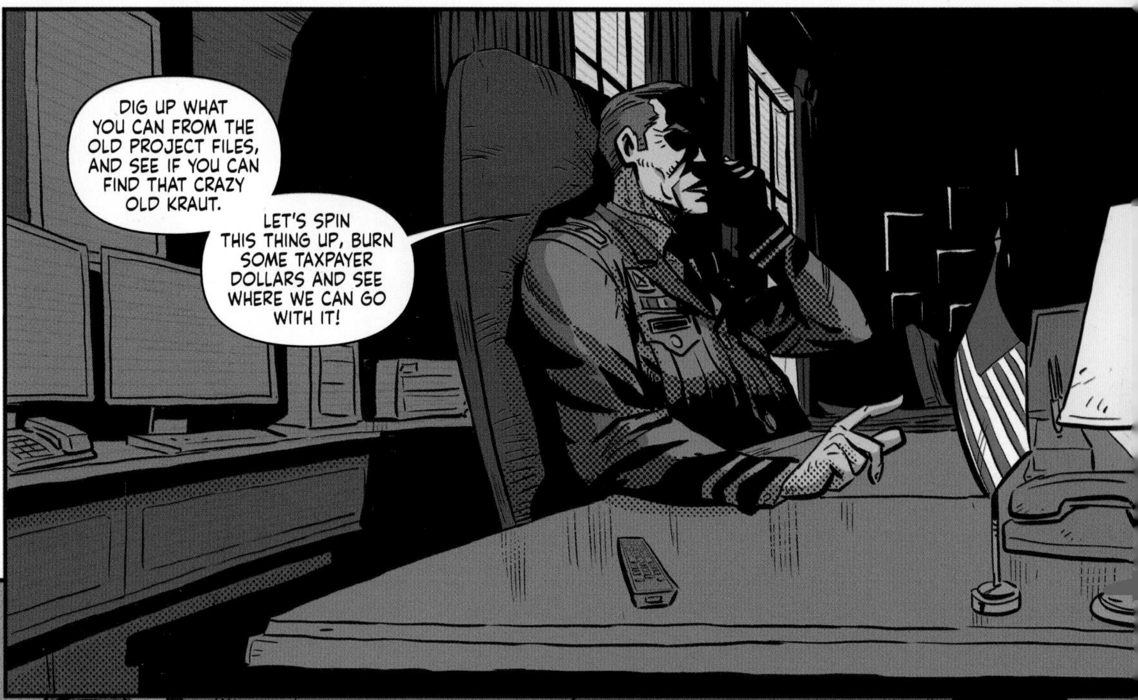
DIG UP WHAT YOU CAN FROM THE OLD PROJECT FILES, AND SEE IF YOU CAN FIND THAT CRAZY OLD KRAUT.
LET'S SPIN THIS THING UP, BURN SOME TAXPAYER DOLLARS AND SEE WHERE WE CAN GO WITH IT!
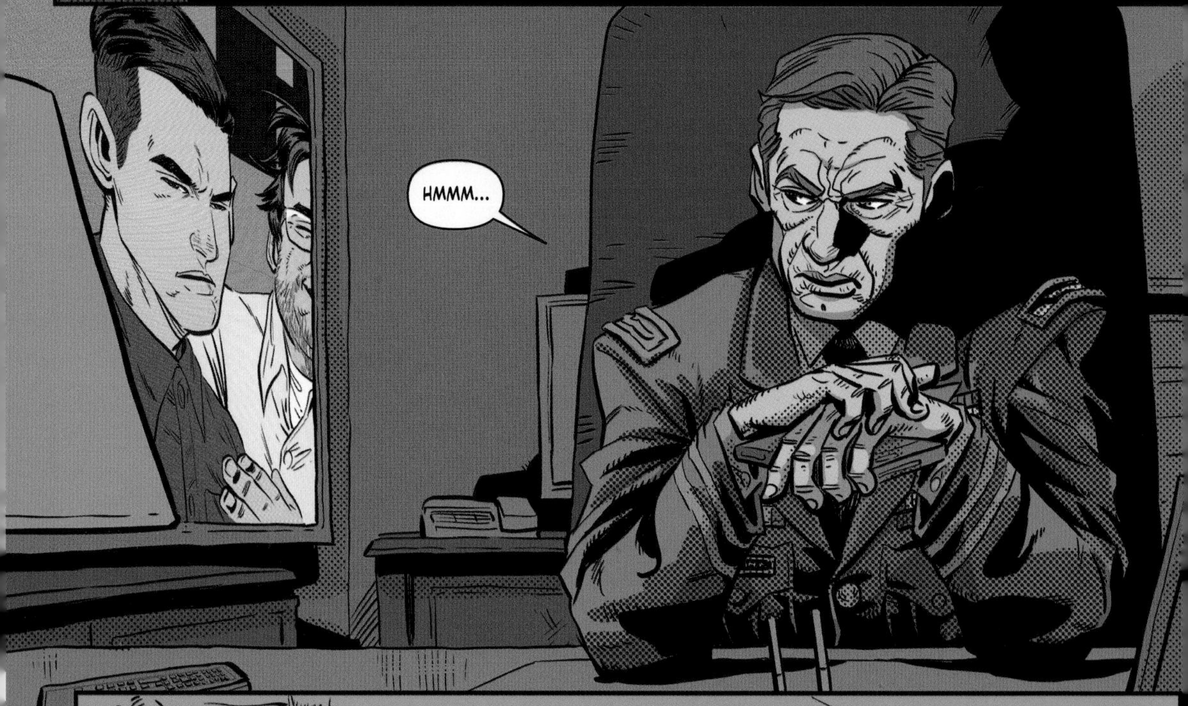
HMMM...
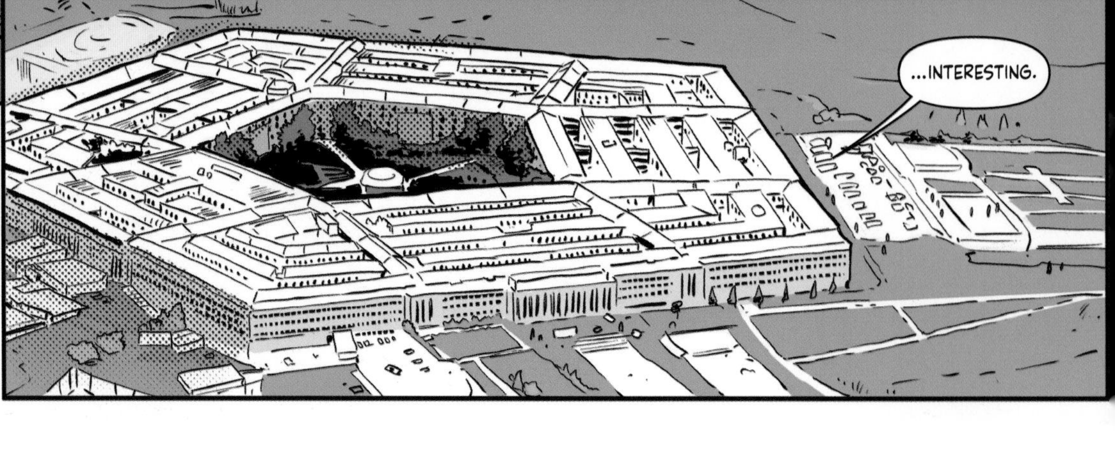
...INTERESTING.

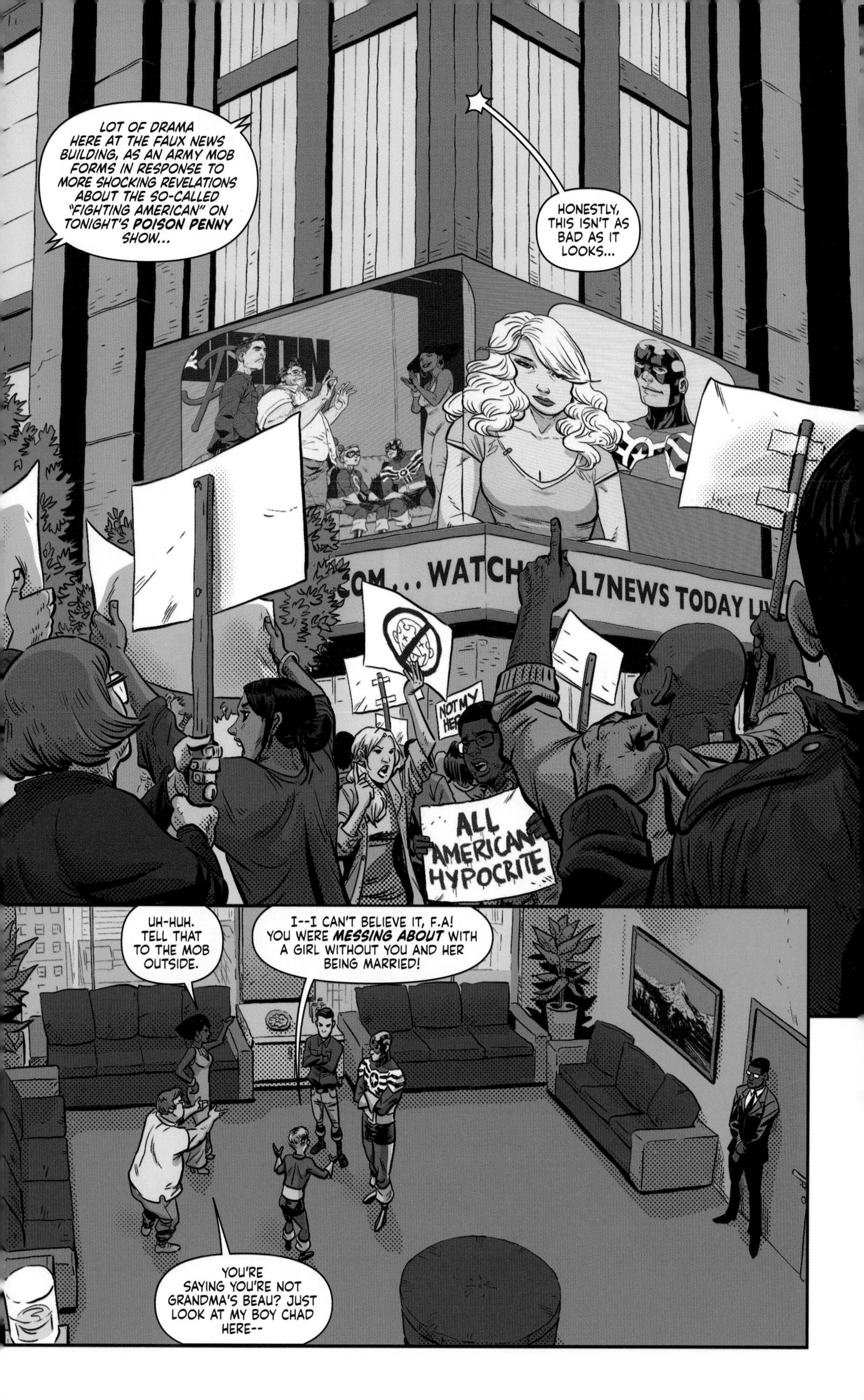
LOT OF DRAMA HERE AT THE FAUX NEWS BUILDING, AS AN ARMY MOB FORMS IN RESPONSE TO MORE SHOCKING REVELATIONS ABOUT THE SO-CALLED "FIGHTING AMERICAN" ON TONIGHT'S **POISON PENNY** SHOW...
HONESTLY, THIS ISN'T AS BAD AS IT LOOKS...
ALL AMERICAN HYPOCRITE
UH-HUH. TELL THAT TO THE MOB OUTSIDE.
I--I CAN'T BELIEVE IT, F.A! YOU WERE ***MESSING ABOUT*** WITH A GIRL WITHOUT YOU AND HER BEING MARRIED!
YOU'RE SAYING YOU'RE NOT GRANDMA'S BEAU? JUST LOOK AT MY BOY CHAD HERE--

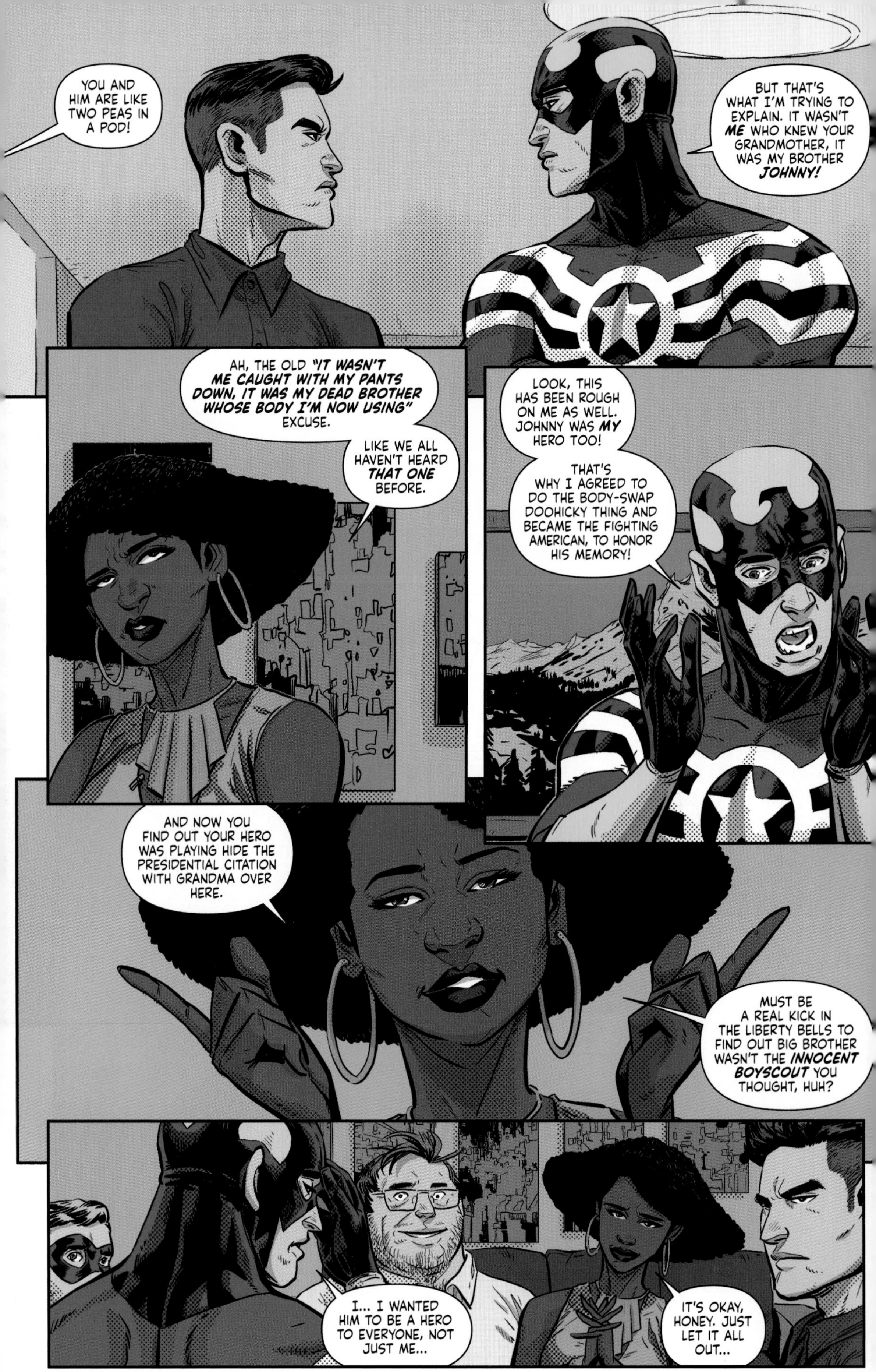
YOU AND HIM ARE LIKE TWO PEAS IN A POD!
BUT THAT'S WHAT I'M TRYING TO EXPLAIN. IT WASN'T ME WHO KNEW YOUR GRANDMOTHER, IT WAS MY BROTHER JOHNNY!
AH, THE OLD "IT WASN'T ME CAUGHT WITH MY PANTS DOWN, IT WAS MY DEAD BROTHER WHOSE BODY I'M NOW USING" EXCUSE.
LIKE WE ALL HAVEN'T HEARD THAT ONE BEFORE.
LOOK, THIS HAS BEEN ROUGH ON ME AS WELL. JOHNNY WAS MY HERO TOO!
THAT'S WHY I AGREED TO DO THE BODY-SWAP DOOHICKY THING AND BECAME THE FIGHTING AMERICAN, TO HONOR HIS MEMORY!
AND NOW YOU FIND OUT YOUR HERO WAS PLAYING HIDE THE PRESIDENTIAL CITATION WITH GRANDMA OVER HERE.
MUST BE A REAL KICK IN THE LIBERTY BELLS TO FIND OUT BIG BROTHER WASN'T THE INNOCENT BOYSCOUT YOU THOUGHT, HUH?
I... I WANTED HIM TO BE A HERO TO EVERYONE, NOT JUST ME...
IT'S OKAY, HONEY. JUST LET IT ALL OUT...

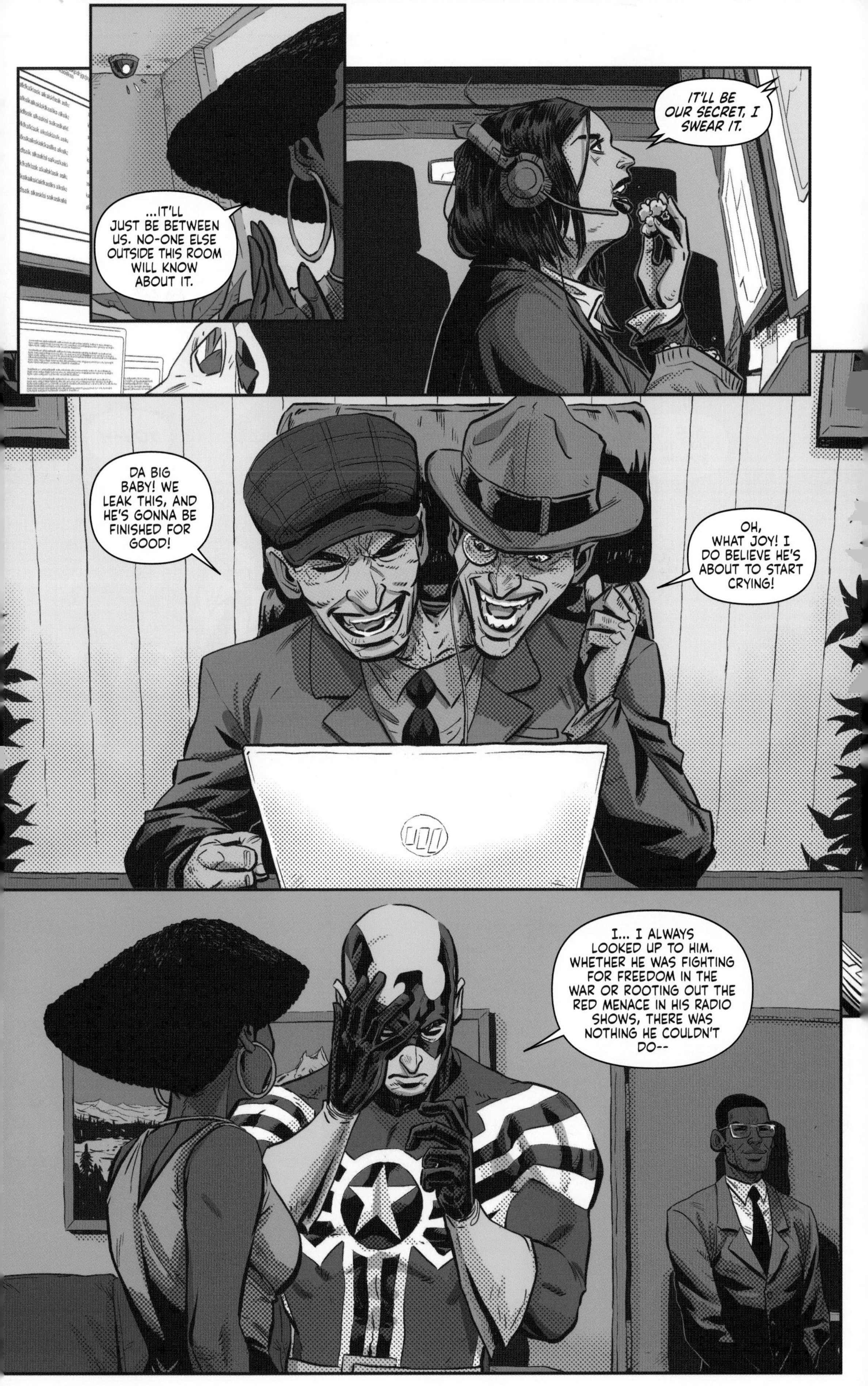
...IT'LL JUST BE BETWEEN US. NO-ONE ELSE OUTSIDE THIS ROOM WILL KNOW ABOUT IT.
IT'LL BE OUR SECRET, I SWEAR IT.
DA BIG BABY! WE LEAK THIS, AND HE'S GONNA BE FINISHED FOR GOOD!
OH, WHAT JOY! I DO BELIEVE HE'S ABOUT TO START CRYING!
I... I ALWAYS LOOKED UP TO HIM. WHETHER HE WAS FIGHTING FOR FREEDOM IN THE WAR OR ROOTING OUT THE RED MENACE IN HIS RADIO SHOWS, THERE WAS NOTHING HE COULDN'T DO--

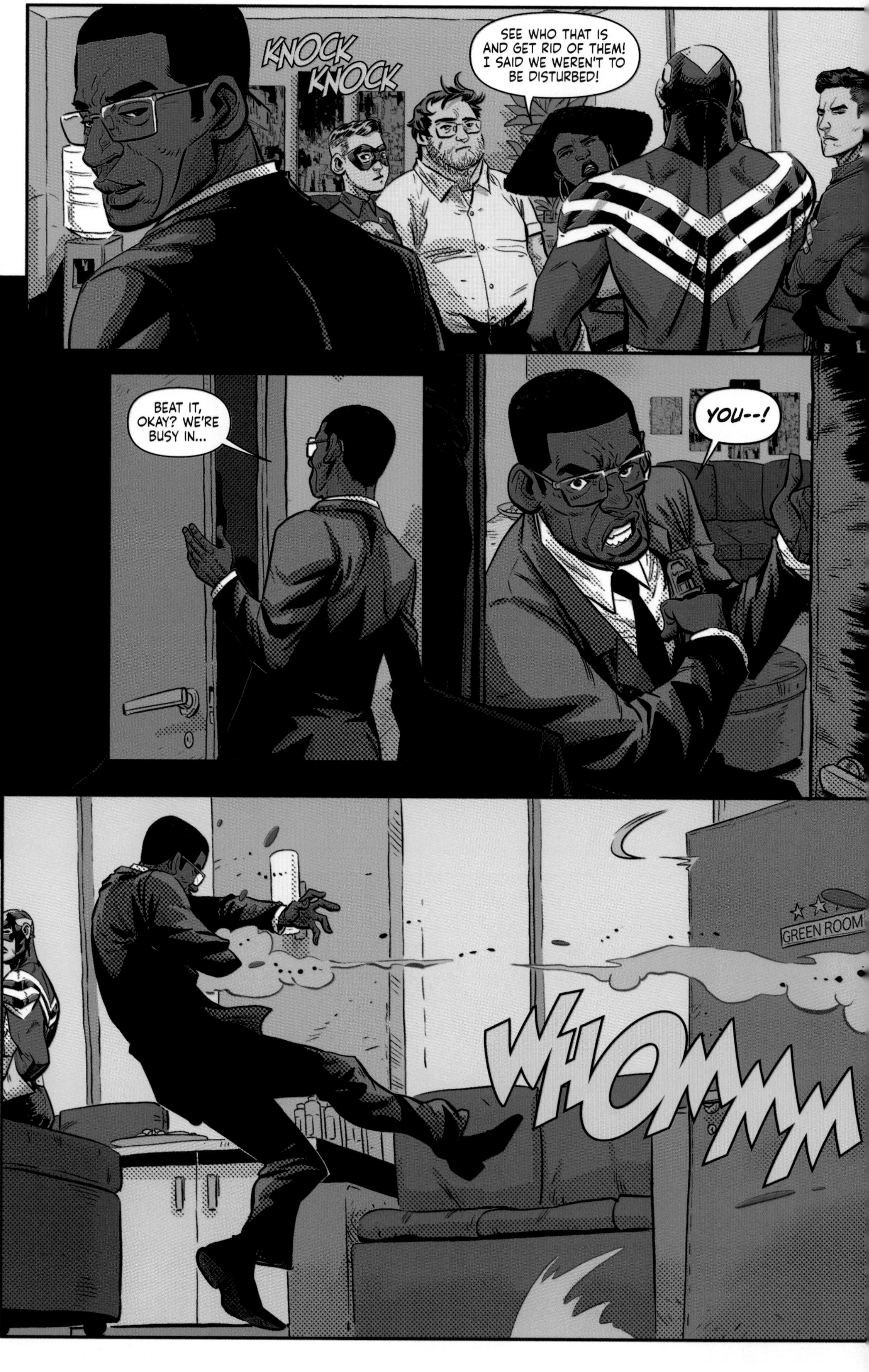
KNOCK KNOCK
SEE WHO THAT IS AND GET RID OF THEM! I SAID WE WEREN'T TO BE DISTURBED!
BEAT IT, OKAY? WE'RE BUSY IN...
YOU--!
GREEN ROOM
WHOMMM

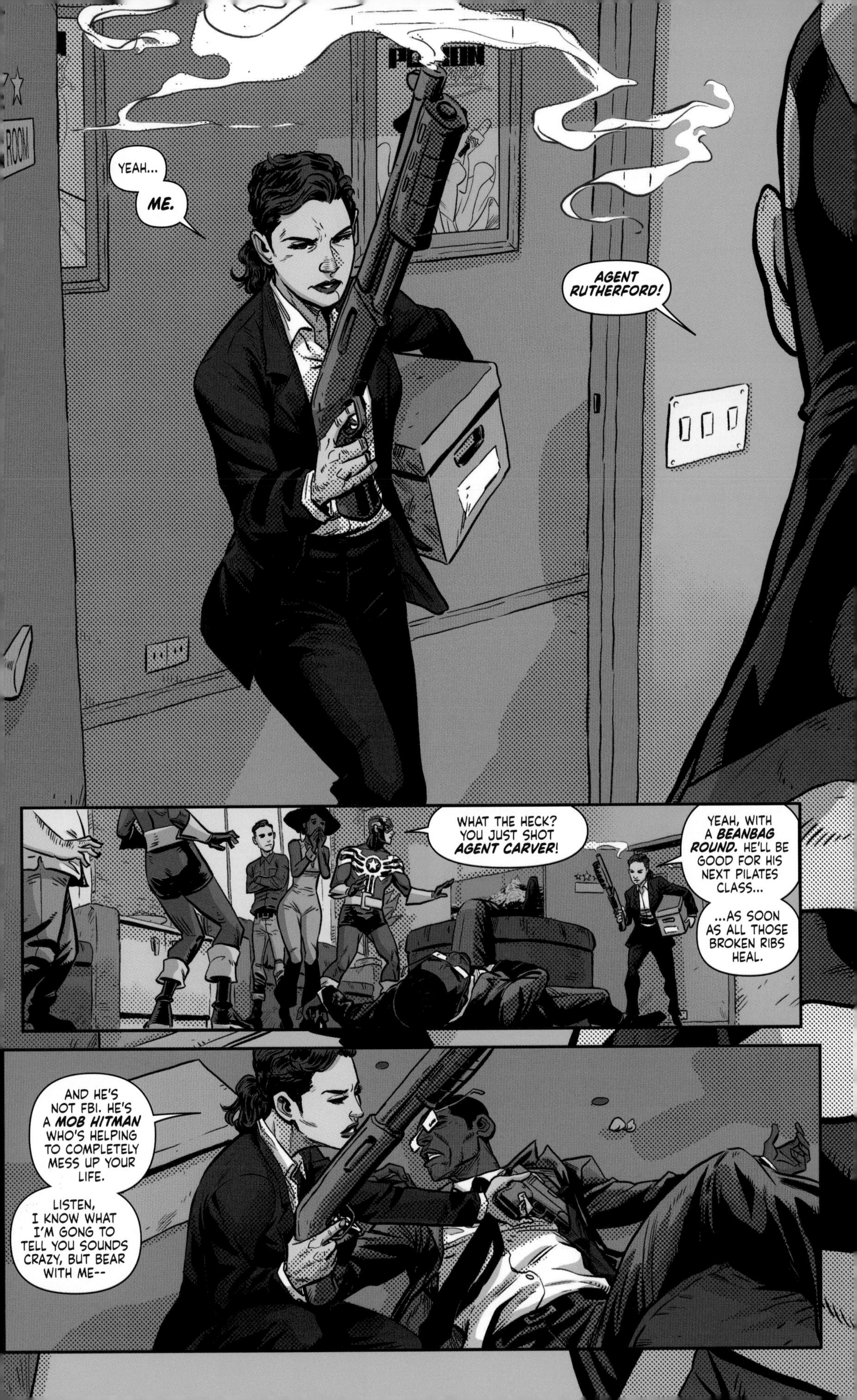
YEAH... ME.
AGENT RUTHERFORD!
WHAT THE HECK? YOU JUST SHOT AGENT CARVER!
YEAH, WITH A BEANBAG ROUND. HE'LL BE GOOD FOR HIS NEXT PILATES CLASS...
...AS SOON AS ALL THOSE BROKEN RIBS HEAL.
AND HE'S NOT FBI. HE'S A MOB HITMAN WHO'S HELPING TO COMPLETELY MESS UP YOUR LIFE.
LISTEN, I KNOW WHAT I'M GONG TO TELL YOU SOUNDS CRAZY, BUT BEAR WITH ME--

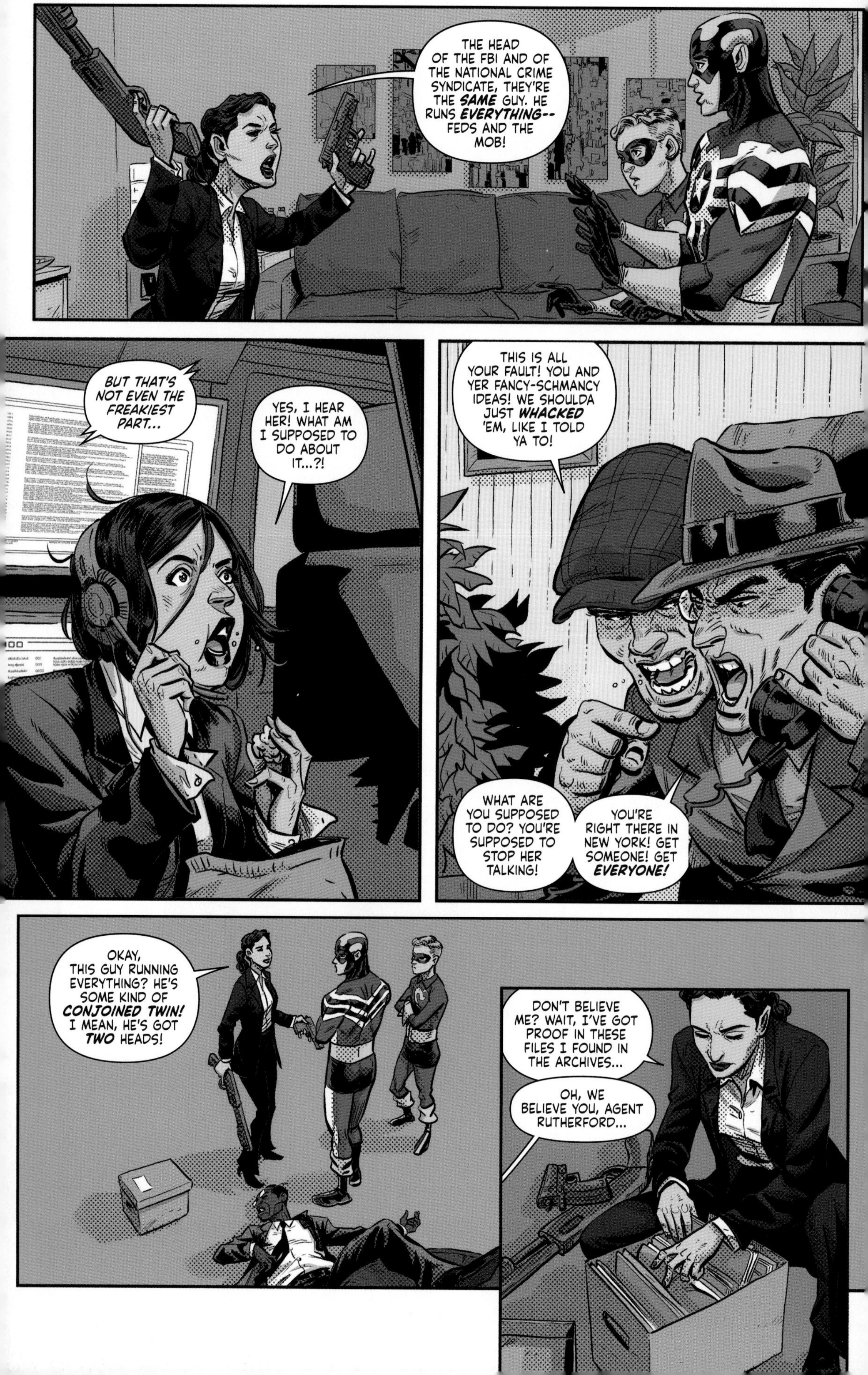
THE HEAD OF THE FBI AND OF THE NATIONAL CRIME SYNDICATE, THEY'RE THE SAME GUY. HE RUNS EVERYTHING-- FEDS AND THE MOB!
BUT THAT'S NOT EVEN THE FREAKIEST PART...
YES, I HEAR HER! WHAT AM I SUPPOSED TO DO ABOUT IT...?!
THIS IS ALL YOUR FAULT! YOU AND YER FANCY-SCHMANCY IDEAS! WE SHOULDA JUST WHACKED 'EM, LIKE I TOLD YA TO!
WHAT ARE YOU SUPPOSED TO DO? YOU'RE SUPPOSED TO STOP HER TALKING!
YOU'RE RIGHT THERE IN NEW YORK! GET SOMEONE! GET EVERYONE!
OKAY, THIS GUY RUNNING EVERYTHING? HE'S SOME KIND OF CONJOINED TWIN! I MEAN, HE'S GOT TWO HEADS!
DON'T BELIEVE ME? WAIT, I'VE GOT PROOF IN THESE FILES I FOUND IN THE ARCHIVES...
OH, WE BELIEVE YOU, AGENT RUTHERFORD...

YOU HEAR THAT, SPEEDBOY? THE *DOUBLE DOSE OF CRIMINAL CUNNING* IS BACK!

DOUBLE-HEADER! I'LL GIVE THAT TWIN-HEADED HOODLUM WHAT FOR--!

WAIT, ARE WE...

I-- I'M NOT SURE...

PARTNERS AGAIN? CAN'T TAKE ON THAT TWO-HEADED SNAKE ON MY OWN!

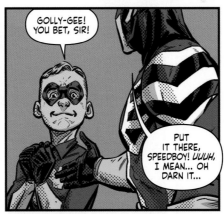

GOLLY-GEE! YOU BET, SIR!

PUT IT THERE, SPEEDBOY! *UUUH,* I MEAN... OH DARN IT...

IT DOESN'T MATTER, SIR. I'M GOOD WITH *SPEEDBOY.*

I DON'T EVEN LIKE MY REAL NAME, ANYWAY!

UUUGH. TONIGHT'S SPECIAL--OVER-COOKED SCHMALTZ WITH A DOUBLE ORDER OF BARF ON THE SIDE.

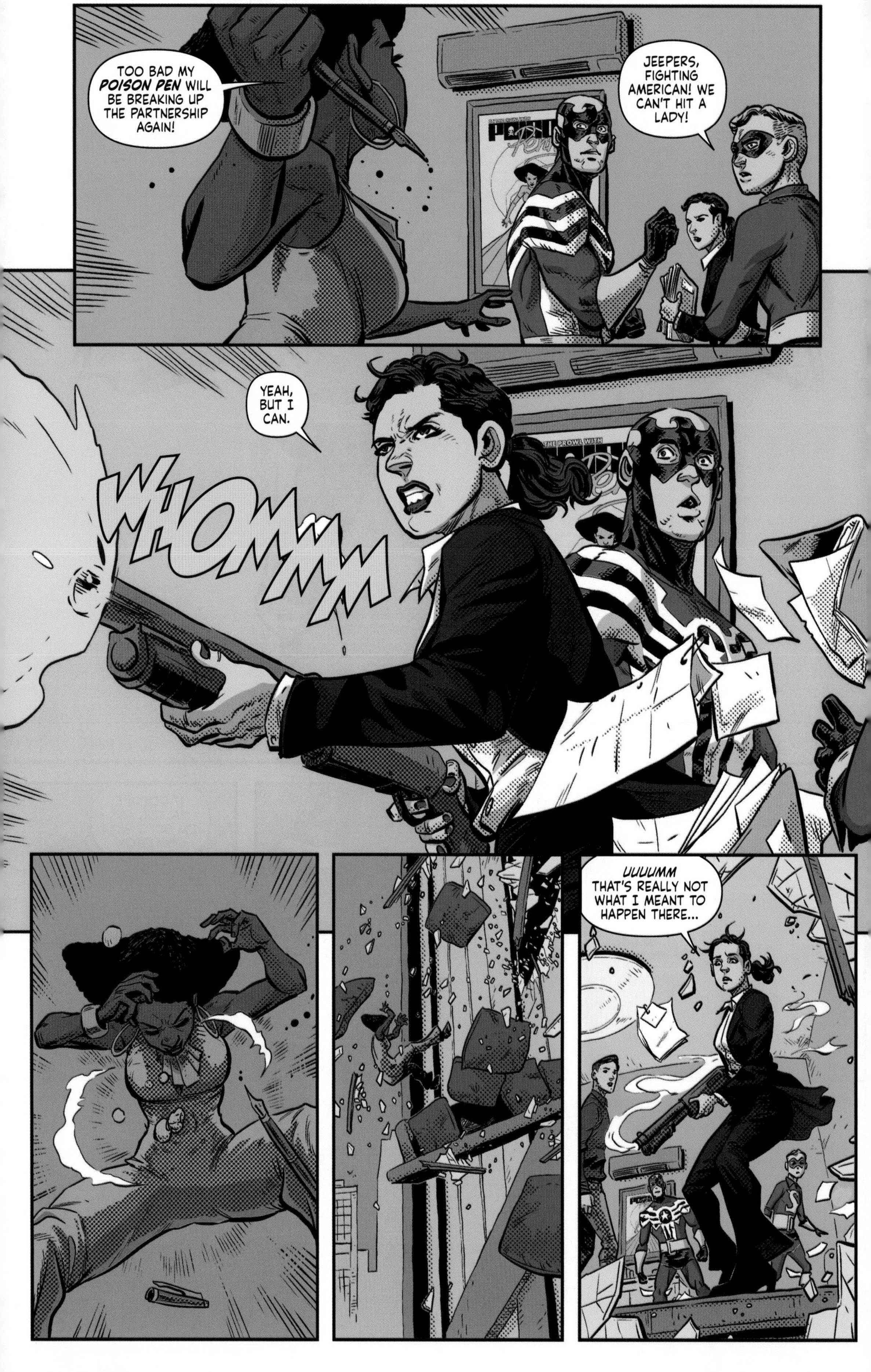
TOO BAD MY POISON PEN WILL BE BREAKING UP THE PARTNERSHIP AGAIN!
JEEPERS, FIGHTING AMERICAN! WE CAN'T HIT A LADY!
YEAH, BUT I CAN.
WHOMMM
UUUUMM THAT'S REALLY NOT WHAT I MEANT TO HAPPEN THERE...

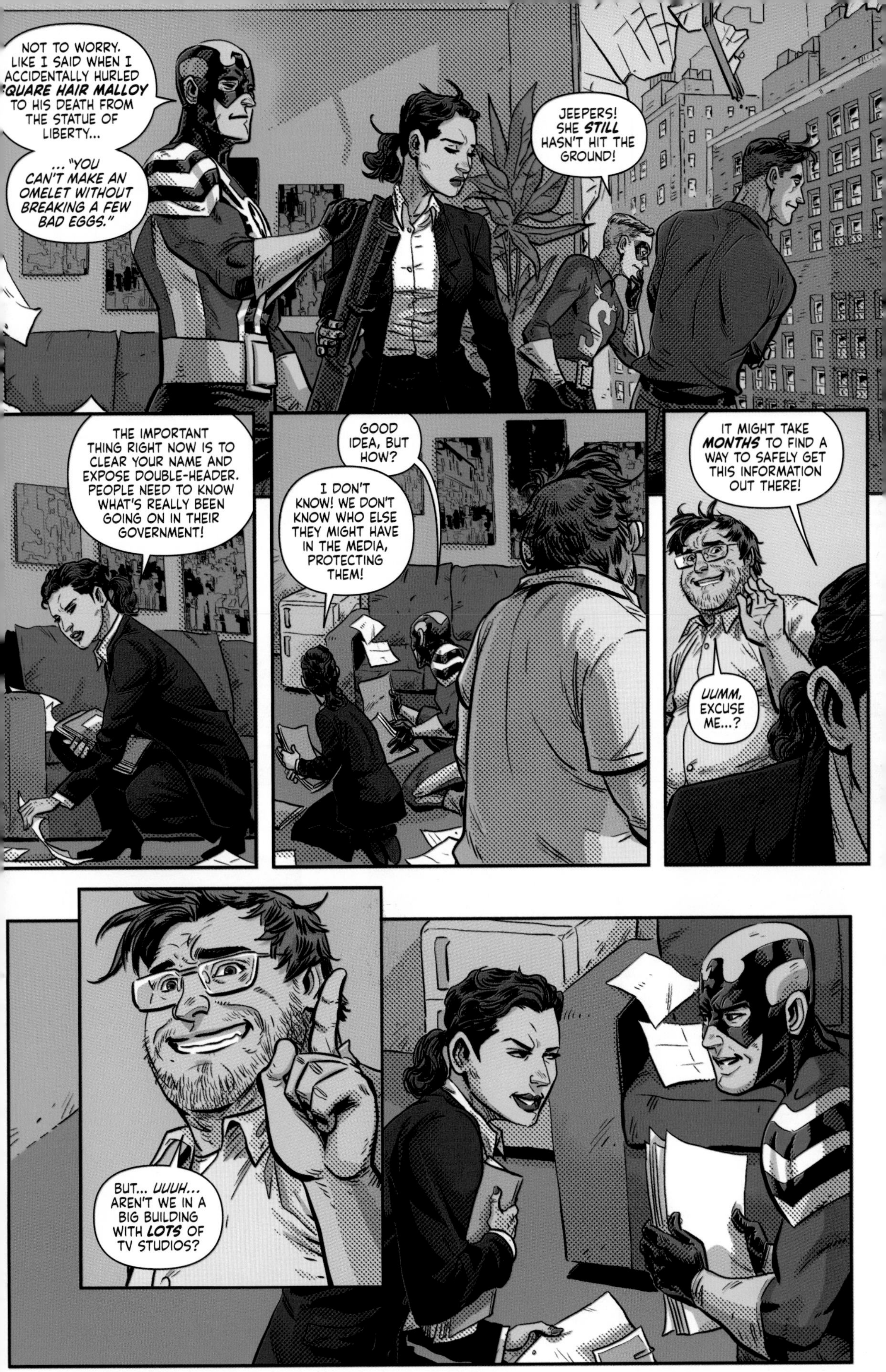
NOT TO WORRY. LIKE I SAID WHEN I ACCIDENTALLY HURLED SQUARE HAIR MALLOY TO HIS DEATH FROM THE STATUE OF LIBERTY...
..."YOU CAN'T MAKE AN OMELET WITHOUT BREAKING A FEW BAD EGGS."
JEEPERS! SHE STILL HASN'T HIT THE GROUND!
THE IMPORTANT THING RIGHT NOW IS TO CLEAR YOUR NAME AND EXPOSE DOUBLE-HEADER. PEOPLE NEED TO KNOW WHAT'S REALLY BEEN GOING ON IN THEIR GOVERNMENT!
GOOD IDEA, BUT HOW?
I DON'T KNOW! WE DON'T KNOW WHO ELSE THEY MIGHT HAVE IN THE MEDIA, PROTECTING THEM!
IT MIGHT TAKE MONTHS TO FIND A WAY TO SAFELY GET THIS INFORMATION OUT THERE!
UUMM, EXCUSE ME...?
BUT... UUUH... AREN'T WE IN A BIG BUILDING WITH LOTS OF TV STUDIOS?

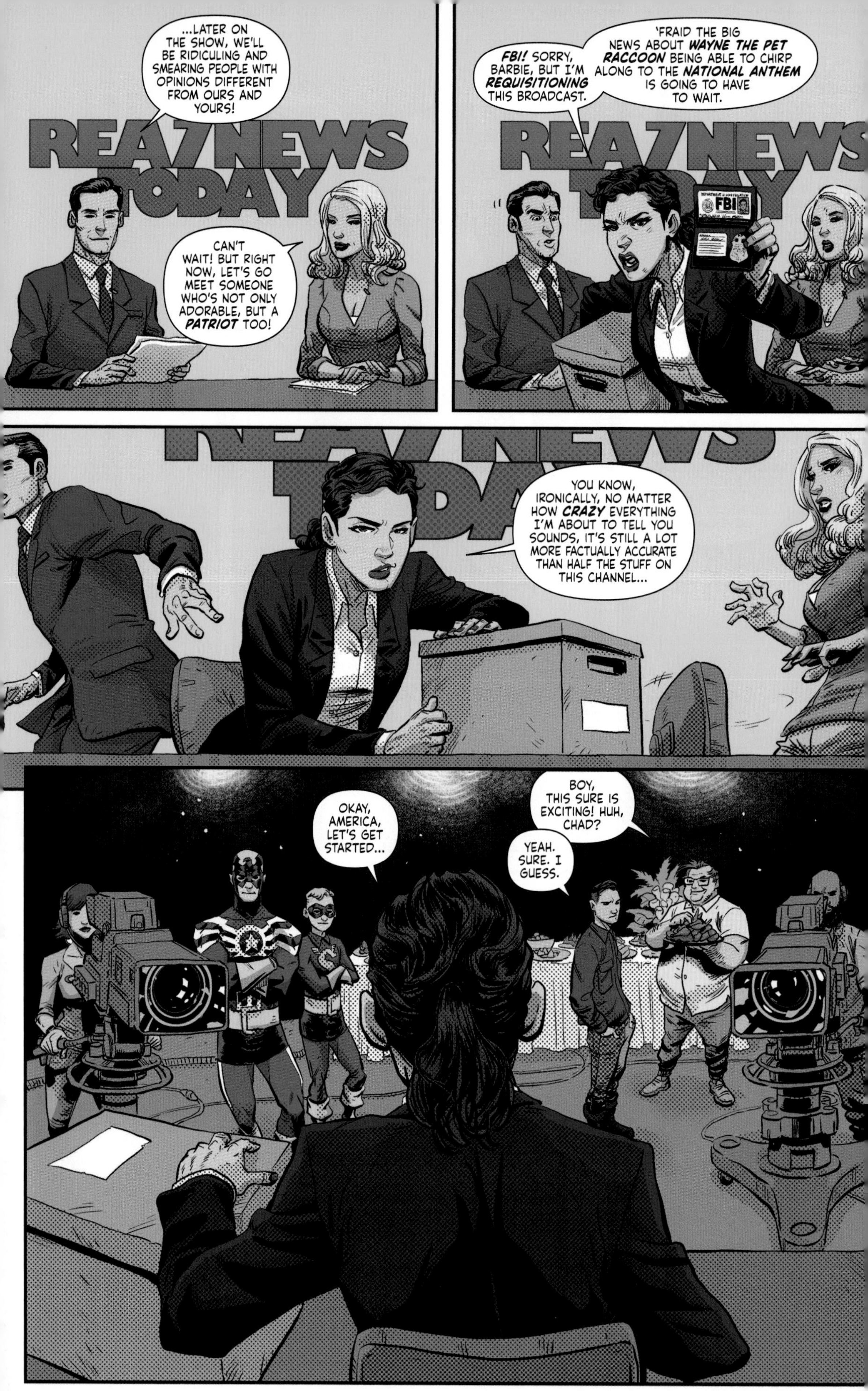
...LATER ON THE SHOW, WE'LL BE RIDICULING AND SMEARING PEOPLE WITH OPINIONS DIFFERENT FROM OURS AND YOURS!
REA7NEWS TODAY
CAN'T WAIT! BUT RIGHT NOW, LET'S GO MEET SOMEONE WHO'S NOT ONLY ADORABLE, BUT A PATRIOT TOO!
FBI! SORRY, BARBIE, BUT I'M REQUISITIONING THIS BROADCAST.
'FRAID THE BIG NEWS ABOUT WAYNE THE PET RACCOON BEING ABLE TO CHIRP ALONG TO THE NATIONAL ANTHEM IS GOING TO HAVE TO WAIT.
FBI
YOU KNOW, IRONICALLY, NO MATTER HOW CRAZY EVERYTHING I'M ABOUT TO TELL YOU SOUNDS, IT'S STILL A LOT MORE FACTUALLY ACCURATE THAN HALF THE STUFF ON THIS CHANNEL...
OKAY, AMERICA, LET'S GET STARTED...
BOY, THIS SURE IS EXCITING! HUH, CHAD?
YEAH. SURE. I GUESS.

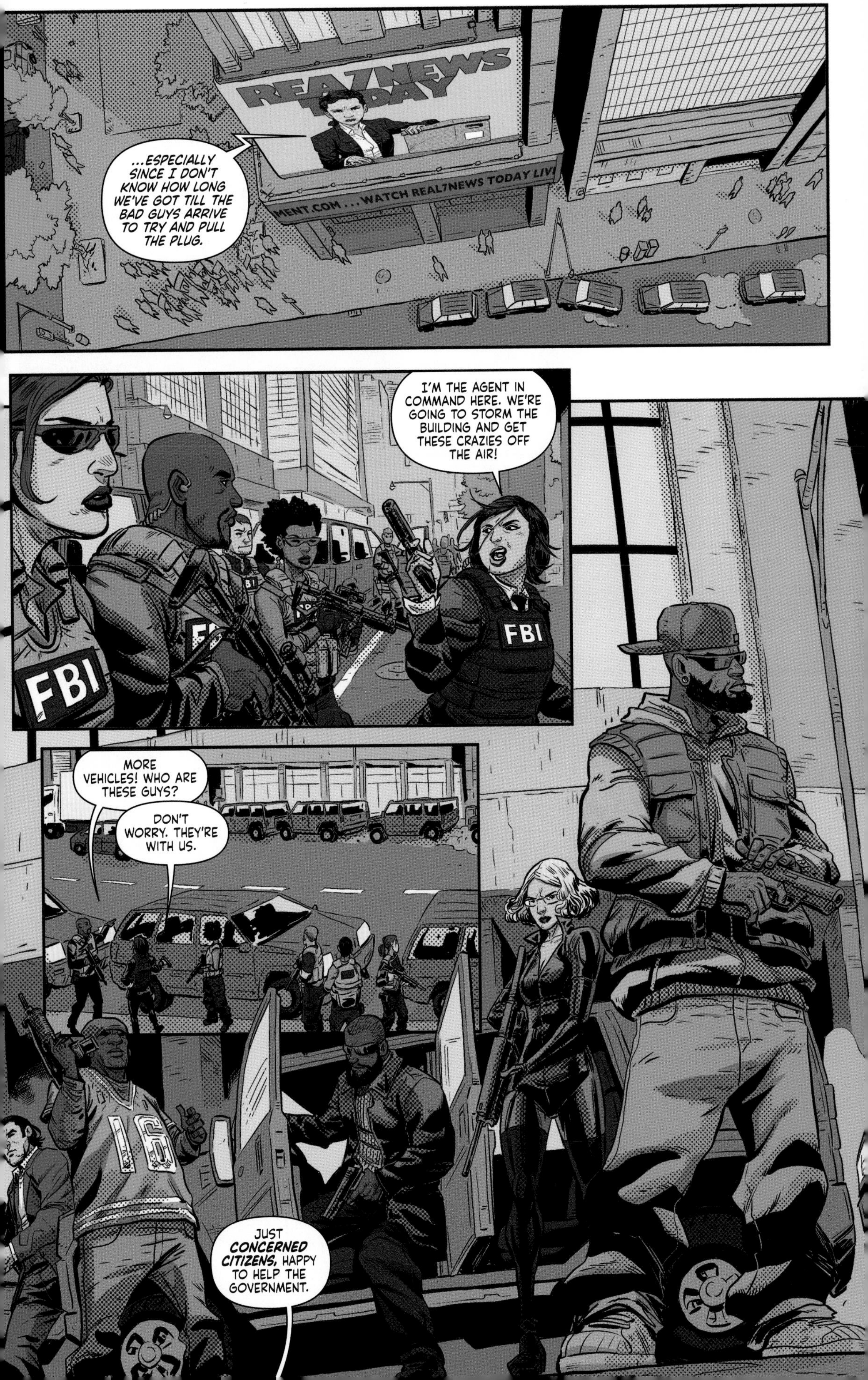
REAL7NEWS TODAY
...ESPECIALLY SINCE I DON'T KNOW HOW LONG WE'VE GOT TILL THE BAD GUYS ARRIVE TO TRY AND PULL THE PLUG.
MENT.COM . . . WATCH REAL7NEWS TODAY LIVE
I'M THE AGENT IN COMMAND HERE. WE'RE GOING TO STORM THE BUILDING AND GET THESE CRAZIES OFF THE AIR!
FBI
FBI
FBI
MORE VEHICLES! WHO ARE THESE GUYS?
DON'T WORRY. THEY'RE WITH US.
JUST *CONCERNED CITIZENS,* HAPPY TO HELP THE GOVERNMENT.

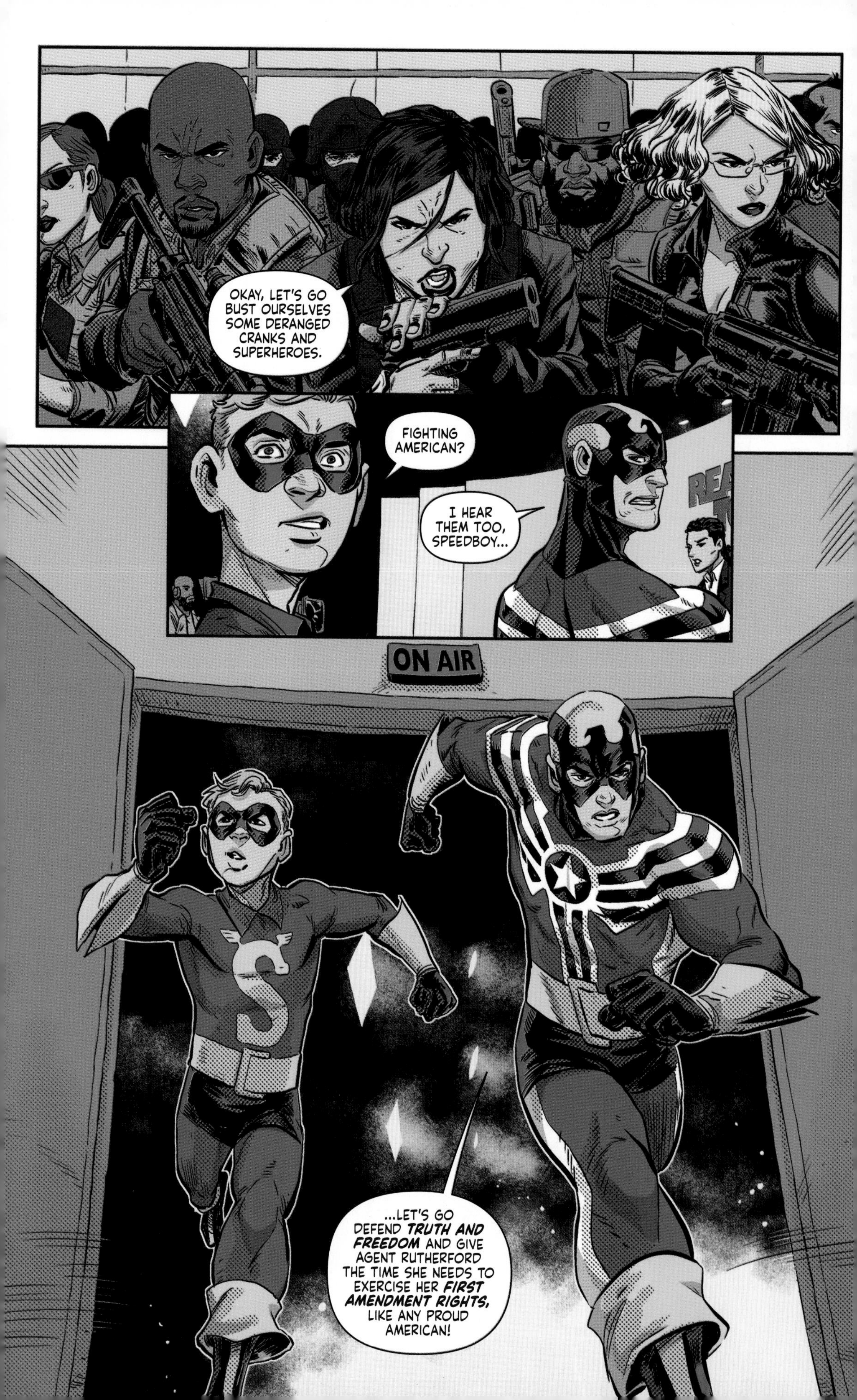
OKAY, LET'S GO BUST OURSELVES SOME DERANGED CRANKS AND SUPERHEROES.
FIGHTING AMERICAN?
I HEAR THEM TOO, SPEEDBOY...
ON AIR
...LET'S GO DEFEND TRUTH AND FREEDOM AND GIVE AGENT RUTHERFORD THE TIME SHE NEEDS TO EXERCISE HER FIRST AMENDMENT RIGHTS, LIKE ANY PROUD AMERICAN!

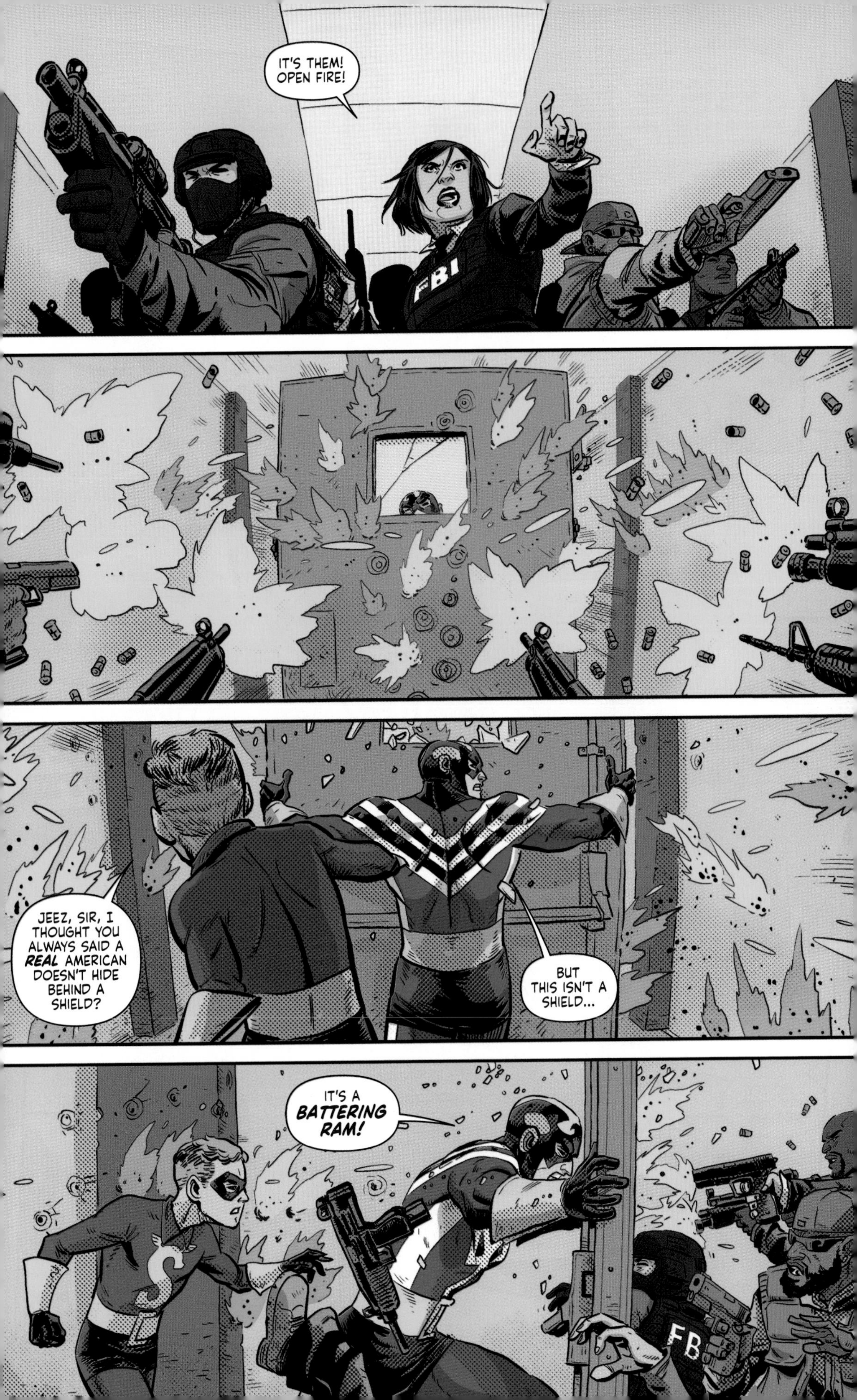
IT'S THEM! OPEN FIRE!
FBI
JEEZ, SIR, I THOUGHT YOU ALWAYS SAID A *REAL* AMERICAN DOESN'T HIDE BEHIND A SHIELD?
BUT THIS ISN'T A SHIELD...
IT'S A *BATTERING RAM!*
FB

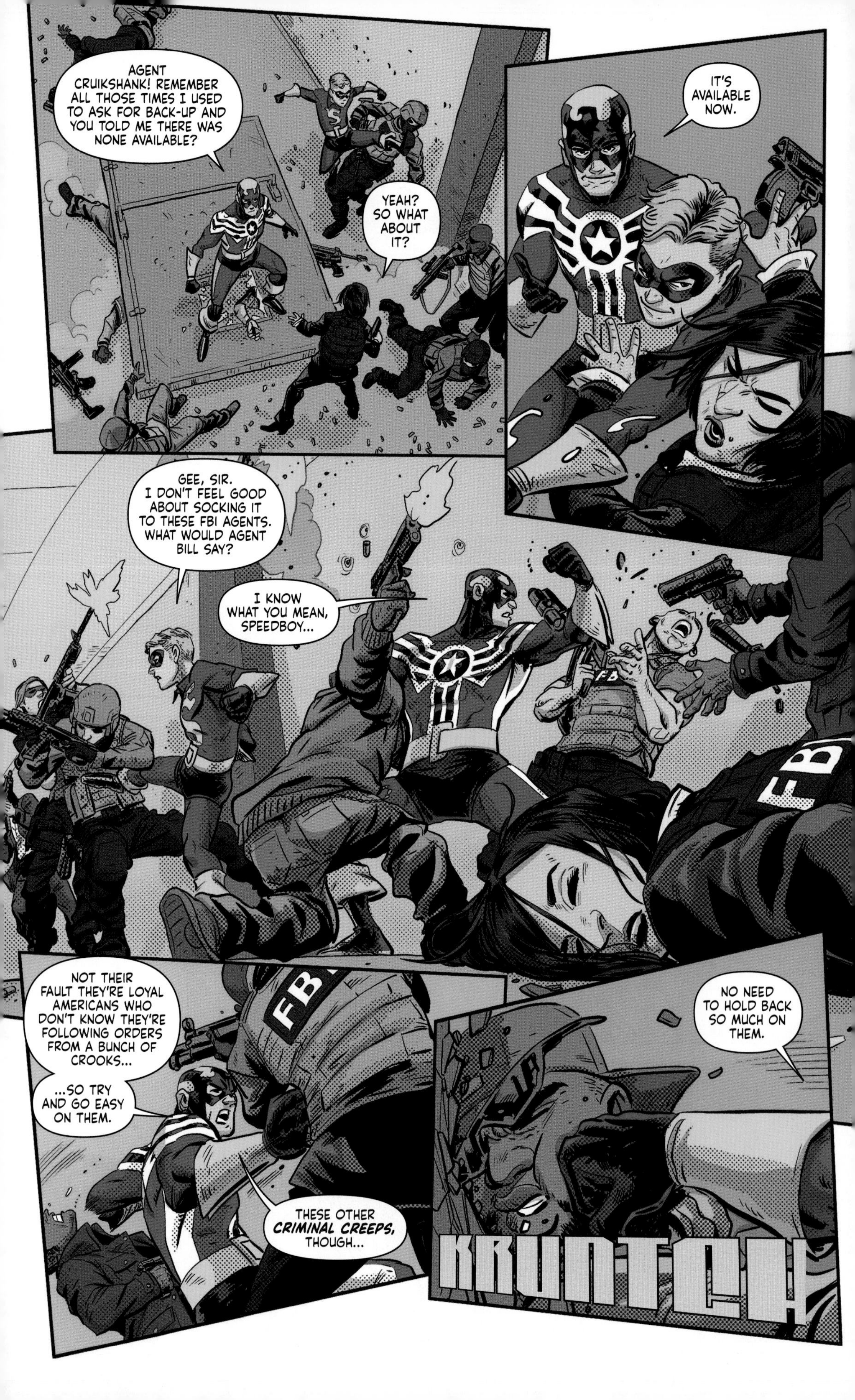
AGENT CRUIKSHANK! REMEMBER ALL THOSE TIMES I USED TO ASK FOR BACK-UP AND YOU TOLD ME THERE WAS NONE AVAILABLE?
YEAH? SO WHAT ABOUT IT?
IT'S AVAILABLE NOW.
GEE, SIR. I DON'T FEEL GOOD ABOUT SOCKING IT TO THESE FBI AGENTS. WHAT WOULD AGENT BILL SAY?
I KNOW WHAT YOU MEAN, SPEEDBOY...
FBI
FBI
NOT THEIR FAULT THEY'RE LOYAL AMERICANS WHO DON'T KNOW THEY'RE FOLLOWING ORDERS FROM A BUNCH OF CROOKS...
...SO TRY AND GO EASY ON THEM.
FBI
THESE OTHER *CRIMINAL CREEPS,* THOUGH...
NO NEED TO HOLD BACK SO MUCH ON THEM.
KRUNTCH

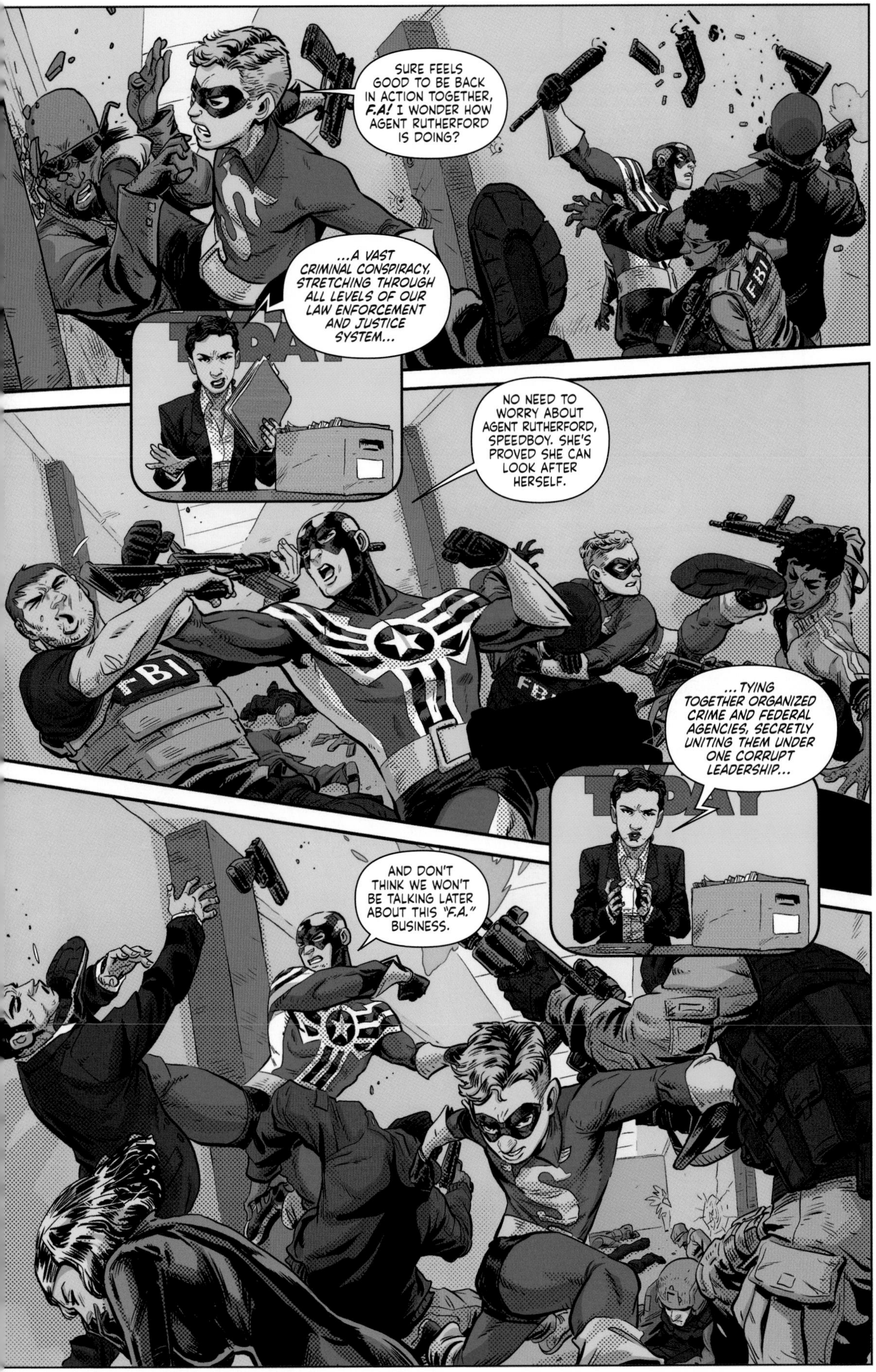
SURE FEELS GOOD TO BE BACK IN ACTION TOGETHER, **F.A!** I WONDER HOW AGENT RUTHERFORD IS DOING?
...A VAST CRIMINAL CONSPIRACY, STRETCHING THROUGH ALL LEVELS OF OUR LAW ENFORCEMENT AND JUSTICE SYSTEM...
NO NEED TO WORRY ABOUT AGENT RUTHERFORD, SPEEDBOY. SHE'S PROVED SHE CAN LOOK AFTER HERSELF.
FBI
...TYING TOGETHER ORGANIZED CRIME AND FEDERAL AGENCIES, SECRETLY UNITING THEM UNDER ONE CORRUPT LEADERSHIP...
AND DON'T THINK WE WON'T BE TALKING LATER ABOUT THIS *"F.A."* BUSINESS.

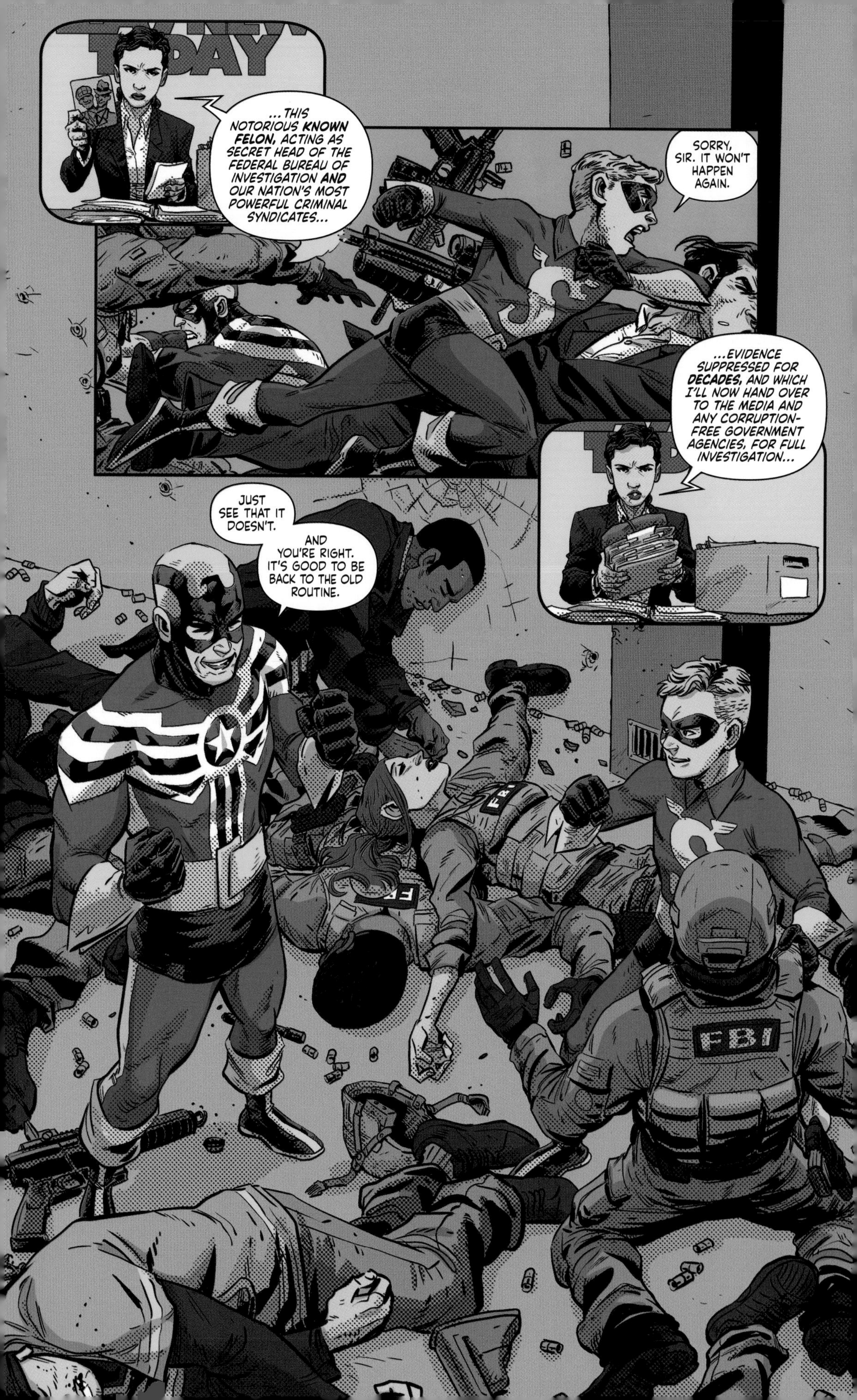

...THIS NOTORIOUS **KNOWN FELON,** ACTING AS SECRET HEAD OF THE FEDERAL BUREAU OF INVESTIGATION **AND** OUR NATION'S MOST POWERFUL CRIMINAL SYNDICATES...
SORRY, SIR. IT WON'T HAPPEN AGAIN.
...EVIDENCE SUPPRESSED FOR **DECADES,** AND WHICH I'LL NOW HAND OVER TO THE MEDIA AND ANY CORRUPTION-FREE GOVERNMENT AGENCIES, FOR FULL INVESTIGATION...
JUST SEE THAT IT DOESN'T.
AND YOU'RE RIGHT. IT'S GOOD TO BE BACK TO THE OLD ROUTINE.
FBI

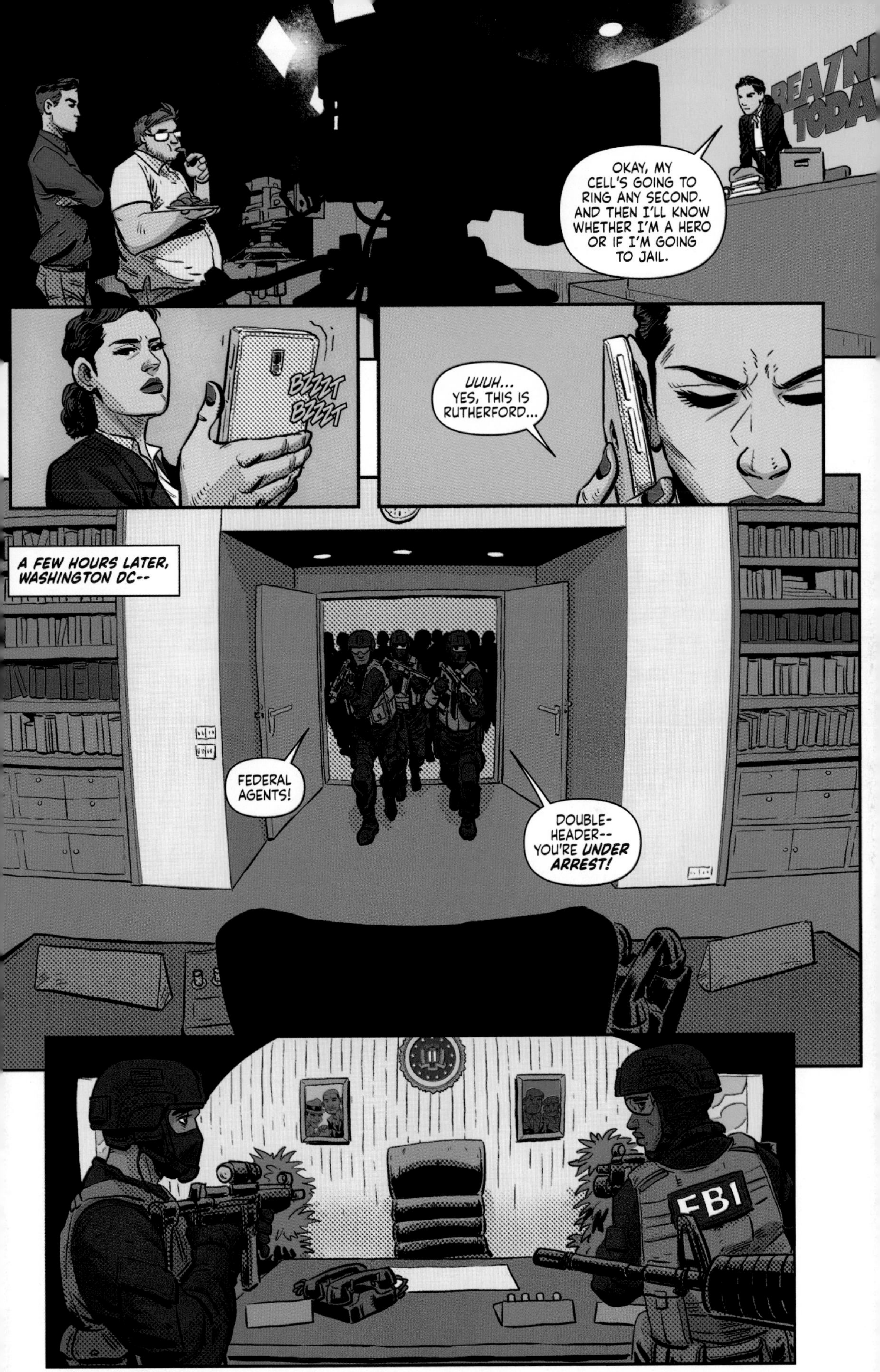

OKAY, MY CELL'S GOING TO RING ANY SECOND. AND THEN I'LL KNOW WHETHER I'M A HERO OR IF I'M GOING TO JAIL.
BZZZT BZZZT
UUUH... YES, THIS IS RUTHERFORD...
A FEW HOURS LATER, WASHINGTON DC--
FEDERAL AGENTS!
DOUBLE-HEADER-- YOU'RE UNDER ARREST!
FBI

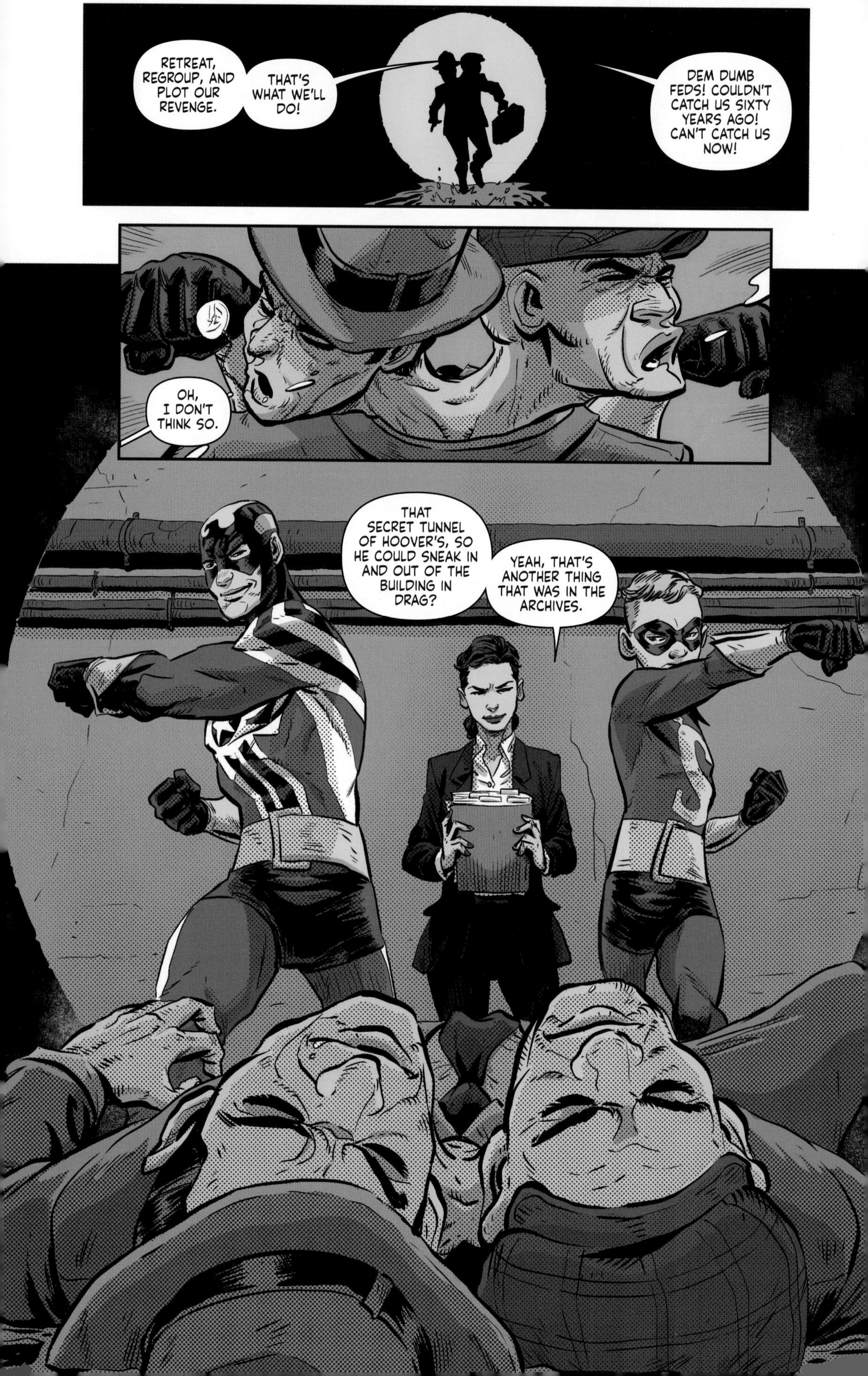
RETREAT, REGROUP, AND PLOT OUR REVENGE.
THAT'S WHAT WE'LL DO!
DEM DUMB FEDS! COULDN'T CATCH US SIXTY YEARS AGO! CAN'T CATCH US NOW!
OH, I DON'T THINK SO.
THAT SECRET TUNNEL OF HOOVER'S, SO HE COULD SNEAK IN AND OUT OF THE BUILDING IN DRAG?
YEAH, THAT'S ANOTHER THING THAT WAS IN THE ARCHIVES.

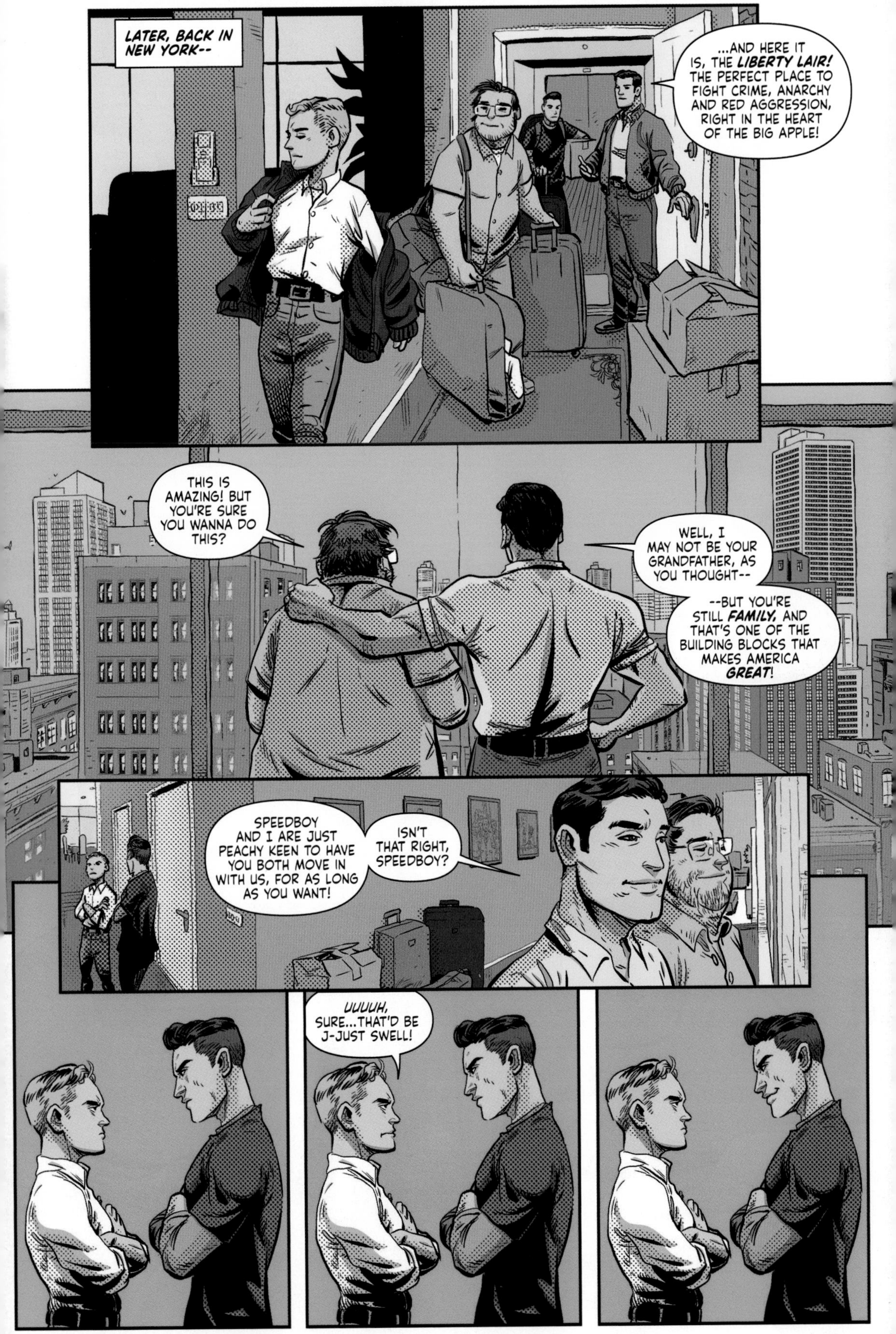
LATER, BACK IN NEW YORK--
...AND HERE IT IS, THE *LIBERTY LAIR!* THE PERFECT PLACE TO FIGHT CRIME, ANARCHY AND RED AGGRESSION, RIGHT IN THE HEART OF THE BIG APPLE!
THIS IS AMAZING! BUT YOU'RE SURE YOU WANNA DO THIS?
WELL, I MAY NOT BE YOUR GRANDFATHER, AS YOU THOUGHT--
--BUT YOU'RE STILL *FAMILY,* AND THAT'S ONE OF THE BUILDING BLOCKS THAT MAKES AMERICA *GREAT*!
SPEEDBOY AND I ARE JUST PEACHY KEEN TO HAVE YOU BOTH MOVE IN WITH US, FOR AS LONG AS YOU WANT!
ISN'T THAT RIGHT, SPEEDBOY?
UUUUH, SURE...THAT'D BE J-JUST SWELL!

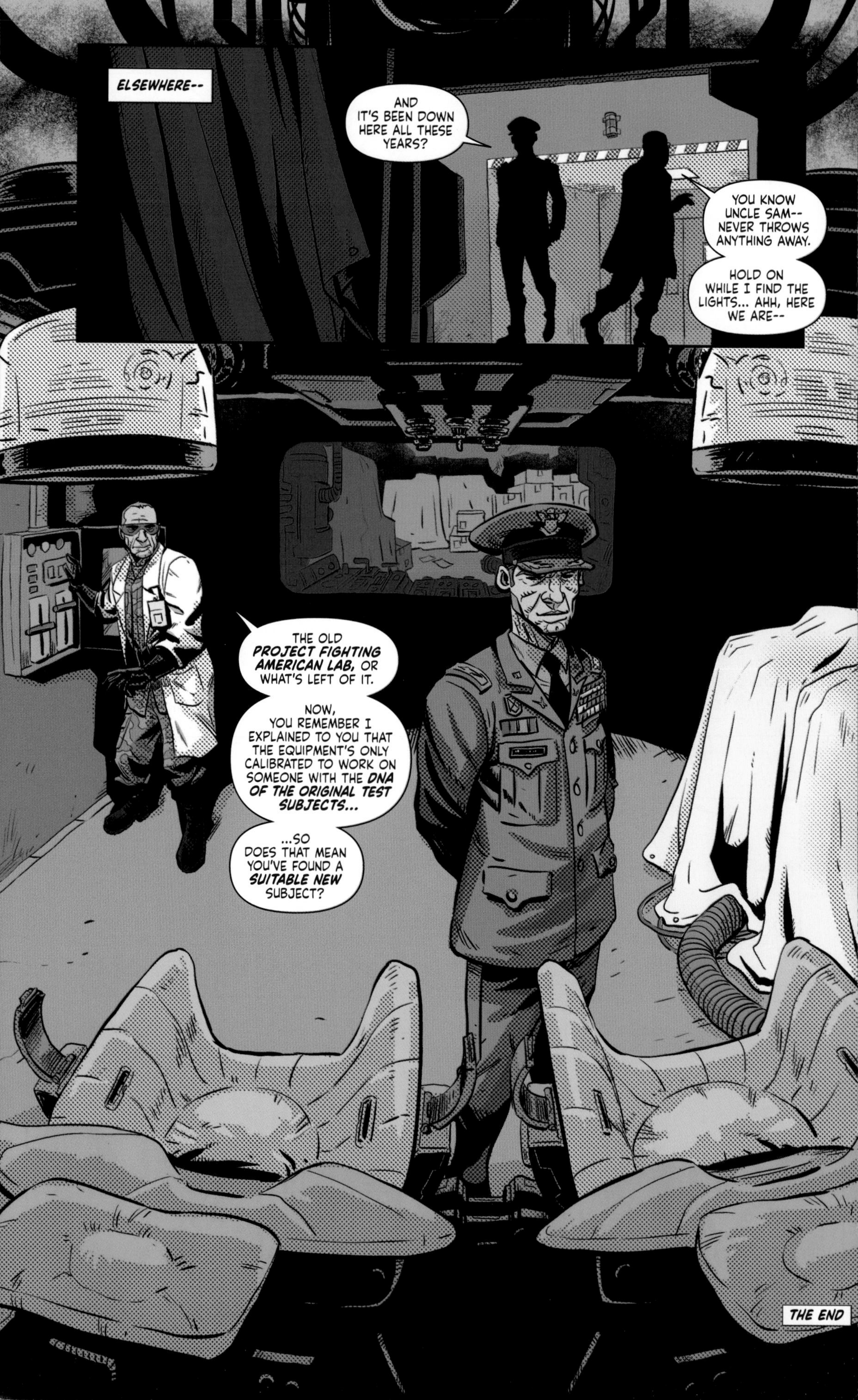
ELSEWHERE--
AND IT'S BEEN DOWN HERE ALL THESE YEARS?
YOU KNOW UNCLE SAM-- NEVER THROWS ANYTHING AWAY.
HOLD ON WHILE I FIND THE LIGHTS... AHH, HERE WE ARE--
THE OLD PROJECT FIGHTING AMERICAN LAB, OR WHAT'S LEFT OF IT.
NOW, YOU REMEMBER I EXPLAINED TO YOU THAT THE EQUIPMENT'S ONLY CALIBRATED TO WORK ON SOMEONE WITH THE DNA OF THE ORIGINAL TEST SUBJECTS...
...SO DOES THAT MEAN YOU'VE FOUND A SUITABLE NEW SUBJECT?
THE END

BONUS MATERIAL

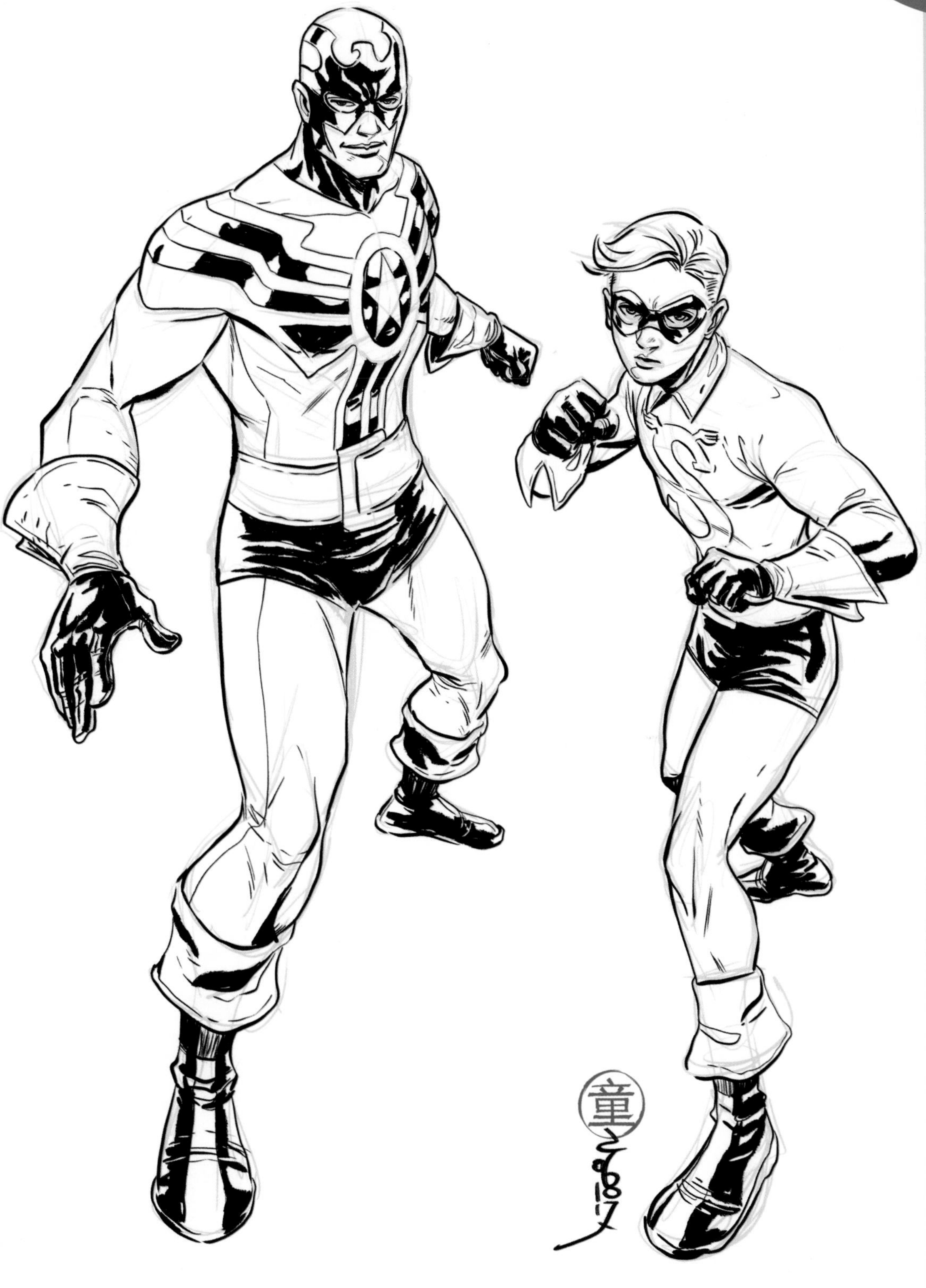

The following pages showcase Andie Tong's character sketches starting with Fighting American and Speedboy.

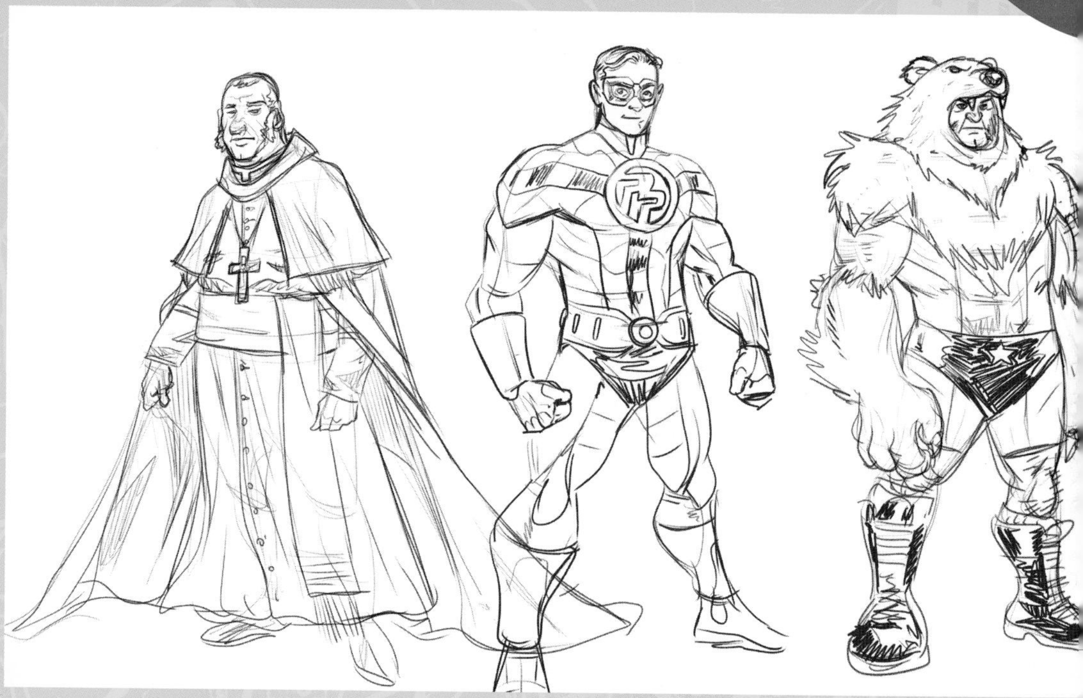

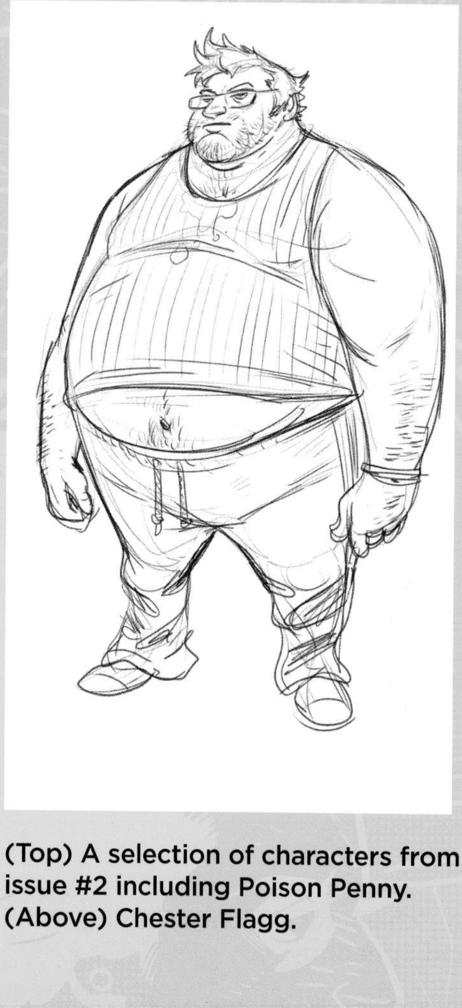

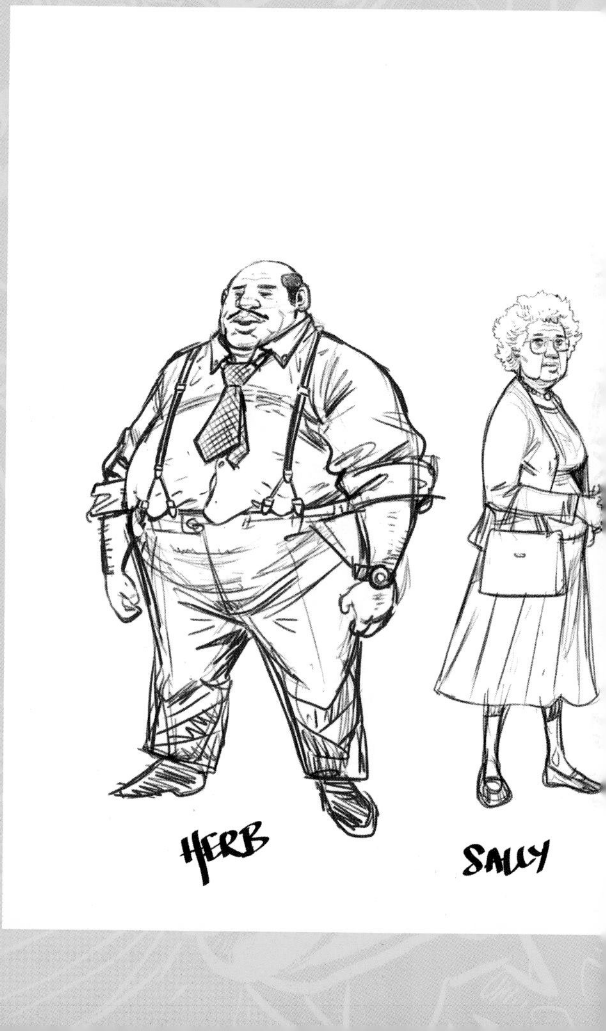
HERB
SALLY

(Top) A selection of characters from issue #2 including Poison Penny.
(Above) Chester Flagg.

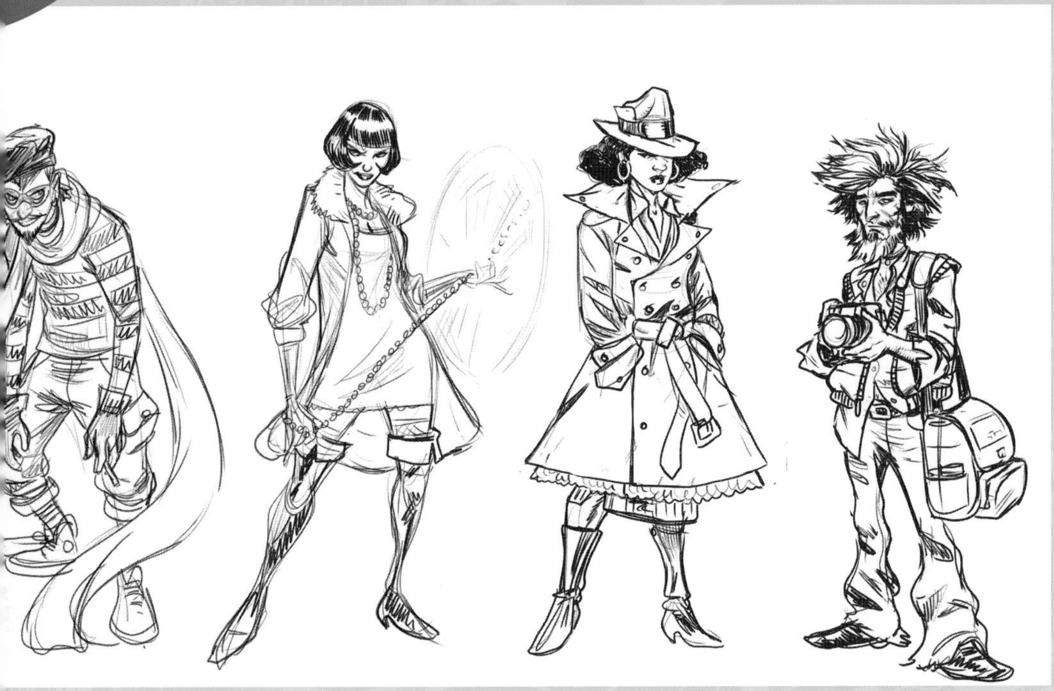

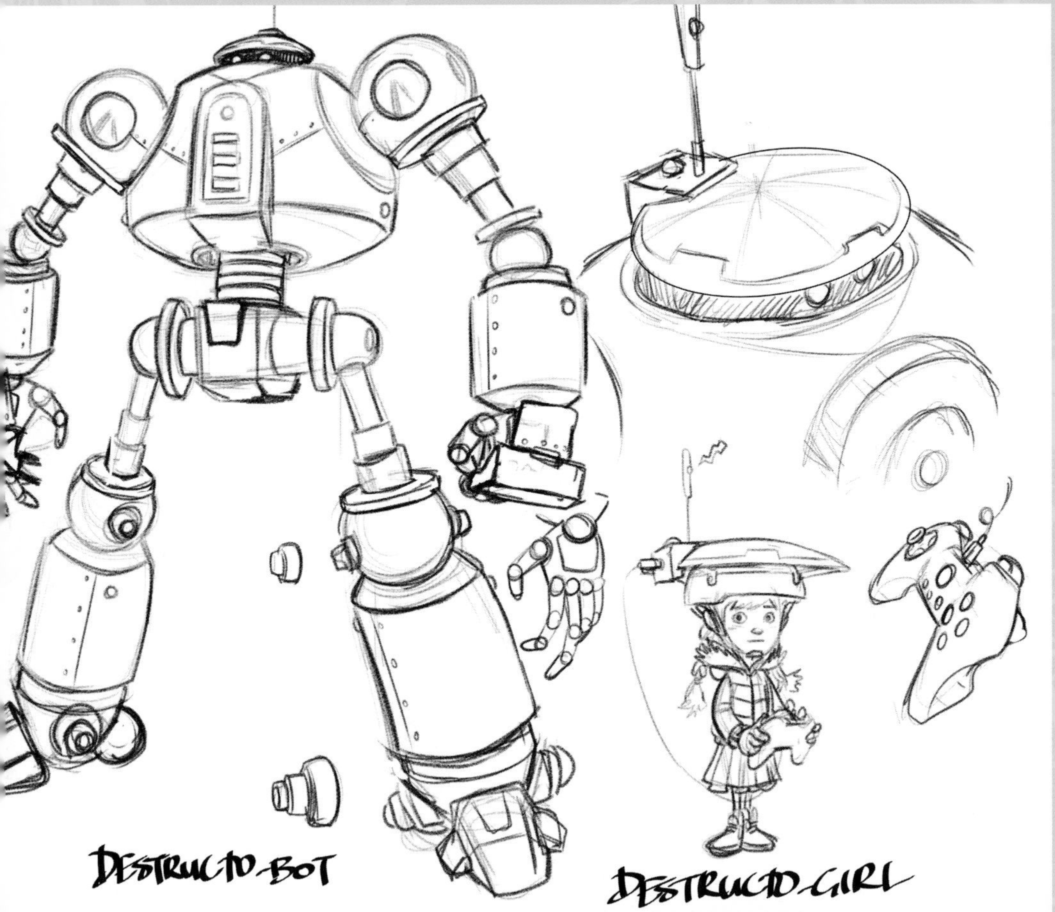
DESTRUCTO-BOT
DESTRUCTO-GIRL

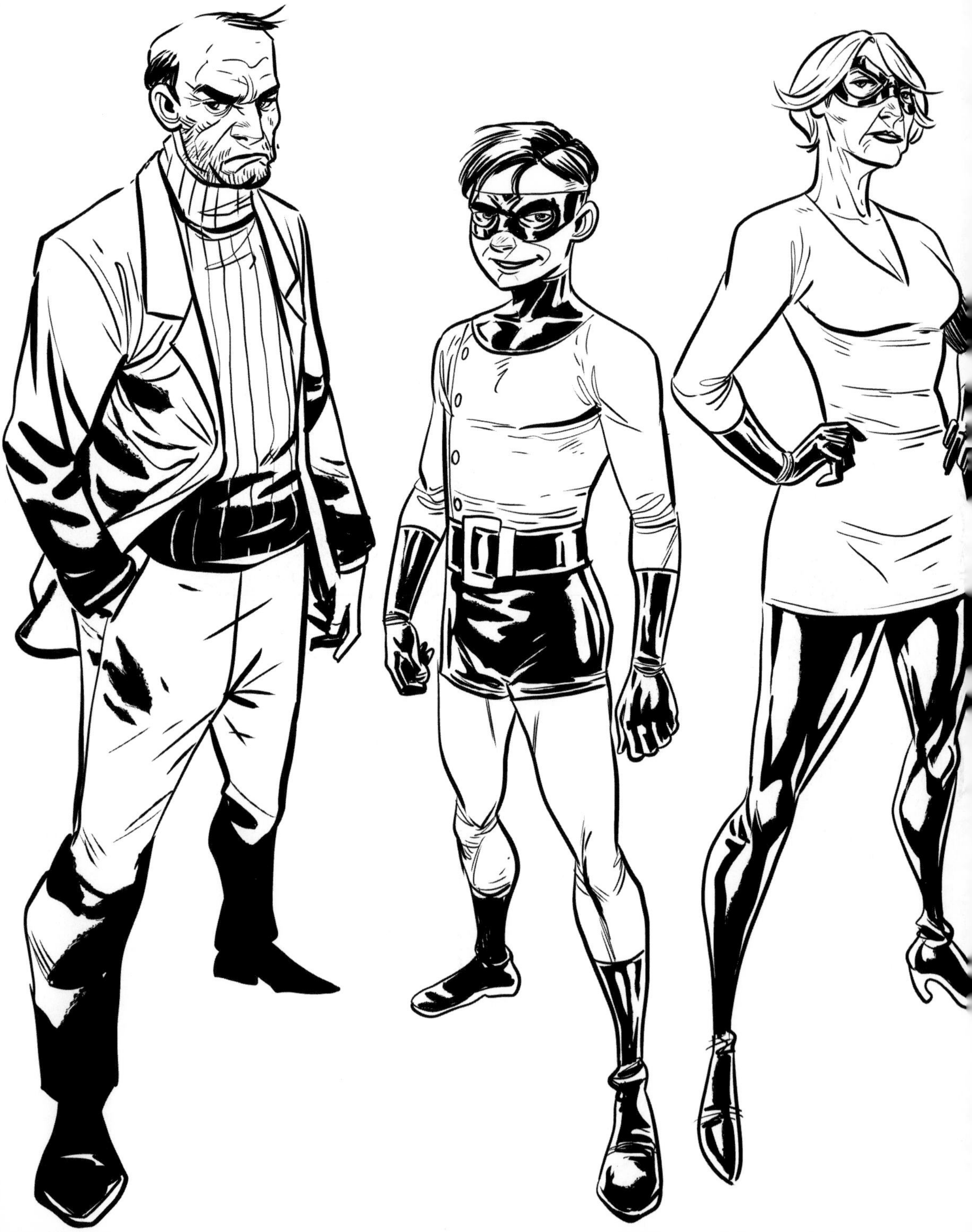

Poison Ivan, Chaos Lad and Madam Chaos

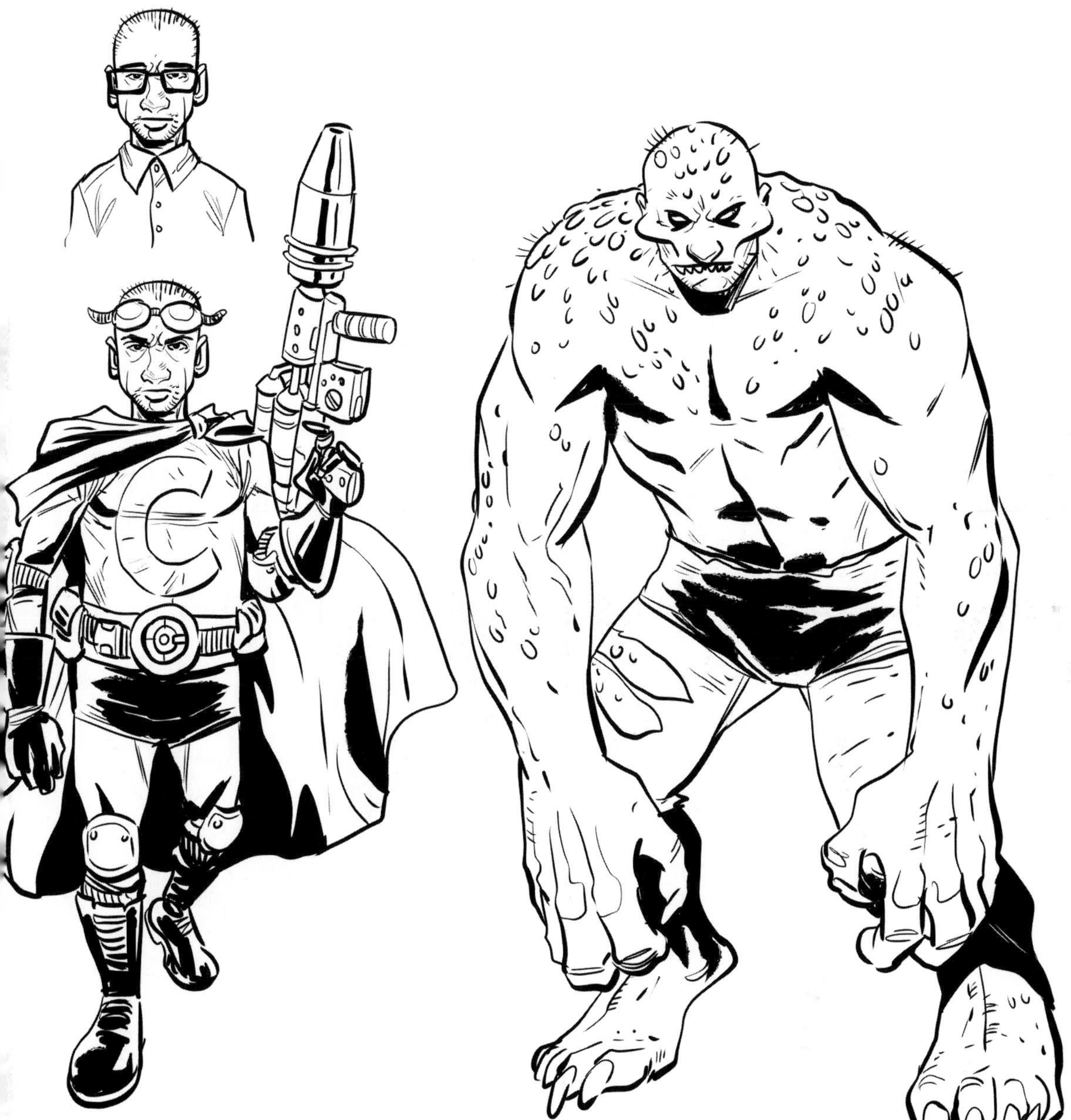

(Top left) Matt aka Captain ZombieMaster (bottom left) and Matt on Transformo Pills (right)

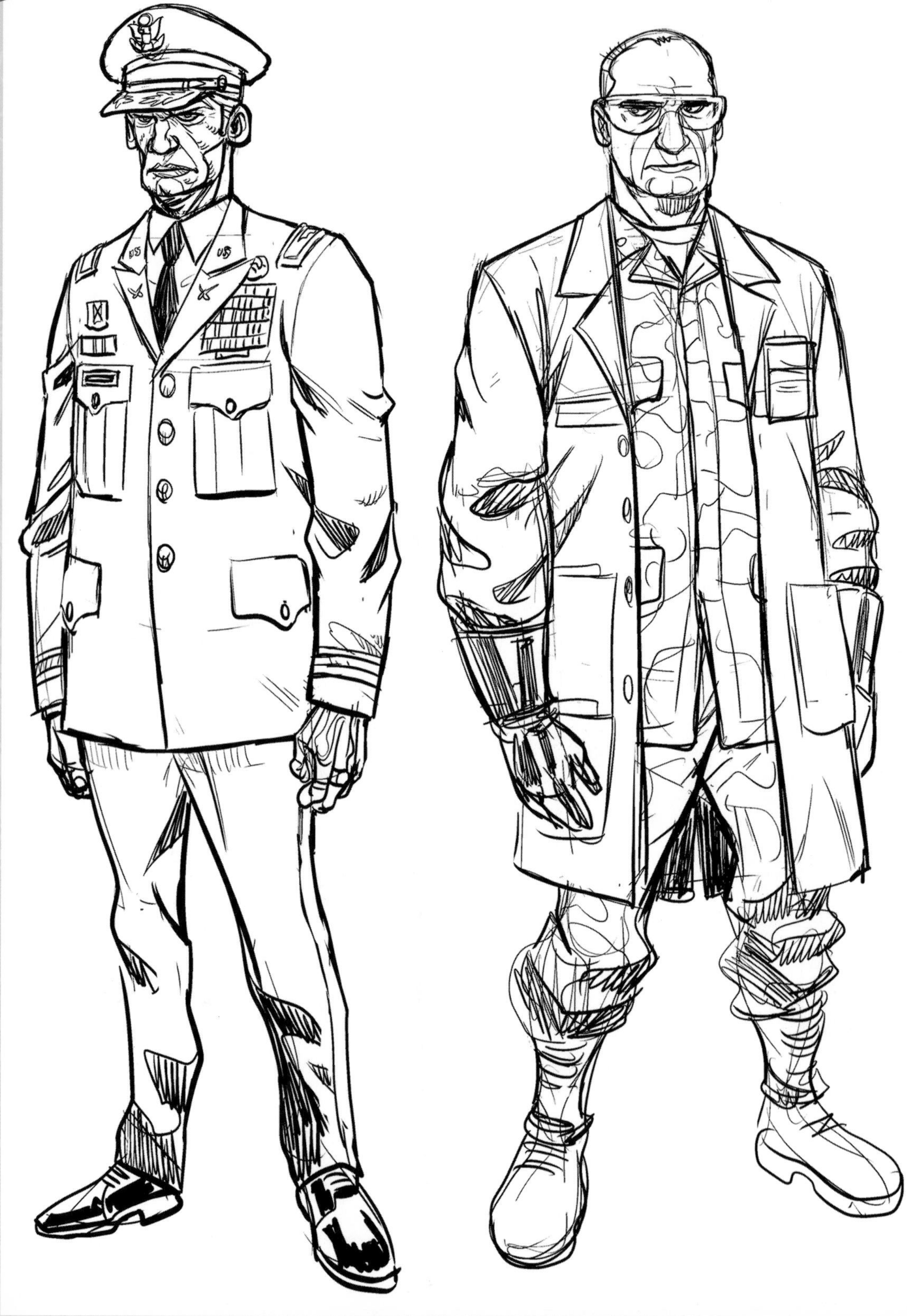

Colonel Octavius West and Doctor Gustav Snafknacker

COVER GALLERY

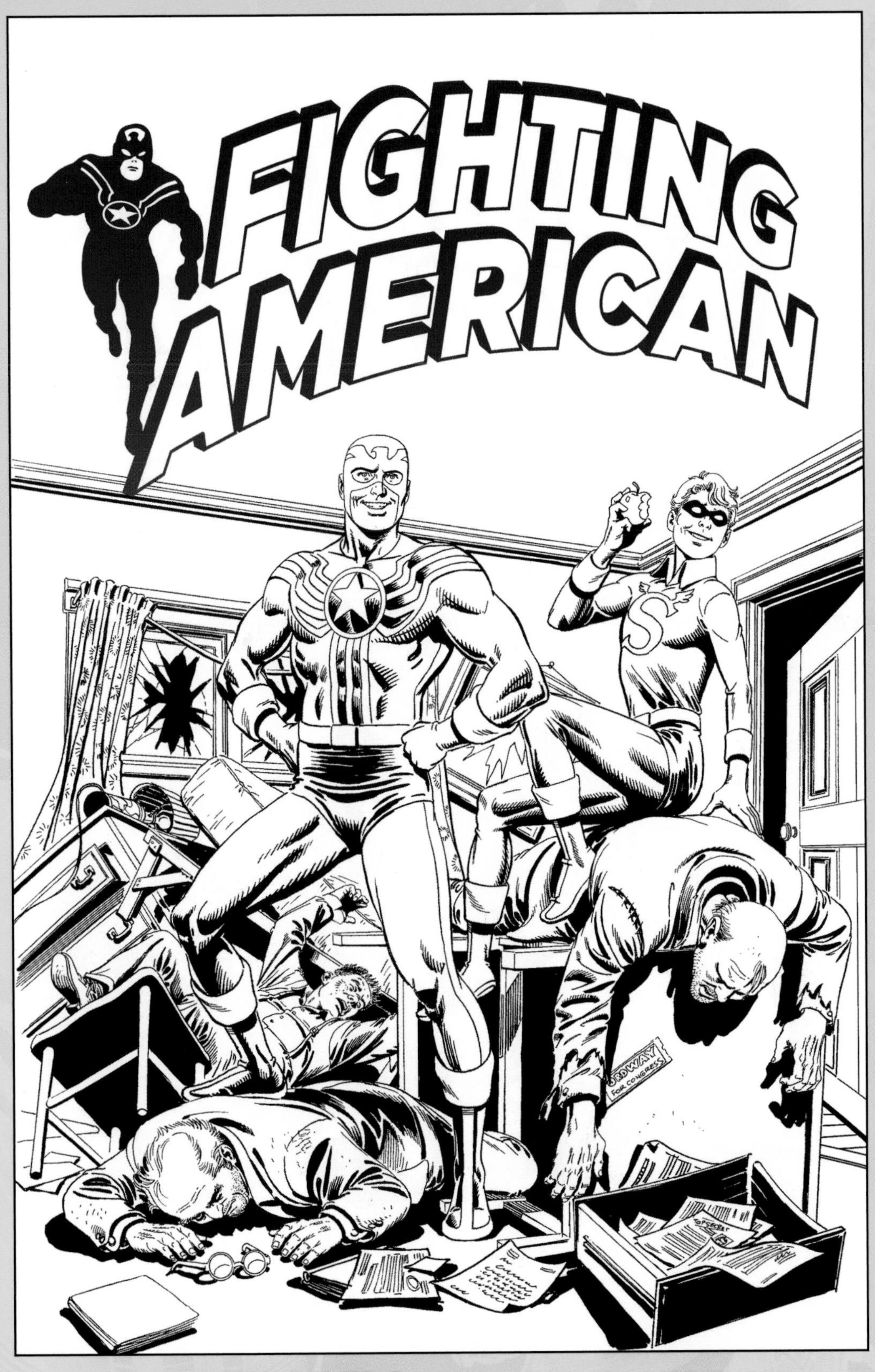
FIGHTING AMERICAN
ORDWAY FOR CONGRESS

ISSUE 1 COVER A ORIGINAL ART BY JERRY ORDWAY

COVER GALLERY

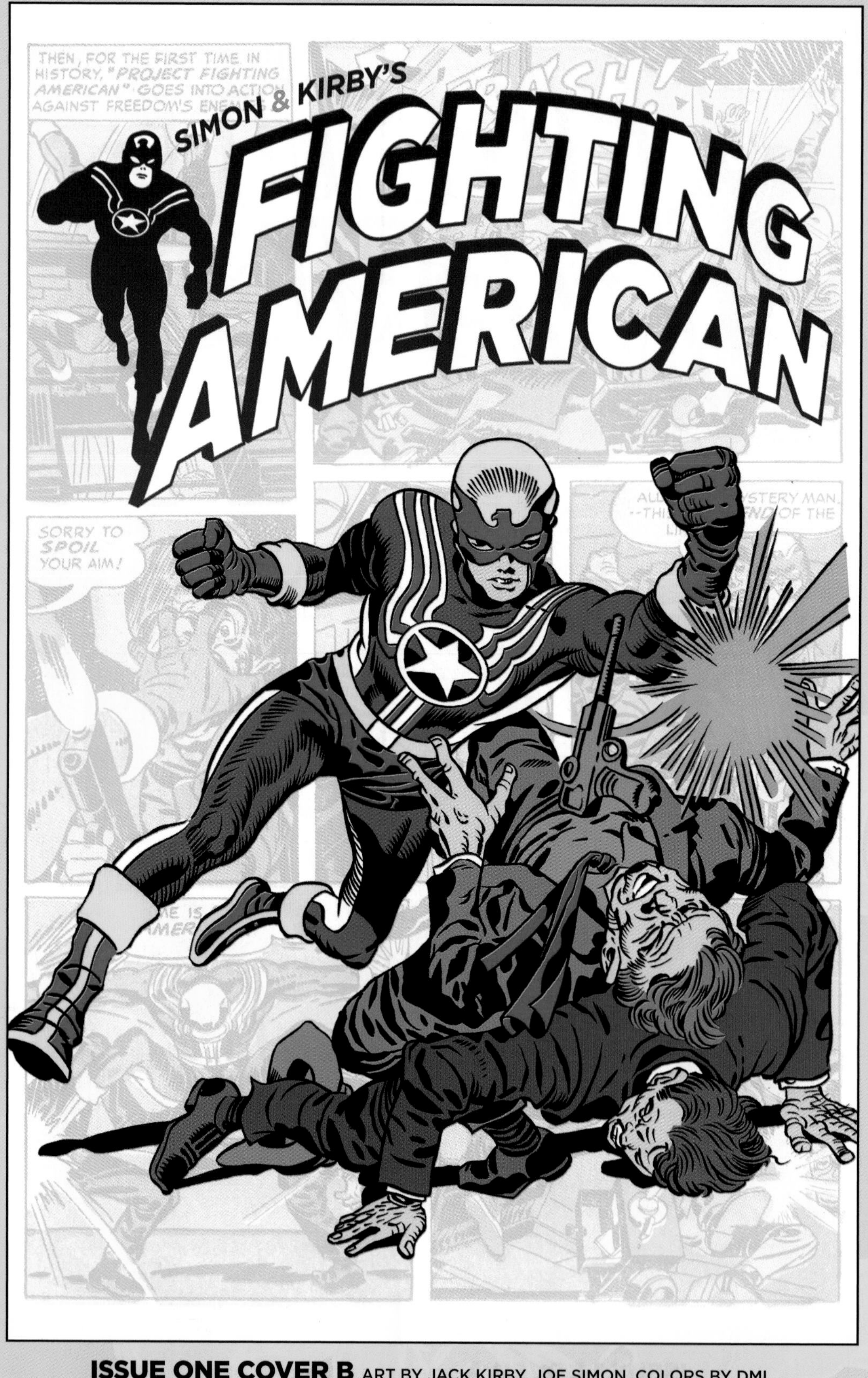
SIMON & KIRBY'S
FIGHTING AMERICAN
SORRY TO SPOIL YOUR AIM!

ISSUE ONE COVER B ART BY JACK KIRBY, JOE SIMON, COLORS BY DML

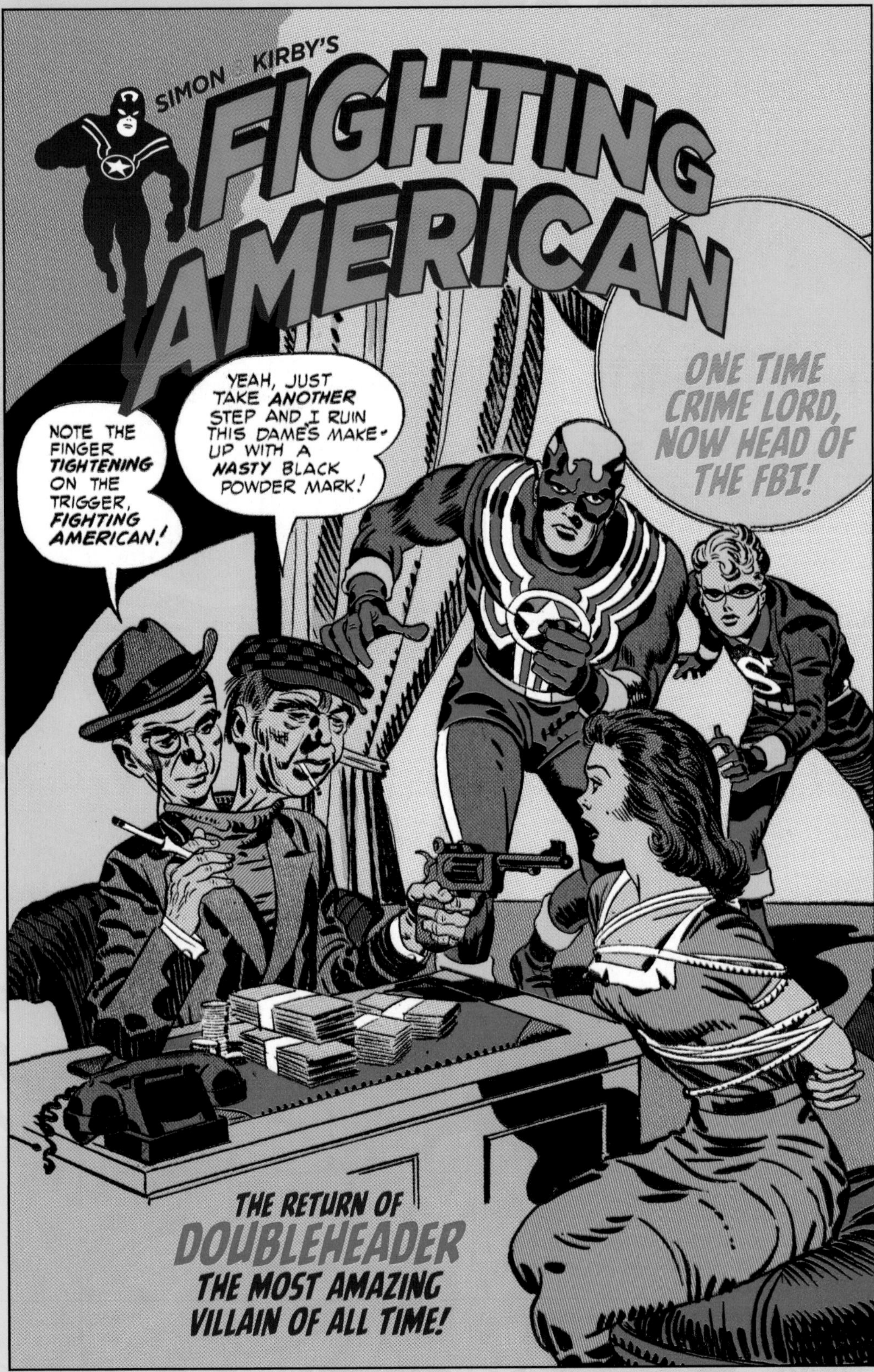
SIMON & KIRBY'S
FIGHTING AMERICAN
NOTE THE FINGER TIGHTENING ON THE TRIGGER, FIGHTING AMERICAN!
YEAH, JUST TAKE ANOTHER STEP AND I RUIN THIS DAME'S MAKE-UP WITH A NASTY BLACK POWDER MARK!
ONE TIME CRIME LORD, NOW HEAD OF THE FBI!
THE RETURN OF DOUBLEHEADER THE MOST AMAZING VILLAIN OF ALL TIME!

ISSUE TWO COVER B ART BY JACK KIRBY, JOE SIMON, COLORS BY TRACY BAILEY

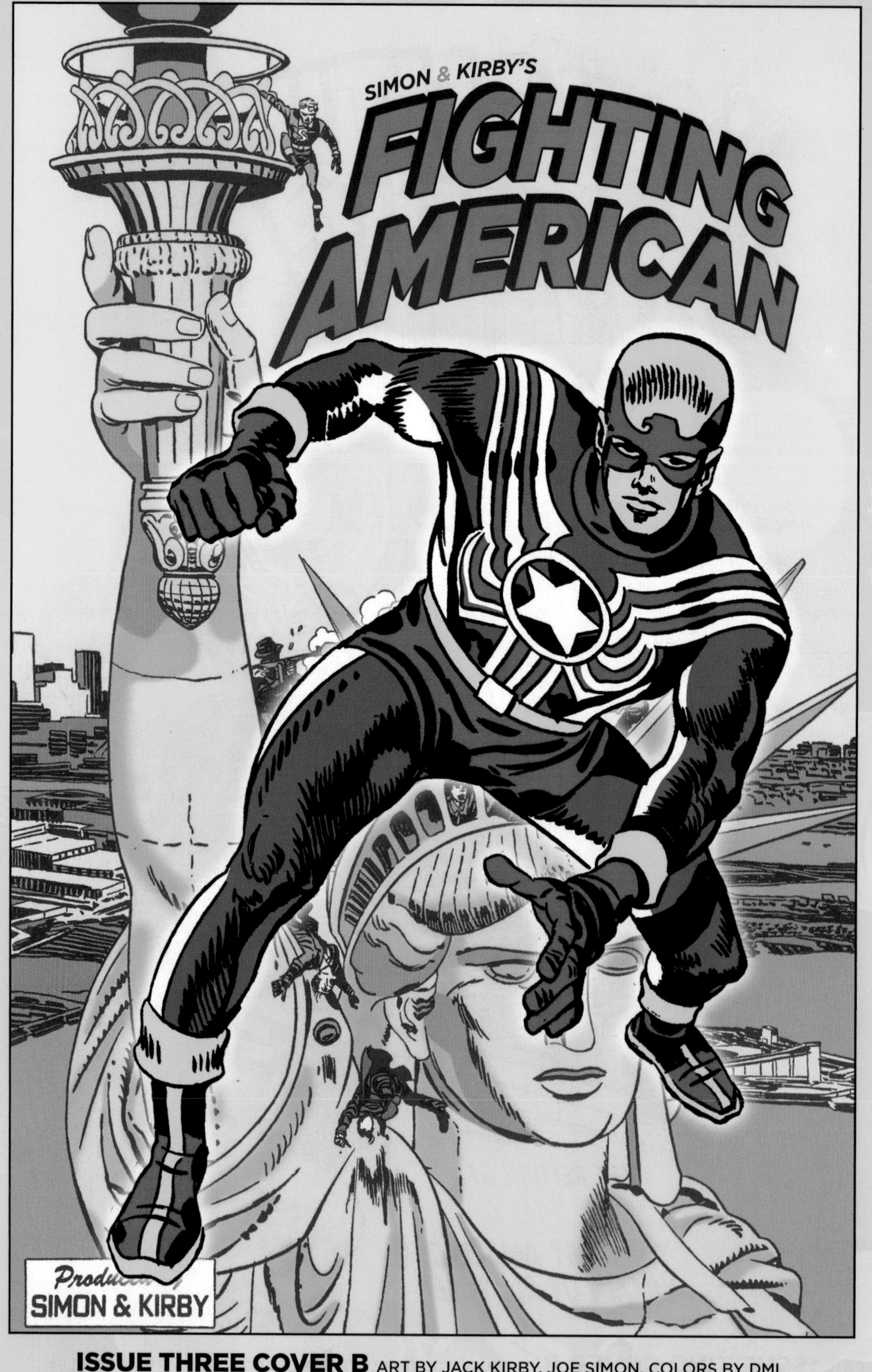
SIMON & KIRBY'S
FIGHTING AMERICAN
Produced by
SIMON & KIRBY

ISSUE THREE COVER B ART BY JACK KIRBY, JOE SIMON, COLORS BY DML